Carolyn Walker

with Paul Harvey

English for
BUSINESS
STUDIES

in Higher Education Studies
Teacher's Book

Series editor: Terry Phillips

Published by
Garnet Publishing Ltd.
8 Southern Court
South Street
Reading RG1 4QS, UK

First published 2008
Reprinted 2008, 2010

ISBN 978 1 85964 944 2

British Cataloguing-in-Publication Data
A catalogue record for this book is available from
the British Library.

Production
Series editor: Terry Phillips
Project management: Louise Elkins, Martin Moore
Editorial team: Jane Gregory, Rebecca Snelling
Academic review: Ian Crawford
Design: Henry Design Associates and Mike Hinks
Photography: Sally Henry and Trevor Cook; Alamy (David R.
Frazier Photolibrary, Inc); Corbis (Serge Attal, James Leynse,
Frederic Pitchall, Steve Raymer); Shutterstock, Clipart.com,
Digital Vision, Stockbyte
water frame spinning machine on page 66 © The Baldwin
Online Children's Literature Project at mainlesson.com;
images 2, 3 & 4 at top of page 113 © Alum Bay Glass;
images 5 & 6 on page 113 and image 1 on page 124 ©
Dartington Crystal

Audio recorded at Motivation Sound Studios produced by
EFS Television Production Ltd

The author and publisher would like to thank Google for
permission to reproduce the results listings on page 72.
Every effort has been made to trace copyright holders and
we apologize in advance for any unintentional omission. We
will be happy to insert the appropriate acknowledgements
in any subsequent editions.

Printed and bound in Lebanon by International Press:
interpress@int-press.com

Contents

Book map

Unit	Topics
1 The business of business Listening · Speaking	• types of business • the history of business
2 The organization of work Reading · Writing	• how organizations are structured (hierarchies, teams, etc.) • leadership and teams
3 Getting the work done Listening · Speaking	• productivity • theories of motivation • Management by Objectives
4 The world of technology Reading · Writing	• computers for research • technological change
5 People and markets Listening · Speaking	• definition of marketing • importance of marketing • types of market • market research
6 Products and strategies Reading · Writing	• the role of the product • product life cycles • product portfolios
7 Operations: producing the goods Listening · Speaking	• the production process: input/transformation/output • value added • types of production: job/batch/flow • scheduling
8 Operations: efficiency, costs and quality Reading · Writing	• efficiency in operations managment • Japanese management practices: 'lean' production techniques, TQM
9 Managing financial accounts Listening · Speaking	• accounting: management accounting · financial accounting • documentation: balance sheet · profit and loss account • cash flow statement
10 Funding company activities Reading · Writing	• sources of business finance • short- and long-term finance • start-up and expansion finance
11 External influences Listening · Speaking	• external influences on businesses: national · international · political · economic • environmental issues
12 Strategy and change Reading · Writing	• company performance: SWOT analysis • management of change • case study: responding to external factors

Vocabulary focus	Skills focus		Unit
• words from general English with a special meaning in business • prefixes and suffixes	Listening	• preparing for a lecture • predicting lecture content from the introduction • understanding lecture organization • choosing an appropriate form of notes • making lecture notes	**1**
	Speaking	• speaking from notes	
• English–English dictionaries: headwords · definitions · parts of speech · phonemes · stress markers · countable/uncountable · transitive/intransitive	Reading	• using research questions to focus on relevant information in a text • using topic sentences to get an overview of the text	**2**
	Writing	• writing topic sentences • summarizing a text	
• stress patterns in multi-syllable words • prefixes	Listening	• preparing for a lecture • predicting lecture content • making lecture notes • using different information sources	**3**
	Speaking	• reporting research findings • formulating questions	
• computer jargon • abbreviations and acronyms • discourse and stance markers • verb and noun suffixes	Reading	• identifying topic development within a paragraph • using the Internet effectively • evaluating Internet search results	**4**
	Writing	• reporting research findings	
• word sets: synonyms, antonyms, etc. • the language of trends • common lecture language	Listening	• understanding 'signpost language' in lectures • using symbols and abbreviations in note-taking	**5**
	Speaking	• making effective contributions to a seminar	
• synonyms, replacement subjects, etc. for sentence-level paraphrasing	Reading	• locating key information in complex sentences	**6**
	Writing	• reporting findings from other sources: paraphrasing • writing complex sentences	
• compound nouns • fixed phrases from business studies • fixed phrases from academic English • common lecture language	Listening	• understanding speaker emphasis	**7**
	Speaking	• asking for clarification • responding to queries and requests for clarification	
• synonyms • nouns from verbs • definitions • common 'direction' verbs in essay titles (*discuss, analyse, evaluate*, etc.)	Reading	• understanding dependent clauses with passives	**8**
	Writing	• paraphrasing • expanding notes into complex sentences • recognizing different essay types/structures: descriptive · analytical · comparison/evaluation · argument • writing essay plans • writing essays	
• fixed phrases from finance • fixed phrases from academic English	Listening	• using the Cornell note-taking system • recognizing digressions in lectures	**9**
	Speaking	• making effective contributions to a seminar • referring to other people's ideas in a seminar	
• 'neutral' and 'marked' words • fixed phrases from finance • fixed phrases from academic English	Reading	• recognizing the writer's stance and level of confidence or tentativeness • inferring implicit ideas	**10**
	Writing	• writing situation–problem–solution–evaluation essays • using direct quotations • compiling a bibliography/reference list	
• words/phrases used to link ideas (*moreover, as a result*, etc.) • stress patterns in noun phrases and compounds • fixed phrases from academic English • words/phrases related to environmental issues	Listening	• recognizing the speaker's stance • writing up notes in full	**11**
	Speaking	• building an argument in a seminar • agreeing/disagreeing	
• verbs used to introduce ideas from other sources (*X contends/suggests/asserts that* …) • linking words/phrases conveying contrast (*whereas*), result (*consequently*), reasons (*due to*), etc. • words for quantities (*a significant minority*)	Reading	• understanding how ideas in a text are linked	**12**
	Writing	• deciding whether to use direct quotation or paraphrase • incorporating quotations • writing research reports • writing effective introductions/conclusions	

Introduction

The ESAP series

The aim of the titles in the ESAP series is to prepare students for academic study in a particular discipline. In this respect, the series is somewhat different from many ESP (English for Specific Purposes) series, which are aimed at people already working in the field, or about to enter the field. This focus on *study* in the discipline rather than *work* in the field has enabled the authors to focus much more specifically on the skills which a student of business studies needs.

It is assumed that prior to using titles in this series students will already have completed a general EAP (English for Academic Purposes) course such as *Skills in English* (Garnet Publishing, up to the end of at least Level 3), and will have achieved an IELTS level of at least 5.

English for Business Studies

English for Business Studies is designed for students who plan to take a business or management studies course entirely or partly in English. The principal aim of *English for Business Studies* is to teach students to cope with input texts, i.e., listening and reading, in the discipline. However, students will also be expected to produce output texts in speech and writing throughout the course.

The syllabus concentrates on key vocabulary for the discipline and on words and phrases commonly used in academic and technical English. It covers key facts and concepts from the discipline, thereby giving students a flying start for when they meet the same points again in their faculty work. It also focuses on the skills that will enable students to get the most out of lectures and written texts. Finally, it presents the skills required to take part in seminars and tutorials and to produce essay assignments. For a summary of the course content, see the book map on pages 4–5.

Components of the course

The course comprises:
- the student Course Book
- this Teacher's Book, which provides detailed guidance on each lesson, full answer keys, audio transcripts and extra photocopiable resources
- audio CDs with lecture and seminar excerpts

Organization of the course

English for Business Studies has 12 units, each of which is based on a different aspect of business studies.

Odd-numbered units are based on listening (lecture/seminar extracts). Even-numbered units are based on reading.

Each unit is divided into four lessons:

Lesson 1: vocabulary for the discipline; vocabulary skills such as word-building, use of affixes, use of synonyms for paraphrasing

Lesson 2: reading or listening text and skills development

Lesson 3: reading or listening skills extension. In addition, in later reading units, students are introduced to a writing assignment which is further developed in Lesson 4; in later listening units, students are introduced to a spoken language point (e.g., making an oral presentation at a seminar) which is further developed in Lesson 4

Lesson 4: a parallel listening or reading text to that presented in Lesson 2, which students have to use their new skills (Lesson 3) to decode; in addition, written or spoken work is further practised

The last two pages of each unit, *Vocabulary bank* and *Skills bank*, are a useful summary of the unit content.

Each unit provides between four and six hours of classroom activity with the possibility of a further two to four hours on the suggested extra activities. The course will be suitable, therefore, as the core component of a faculty-specific pre-sessional or foundation course of between 50 and 80 hours.

Vocabulary development

English for Business Studies attaches great importance to vocabulary. This is why one lesson out of four is devoted to vocabulary and why, in addition, the first exercise at least in many of the other three lessons is a vocabulary exercise. The vocabulary presented can be grouped into two main areas:
- key vocabulary for business studies
- key vocabulary for academic English

In addition to presenting specific items of vocabulary, the course concentrates on the vocabulary skills and strategies that will help students to make sense of lectures and texts. Examples include:
- understanding prefixes and suffixes and how these affect the meaning of the base word
- guessing words in context
- using an English–English dictionary effectively
- understanding how certain words/phrases link ideas
- understanding how certain words/phrases show the writer/speaker's point of view

Skills development

Listening and reading in the real world involve extracting communicative value in real time – i.e., as the spoken text is being produced or as you are reading written text. Good listeners and readers do not need to go back to listen or read again most of the time. Indeed, with listening to formal speech such as a lecture, there is no possibility of going back. In many ELT materials second, third, even fourth listenings are common. The approach taken in the ESAP series is very different. We set out to teach and practise 'text-attack' skills – i.e., listening and reading strategies that will enable students to extract communicative value at a single listening or reading.

Students also need to become familiar with the way academic 'outputs' such as reports, essays and oral presentations are structured in English. Conventions may be different in their own language – for example, paragraphing conventions, or introduction–main body–conclusion structure. All students, whatever their background, will benefit from an awareness of the skills and strategies that will help them produce written work of a high standard.

Examples of specific skills practised in the course include:

Listening

- predicting lecture content and organization from the introduction
- following signposts to lecture organization
- choosing an appropriate form of lecture notes
- recognizing the lecturer's stance and level of confidence/tentativeness

Reading

- using research questions to focus on relevant information
- using topic sentences to get an overview of the text
- recognizing the writer's stance and level of confidence/tentativeness
- using the Internet effectively

Speaking

- making effective contributions to a seminar
- asking for clarification – formulating questions
- speaking from notes
- summarizing

Writing

- writing notes
- paraphrasing
- reporting findings from other sources – avoiding plagiarism

- recognizing different essay types and structures
- writing essay plans and essays
- compiling a bibliography/reference list

Specific activities

Certain types of activity are repeated on several occasions throughout the course. This is because these activities are particularly valuable in language learning.

Tasks to activate schemata

It has been known for many years, since the research of Bartlett in the 1930s, that we can only understand incoming information, written or spoken, if we can fit it into a schemata. It is essential that we build these schemata in students before exposing them to new information, so all lessons with listening or reading texts begin with one or more relevant activities.

Prediction activities

Before students are allowed to listen to a section of a lecture or read a text, they are encouraged to make predictions about the contents, in general or even specific terms, based on the context, the introduction to the text or, in the case of reading, the topic sentences in the text. This is based on the theory that active listening and reading involve the receiver in being ahead of the producer.

Working with illustrations, diagrams, figures

Many tasks require students to explain or interpret visual material. This is clearly a key task in a field which makes great use of such material to support written text. Students can be taken back to these visuals later on in the course to ensure that they have not forgotten how to describe and interpret them.

Vocabulary tasks

Many tasks ask students to group key business words, to categorize them in some way or to find synonyms or antonyms. These tasks help students to build relationships between words which, research has shown, is a key element in remembering words. In these exercises, the target words are separated into blue boxes so you can quickly return to one of these activities for revision work later.

Gap-fill

Filling in missing words or phrases in a sentence or a text, or labelling a diagram, indicates comprehension both of the missing items and of the context in which they correctly fit. You can vary the activity by, for example, going through the gap-fill text with the whole class first orally, pens down, then setting the same task for individual completion. Gap-fill activities can be photocopied and set as revision at the end of the unit or later, with or without the missing items.

Breaking long sentences into key components

One feature of academic English is the average length of sentences. Traditionally, EFL classes teach students to cope with the complexity of the verb phrase, equating level with more and more arcane verb structures, such as the present perfect modal passive. However, research into academic language, including the corpus research which underlies the *Longman Grammar of Spoken and Written English,* suggests that complexity in academic language does not lie with the verb phrase but rather with the noun phrase and clause joining and embedding. For this reason, students are shown in many exercises later in the course how to break down long sentences into kernel elements, and find the subject, verb and object of each element. This receptive skill is then turned into a productive skill, by encouraging students to think in terms of kernel elements first before building them into complex sentences.

Activities with stance marking

Another key element of academic text is the attitude (or stance) of the writer or speaker to the information which is being imparted. This could be dogmatic, tentative, incredulous, sceptical, and so on. Students must learn the key skill of recognizing words and phrases marked for stance.

Crosswords and other word puzzles

One of the keys to vocabulary learning is repetition. However, the repetition must be active. It is no good if students are simply going through the motions. The course uses crosswords and other kinds of puzzles to bring words back into the students' consciousness through an engaging activity. However, it is understood by the writers that such playful activities are not always seen as serious and academic. The crosswords and other activities are therefore made available as photocopiable resources at the back of the Teacher's Book and can be used at the teacher's discretion, after explaining to the students why they are valuable.

Methodology points

Setting up tasks

The teaching notes for many of the exercises begin with the word *Set ... .* This single word covers a number of vital functions for the teacher, as follows:

- Refer students to the rubric (instructions).
- Check that they understand **what** to do – get one or two students to explain the task in their own words.
- Tell students **how** they are to do the task, if this is not clear in the Course Book instructions – as individual work, pairwork or in groups.
- Go through the example, if there is one. If not, make it clear what the target output is – full sentences, short answers, notes, etc.
- Go through one or two of the items, working with a good student to elicit the required output.

Use of visuals

There is a considerable amount of visual material in the book. This should be exploited in a number of ways:

- before an exercise, to orientate students, to get them thinking about the situation or the task, and to provide an opportunity for a small amount of pre-teaching of vocabulary (be careful not to pre-empt any exercises, though)
- during the exercise, to remind students of important language
- after the activity, to help with related work or to revise the target language

Comparing answers in pairs

This is frequently suggested when students have completed a task individually. It provides all students with a chance to give and explain their answers, which is not possible if the teacher immediately goes through the answers with the whole class.

Self-checking

Learning only takes place after a person has noticed that there is something to learn. This noticing of an individual learning point does not happen at the same time for all students. In many cases, it does not even happen in a useful sense when a teacher has focused on it. So learning occurs to the individual timetable of each student in a group. For this reason, it is important to give students time to notice mistakes in their own work and try to correct them individually. Take every opportunity to get students to self-check to try to force the noticing stage.

Confirmation and correction

Many activities benefit from a learning tension, i.e., a period of time when students are not sure whether something is right or wrong. The advantages of this tension are:

- a chance for all students to become involved in an activity before the correct answers are given

- a higher level of concentration from the students (tension is quite enjoyable!)
- a greater focus on the item as students wait for the correct answer
- a greater involvement in the process – students become committed to their answers and want to know if they are right and, if not, why not

In cases where learning tension of this type is desirable, the teacher's notes say, *Do not confirm or correct (at this point)*.

Feedback

At the end of each task, there should be a feedback stage. During this stage, the correct answers (or a model answer in the case of freer exercises) are given, alternative answers (if any) are accepted, and wrong answers are discussed. Unless students' own answers are required (in the case of very free exercises), answers or model answers are provided in the teacher's notes.

Highlighting grammar

This course is not organized on a grammatical syllabus and does not focus on grammar specifically. It is assumed that students will have covered English grammar to at least upper intermediate level in their general English course. However, at times it will be necessary to focus on the grammar, and indeed occasionally the grammar is a main focus (for example, changing active to passive or vice versa when paraphrasing).

To highlight the grammar:

- focus students' attention on the grammar point, e.g., *Look at the word order in the first sentence.*
- write an example of the grammar point on the board
- ask a student to read out the sentence/phrase
- demonstrate the grammar point in an appropriate way (e.g., numbering to indicate word order; paradigms for verbs; time lines for tenses)
- refer to the board throughout the activity if students are making mistakes

Pronunciation

By itself, the mispronunciation of a single phoneme or a wrong word stress is unlikely to cause a breakdown in communication. However, most L2 users make multiple errors in a single utterance, including errors of word order, tense choice and vocabulary choice. We must therefore try to remove as many sources of error as possible. When you are working with a group of words, make sure that students can pronounce each word with reasonable accuracy in phonemic terms, and with the correct stress for multiple syllable words. Many researchers have found that getting the stress of a word wrong is a bigger cause of miscommunication than getting individual phonemes wrong.

Pair and group activities

Pairwork and group activities are, of course, an opportunity for students to produce spoken language. As mentioned above, this is not the main focus of this course. But the second benefit of these interactional patterns is that they provide an opportunity for the teacher to check three points:

- Are students performing the correct task, in the correct way?
- Do students understand the language of the task they are performing?
- Which elements need to be covered again for the benefit of the class, and which points need to be dealt with on an individual basis with particular students?

Vocabulary and Skills banks

Each unit has clear targets in terms of vocabulary extension and skills development. These are detailed in the checks at the end of the unit (*Vocabulary bank* and *Skills bank*). However, you may wish to refer students to one or both of these pages at the start of work on the unit, so they have a clear idea of the targets. You may also wish to refer to them from time to time during lessons.

1 THE BUSINESS OF BUSINESS

This introductory unit explores what we understand by the term 'business'. Students listen to an extract from a lecture which describes different functions of business management such as operations and finance. They also listen to a series of mini-lectures which introduce different aspects of business, from types of ownership to PEST analysis. The content of the mini-lectures will be explored in more detail in subsequent units.

Skills focus

🎧 Listening

- preparing for a lecture
- predicting lecture content from the introduction
- understanding lecture organization
- choosing an appropriate form of notes
- making lecture notes

Speaking

- speaking from notes

Vocabulary focus

- words from general English with a special meaning in business
- prefixes and suffixes

Key vocabulary

capital (n)	labour	production
consume	limited liability	promotion
consumer	machinery	raw materials
director	manufacturing	research and development (R&D)
durable goods	market (n)	resource (n)
employ	marketing	return (on investment)
employee	non-durable goods	service industry
expand	operations	set up
finance (n)	output (n)	shareholder
human resources	ownership	sole trader
income	partnership	stakeholder
industrial	performance	subcontractor
input (n)	plc	technology
invest	premises	transformation
investment	product	

1.1 Vocabulary

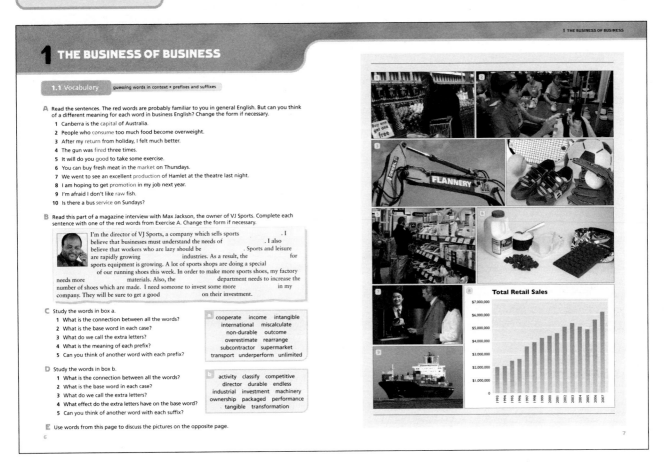

1 THE BUSINESS OF BUSINESS

General note

Read the *Vocabulary bank* at the end of the Course Book unit. Decide when, if at all, to refer students to it. The best time is probably at the very end of the lesson or the beginning of the next lesson, as a summary/revision.

Lesson aims

- identify words for the discipline in context, including words which contain affixes
- gain fluency in the target vocabulary

Introduction

Write the following sentences on the board:

1 *Mind your own business.*
2 *She has her own business.*
3 *He decided to go into business.*

Ask students the meaning of *business* in the three sentences:

- In sentence 1 it has a *general* English meaning – i.e., affairs, concerns, matters. Notice that in this sense the word is uncountable.

- In sentence 2 the meaning is a company or another type of business (examples will be covered later in this unit) and it is a countable noun.

- In sentence 3 the meaning relates to work and the world of buying and selling – or commerce. Here, as in sentence 1, it is an uncountable noun.

Notice that the pronunciation of *business* – /'bɪznəs/ – is not the same as *busyness* /'bɪzinəs/ (being busy, having a lot of things to do). Make sure students can pronounce the difference.

Ask students to think of some phrases with *business* in them. If you like, you can ask them to check in their dictionaries. Ask them to distinguish between those with a general English meaning and those related to commerce. For example:

businessman/woman
business management
to do business
business class
it's not your business
let's get down to business
funny business

Note: Don't spend too long on this.

Language note

The use of *business* to mean specifically commercial activity dates from the 18th century. Before that it had a much more general meaning. Clearly, people in the English-speaking world thought businessmen and businesswomen were busy people. Ask students if the word in their language for *businessman* or *businesswoman* comes from a word like *busy*.

Exercise A

Set for individual work and pairwork checking. Point out that these sentences introduce some important basic vocabulary related to business – although it may not seem like that at first glance. Do the first one as an example, e.g., *In general English the capital of a country is the city where the government is. In business English, it means money, especially money used to start or expand a business.*

Point out that there is often a relationship with the general English meaning, and if you know the general English meaning it can help to guess the business meaning (as in the case of *market* or *raw*). Remind students to change the form if necessary, e.g., from verb to noun. Check students understand grammar or other changes.

Feed back, putting the business English meanings in a table on the board. Tell students to use these structures where possible:

- *a(n) X is (a(n)) …* to define a noun
- *to X is to Y* to define a verb

Make sure students can say the words correctly, e.g.,

- vowel in *raw* /ɔː/, and no /w/ at the end
- short /ɪ/ in *mark<u>e</u>t*
- schwa /ə/ in *produc<u>tio</u>n, promo<u>tio</u>n*
- syllabic /l̩/ (or schwa) in *capit<u>al</u>*

Answers

See table below.

Students may not be familiar with all meanings in general English, e.g., *consume* = eat; *fired* = the past of *fire* as in to shoot a bullet; a *production* = a play in a theatre; *promotion* = a better, more responsible job; *raw* = not cooked; *service* = a supply (of buses).

Exercise B

Set for individual work and pairwork checking. Do the first sentence as an example.

Feed back with the whole class. Ask students for any other words they know which have a special meaning in business.

Answers

Model answers:

I'm the director of VJ Sports, a company which sells sports <u>goods</u>. I believe that businesses must understand the needs of <u>consumers</u>. I also believe that workers who are lazy should be <u>fired</u>. Sports and leisure are rapidly growing <u>service</u> industries. As a result, the <u>market</u> for sports equipment is growing. A lot of sports shops are doing a special <u>promotion</u> of our running shoes this week. In order to make more sports shoes, my factory needs more <u>raw</u> materials. Also, the <u>production</u> department needs to increase the number of shoes which are made. I need someone to invest some more <u>capital</u> in my company. They will be sure to get a good <u>return</u> on their investment.

Word	Meaning	Comments
capital	money, especially for starting or expanding a business	change to uncountable
consumers	the people who buy and use a product	change from verb to noun here. Also possible to use the verb *consume* in a business sense meaning *buy and use*
return	profit from investment or sales	
fired	told to leave their job	another verb is *sack*
goods	products	*goods* is generally a plural noun in business, but can also be found as a singular countable: *a good*
market	demand	has other meanings (see Unit 2)
production	making products for sale	
promotion	special offer, e.g., buy one (pair of shoes) and get another (pair) free	change to countable
raw	not yet processed in the factory	goes with *materials*
service	something that you buy but you can't touch; usually something that is useful to you, such as transport or hotel accommodation	*service industry* is a compound noun

Examples of other possible words from general English in business:

pay (n) – the money that workers receive for their work

packaging – putting products in paper or card so that they look attractive

train (v) – teach someone how to work in a particular job

section – a part of a company or a department

labour – as well as work, it can also refer to the people who work: the *labour force*

enterprise – (uncountable noun) the effort, energy and risk needed to start a business project

head – the head of a company is the director; a director *heads* (v) a company

Exercise C

Set the first question for pairwork. See which pair can work out the answer first.

Set the remainder for pairwork. Feed back, building up the prefixes + meaning on the board.

Answers

Model answers:

1 They all have a base word + extra letters at the beginning/prefixes.
2 See table below.
3 Prefix.
4 See table.
5 See table.

Exercise D

Repeat the procedure from Exercise C.

Answers

Model answers:

1 They all have a base word + extra letters at the end/suffixes.
2 See table on next page.
3 Suffix.
4 See table.
5 See table.

Prefix	Base word	Meaning of prefix	Another word
co	operate	with, together	co-director, co-founder
in	come	movement in	intake
in	tangible	not	inefficient
inter	national	between	intercity
mis	calculate	do wrong	misread
non	-durable	not	non-material
out	come	movement out	outgoings, outturn
over	estimate	do more than enough	overcharge
re	arrange	do again	rethink
sub	contractor	under, lesser	subordinate, subnormal
super	market	over or bigger than	supervise
trans	port*	from one state/place to another	transatlantic
under	perform	under or less than should be	underestimate
un	limited	not, opposite	uninteresting

*in fact, here *port* comes from *portare* = carry, not from *port* = place for ships

Base word	Suffix	Effect/meaning of suffix	Another word
activ	ity	adjective ? noun	ability, liability
class	ify	make into	terrify, purify, identify
competit	ive	? adjective	active
direct	or	a person who does something	sailor
dur	able	can be	replaceable
end	less	without	jobless
industri	al	noun ? adjective	natural, commercial
invest	ment	verb ? noun	management
machiner	y	noun ending	category, industry
owner	ship	in the position of being (an owner)	membership, partnership, friendship, relationship
package	d	noun ? verb – in fact, the two parts of speech have the same form but the inflection shows that the change has occurred; note that this word form can also be an adjective	processed
perform	ance	verb ? noun	insurance
tang	ible	can be	legible
transform	(a)tion	verb ? noun	regulation, production

Language note

Note that with prefixes we rarely change the form of the base word. However, with suffixes, there are often changes to the base word, so students must:

● take off the suffix
● try to reconstruct the base word

Exercise E

Set for pairwork. Try to elicit more than just the words from this lesson. Tell students to use adjectives as well as nouns. They can add other words to complete a description (e.g., *service industry*).

Students may use the following words in their discussion of each picture:

1 **supermarket, non-durable goods, promotion**
2 **production** department
3 **machinery**
4 sports **goods**
5 **consumers, durable** goods
6 **raw** materials (for making chocolate)
7 **service** industry (hospitality/tourism or banking)
8 (sales) **performance/income**
9 (**international**) **transport**

Closure

If you have not done so already, refer students to the *Vocabulary bank* at the end of Unit 1. Tell students to explain how this lesson can help them deal with new words in context. If you wish, make three groups. Group A looks at the first section, *Using related words*. Group B looks at the second section, *Removing prefixes*. Group C looks at the third section, *Removing suffixes*. Then make new groups of three with an ABC in each to explain to each other.

1.2 Listening

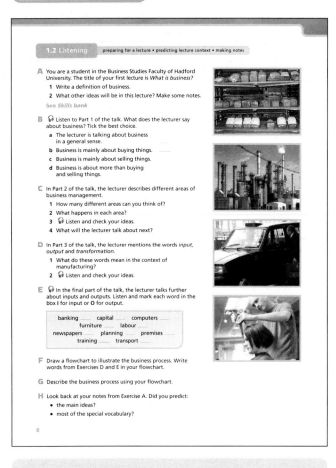

General note

The recording should only be played once, since this reflects what happens in a real lecture. Students should be encouraged to listen for the important points, since this is what a native speaker would take from the text. However, students can be referred to the transcript at the end of the lesson to check their detailed understanding and word recognition, or to try to discover reasons for failing to comprehend.

Read the *Skills bank* at the end of the Course Book unit. Decide when, if at all, to refer students to it. The best time is probably at the very end of the lesson or the beginning of the next lesson, as a summary/revision.

Lesson aims

● prepare for a lecture
● predict lecture content
● make notes

Introduction

1 Show students flashcards of some or all of the words from Lesson 1. Tell students to say the words correctly and quickly as you flash them. Give out each word to one of the students. Say the words again. The student with the word must hold it up. Repeat the process saying the words in context.

2 Refer students to the photos. Briefly elicit ideas of what they depict. (They will look at the different types of business activity in more detail in Exercise E.)

Exercise A

1 Set for pair or group work. Feed back, but do not confirm or correct at this time.

2 Set for pairwork. Elicit some ideas but do not confirm or correct.

Methodology note

You may want to refer students to the *Skills bank – Making the most of lectures* at this point.
Set the following for individual work and pairwork checking. Tell students to cover the points and try to remember what was under each of the Ps – Plan, Prepare, Predict, Produce. Then tell students to work through the points to make sure they are prepared for the lecture they are about to hear.

🎧 Exercise B

Give students time to read the choices. Point out that they are only going to hear the introduction once, as in an authentic lecture situation. Play Part 1. Feed back. If students' answers differ, discuss which is the best answer and why.

Answers

d Business is about more than buying and selling things.

Transcript 🎧 1.1

Part 1

Good morning, everyone, and welcome to the Faculty of Business Studies. I'd like to start today by asking a rather simple question. What is business? Of course, like many simple questions, it's quicker to ask the question than to give an answer.

Right. Let's take the word 'business' first. First, we need to make sure that it is commercial business we are talking about here, because the word 'business' can mean something more general. So what happens in commercial business? People sell things, don't they? I think everyone would agree with that. And other people buy these things, don't they? So, if I advertise my car in the newspaper, and someone buys it, is that 'business'? The answer is no – business is about a lot more than this.

🎧 Exercise C

1/2 Set for pairwork discussion before listening. Tell students to make notes.

3/4 Play Part 2 for students to check their ideas and listen for question 4. Feed back, building up a diagram on the board. Explain that this is a classification diagram. Finally, check the answer to question 4.

Answers

Model answers:

1/2
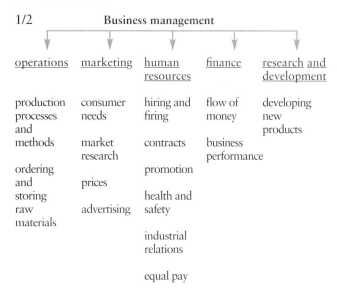

4 The lecturer is now going to answer the question: 'What does a business do?'/'What are the activities that a business organization engages in?'

Transcript 🎧 1.2

Part 2

So what does business involve? What do people in business do? Well, let's take a company that makes chocolate. Someone has to look after the production processes, from ordering and storing the raw materials – the cocoa beans, sugar and so on – to controlling the number of chocolate bars produced in the factory and deciding on the best production methods. This is the area of operations management.

Another important aspect is finding out what the consumers want through market research. Then prices have to be fixed, and the chocolate

advertised and promotions planned. These functions are performed by the marketing department.

Businesses employ people, of course, so some people work in the area of human resources, which is concerned with looking after the employees. This means hiring and firing people, making contracts, questions of health and safety, industrial relations, equal pay, and so on.

Naturally, money is a key element in business and so financial management is a highly important function. Finance people pay attention to the flow of money in and out of the business, and also provide information about the business's performance.

Finally, the company may also have a research and development section that concentrates on developing new products.

So we can see that there is a variety of jobs to be done in business, and it's very important, of course, that people doing these different jobs cooperate and work very closely together. For example, if the marketing people do their work well, they may increase the demand for the products. So the operations managers may have to rethink their production methods to produce more goods.

You'll have noticed, I'm sure, that I've been talking about what people *do* in business, and this gives us an idea about how to answer our original question, 'What is business?' So now perhaps we should ask the question a little differently: 'What does a business do?' In other words, we are asking 'What are the activities that a business organization engages in?'

🎧 Exercise D

Write the words on the board. Remind students about the work on prefixes and suffixes in Lesson 1. Set the questions for pairwork. Play Part 3. Feed back.

Answers

Model answers:

Word	Prefix/suffix and meaning		Meaning of whole
input	in	movement in	elements at beginning of a process
output	out	movement out	results of a process
transformation	trans	from one place or state to another	a process in which something is changed
	ation	noun ending	

Transcript 🎧 1.3
Part 3

We can look at business activity from the point of view of a process in which something is changed from one state to another. Taking the chocolate company as our example, what has to happen in order that you can buy a bar of chocolate from a shop? The answer is that the company buys in *raw materials* – the cocoa, sugar, etc. – and then in the factory the workers use them to make the chocolate bars. Then the bars are packaged and sent to a shop so you can buy one.

However, we can think of raw materials as *inputs* – that is, they are needed to go into the manufacturing process. These raw materials go through a transformation during the production processes – they are mixed together and they turn into solid chocolate. Finally, at the end of the manufacturing process, they come out as nicely packaged bars of chocolate. So we can call the chocolate bars the *outputs*.

So you can see that at a simple level, we have a basic model which explains the manufacturing process.

Methodology note

Up to this point, you have not mentioned how students should record information. Have a look around to see what students are doing. If some are using good methods, make a note and mention that later in the unit.

🎧 Exercise E

Point out that we often give examples of things to help clarify definitions. Give students plenty of time to look at the words in the box, then play Part 4. Feed back.

Answers

banking	O
capital	I
computers	O
furniture	O
labour	I
newspapers	O
planning	I
premises	I
training	I
transport	O

Note: Some things can of course seen as inputs if a company has to spend money on them in order to operate (e.g., banking, computers).

Transcript 🎧 1.4
Part 4

Actually, we can use this model (input – transformation – output) to look at all aspects of business. To do this, we have to apply these concepts to more than just the transformation of raw materials into finished products.

Let's take inputs first. Actually, the list of what we could put into this category is almost endless. Think about it. Suppose you want to start a business and you have what seems like a good idea. Let's say you want to set up a food bar selling lunchtime sandwiches and snacks. Before you even start making the food, you will have to:

- carry out some market research
- make a business plan
- learn about food regulations and hygiene
- design the food items and the food-making process
- find money to start the business
- buy or rent a suitable building
- rearrange the building to suit the business
- invest in equipment and machinery
- buy and store the raw materials
- hire and train staff to help make and sell the food

and so on. So we can see that inputs include more things than just raw materials. There are planning and decisions, time and space, investment, equipment, training – all the skills and abilities of the people involved. One view groups these different kinds of inputs into four main *factors of production*: firstly, land – which includes both the buildings or premises and natural resources; secondly, labour – that is, the people who work in the business; thirdly, capital – which includes both the money invested and also the equipment and machinery owned by the business; and finally, enterprise. Enterprise refers to the fact that someone – an entrepreneur – has to develop a business idea and then work to put it into effect.

Next let's think about outputs. One type of output is *consumer goods*. These are sold to the general public. If they are things that last a long time, such as furniture, cars, computers, etc., they are called *durable* goods. Or if they can be consumed soon after purchase, like food, newspapers, petrol, we call these things *non-durable*.

Another rather different kind of output is *services*. By this I mean things like banking, transport, hairdressing, and so on. Recently services have become a very important area of business activity. Services are intangible. In other words, you can't touch them and they don't last like durable goods. They are not things that you can own or use. Instead, a service provides people with some kind of non-material benefit or help.

Exercise F

Set for individual work and pairwork checking. Feed back, building up a flowchart on the board. Ask for further examples of inputs and outputs.

Answer

Possible answer:

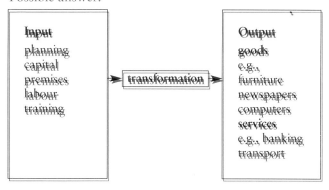

Exercise G

Set for pairwork. Tell students to think of a sentence for each box in the flowchart. Feed back with the whole class, writing suitable sentences on the board.

Answer

Possible answer:

In the business process, various types of inputs are required, such as planning and capital. These inputs are transformed into outputs of different kinds. Outputs can be goods such as furniture, or they can be services such as banking.

Exercise H

Refer students back to their notes from Exercise A.

Closure

1 Look at the pictures of the various business activities. Ask for suggestions for inputs and outputs for each one.

Possible answers:

Bakery. Inputs: flour, yeast, ovens, electricity, baker's skills, etc. Output: bread.

Oil refinery. Inputs: crude oil, chemicals, machinery, etc. Output: petrol.

Taxi. Inputs: car, petrol, driving skills and knowledge, time, etc. Output: transport.

Hairdresser. Inputs: hairdressing equipment, shampoo/hair dye, etc., skills of hairdresser, work of other staff, premises, etc. Output: haircut/style.

2 Refer students to the *Skills bank* if you have not done so already and work through the section *Making the most of lectures*.

1.3 Extending skills

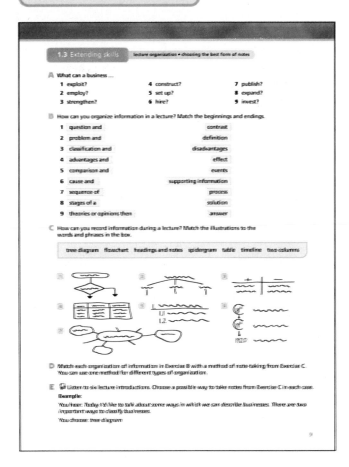

Lesson aims

- identify different types of lecture organization
- use the introduction to a lecture to decide the best form of notes to use

Introduction

Revise the four Ps of preparing for and attending a lecture: Plan, Prepare, Predict, Produce. You could put students into four groups, each group working on one of the stages, then feeding back to the rest of the class.

Exercise A

These words will occur in the listening texts. Set for pairwork. Feed back orally. The more students can say about these words, the better. Accept anything correct but let students explain their choice if they choose a combination not given below.

Answers

Possible answers:

1	exploit	natural resources, opportunities
2	employ	workers, staff, employees
3	strengthen	the business
4	construct	buildings, ships
5	set up	a new business, a factory
6	hire	equipment, staff
7	publish	accounts, books, magazines
8	expand	the business, their operation
9	invest	money

Exercise B

Point out that you can understand a lecture better if you can predict the order of information. Point out also that there are many pairs and patterns in presenting information, e.g., question and answer, or a sequence of events in chronological order.

Set for pairwork. Feed back orally. Check pronunciation. Point out that lecturers may not actually use these words, but if you recognize that what a lecturer is saying is the first of a pair, or the beginning of a sequence, you are ready for the second or next stage later in the lecture.

Answers

1	question and	answer
2	problem and	solution
3	classification and	definition
4	advantages and	disadvantages
5	comparison and	contrast
6	cause and	effect
7	sequence of	events
8	stages of a	process
9	theories or opinions then	supporting information

Exercise C

Identify the first form of notes – a flowchart. Set the rest for individual work and pairwork checking. Feed back, using an OHT or other visual medium if possible.

Answers

1 flowchart
2 tree diagram
3 two columns
4 table
5 headings and notes
6 timeline
7 spidergram

Methodology note

You might like to make larger versions of the illustrations of different note types and pin them up in the classroom for future reference.

Exercise D

Work through the first one as an example. Set for pairwork.

Feed back orally and encourage discussion. Demonstrate how each method of note-taking in Exercise C can be matched with an organizational structure. Point out that:

- a tree diagram is useful for hierarchically arranged information, such as when the information moves from general to specific/examples
- spidergram is more fluid and flexible, and can be used to show connections between things, such as interactions or causes and effects, by using arrows

Answers

Possible answers:

1 question and answer = headings and notes
2 problem and solution = headings and notes or two-column table
3 classification and definition = tree diagram or spidergram
4 advantages and disadvantages = two-column table
5 comparison and contrast = table
6 cause and effect = spidergram
7 sequence of events = timeline or flowchart
8 stages of a process = flowchart (or circle if it is a cycle)
9 theories or opinions then supporting information = headings and notes or two-column table

🎧 Exercise E

Explain that students are going to hear the introductions to several different lectures. They do not have to take notes, only decide what kind of information organization they are going to hear. Work through the example.

Play each introduction. Pause after each one and allow students to discuss then feed back.

After the first four, explain that sometimes lecturers move from one information organization to another, e.g., classification then cause and effect. Play the final two.

Feed back. Students may suggest different answers in some cases. Discuss.

Answers

Possible answers:

1 tree diagram (classification and definition)
2 table (comparison and contrast)
3 spidergram (classification and definition)
4 timeline (sequence of events)
5 spidergram (classification and definition then cause and effect)
6 timeline (sequence of events) then flowchart (stages of a process)

Transcript 🎧 1.5

Introduction 1

Today I'd like to talk about some ways in which we can describe businesses. There are two important ways to classify businesses. Firstly, there is the type of production that the business is engaged in. In other words, what kinds of goods or services does it produce? Secondly, we can look at the type of business ownership. That means we need to see who owns it, how many owners there are, and so on.

Introduction 2

OK, today I'd like to follow on from last week's discussion by looking in a bit more detail at business ownership. In particular, I want to compare sole traders and partnerships. What are their advantages and disadvantages? Is it better to be your own boss or is it better to have a partner?

Introduction 3

Good morning, everyone. There are many people who are interested in businesses, both inside and outside the businesses themselves. The different types of people who have an interest in businesses and their activities are called the *stakeholders*. So who are these stakeholders? What is their interest in a business? In what ways do businesses and stakeholders interact? We will have a look at each group of stakeholders in turn.

Introduction 4

In today's lecture I'm going to look at the history of management. The study of business management is a relatively new subject, compared with, say, mathematics or philosophy – it is often said to have begun in the late 18th century or early 19th century. But it may surprise you to know that the roots of many of today's management ideas can be found in practices and activities that took place a very long time ago, as early as 3000 BCE.

Introduction 5

This week I want to examine some of the effects of the external environment on businesses. Businesses need to keep an eye on what is happening outside the walls of their factories and offices. Why? Because they will have to adapt to changes which are outside their control. I'm going to look at four types of external influence. Then I'll talk about the effects on business of one type of external influence.

Introduction 6

As we all know, money makes the world go round. In today's talk I want to consider the importance of the role of money by first tracing its development from ancient times to the present day. Then we'll look at the flow of money through a business.

Closure

1 Test students on the pairs from Exercise B. Correct pronunciation again if necessary.

2 Refer students to the *Skills bank – Making perfect lecture notes*.

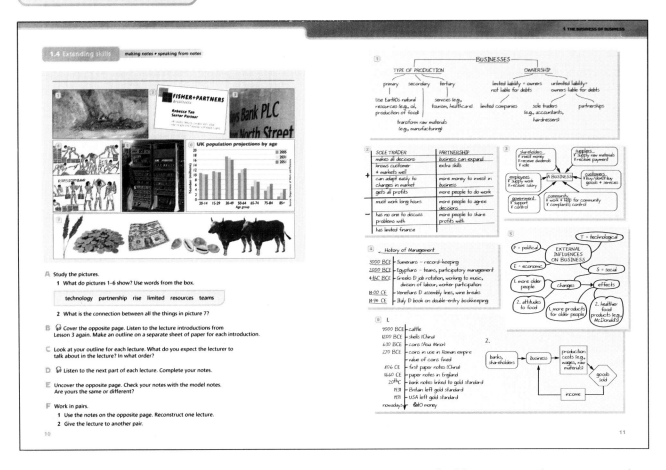

Lesson aims

- make outline notes from lecture introductions
- make notes from a variety of lecture types
- speak from notes

Further practice in:

- predicting lecture content

Introduction

Elicit as much information from the lecture notes in Lesson 2 as possible. If necessary, prompt students by reading parts of the transcript and pausing for students to complete in their own words.

Exercise A

Set for individual work and pairwork checking. Feed back orally but do not confirm or correct. Point out that students are going to hear about all these things in today's lesson. You will return to these illustrations at the end.

For reference, the illustrations show:

1 extracting natural **resources**

2 (someone who works for) a **partnership**

3 plc (= public **limited** company)

4 Egyptians building a pyramid in **teams** = early management technique

5 an early computer = new (at the time) **technology**

6 **rise** in older age groups over the next 50 years in the UK

7 different forms of money: barley, gold coins, banknotes, cowrie shells, cattle

Methodology note

It is best that students close the book at this stage, so they are not tempted to look at the model notes. You can give the instructions for the next few stages orally as required.

🎧 Exercise B

Make sure students understand that they are going to hear the introductions from Lesson 3 again. Ask them briefly if they can remember any of the content from the introductions. Spend a few moments on this if students are able to contribute. Elicit the suggestions for types of notes (Lesson 3, Exercise E).

Explain that this time they must create an outline using an appropriate type of notes. (You can refer them again to the *Skills bank – Making perfect lecture notes*.)

Make sure students understand that they don't need to write a lot at this stage – outlines may consist of just a few words, e.g., the start of a spidergram, the first part of a table or diagram. Play each introduction in turn and give students time to choose a note-type, make the outline and check it with other students.

Feed back, getting all the outlines on the board – you may wish to copy them from the first part of the model notes on the right-hand page, or you may prefer to follow your students' suggestions. Clarify the meaning of new words and check pronunciation.

Transcript 🎧 1.5
Introduction 1
Today I'd like to talk about some ways in which we can describe businesses. There are two important ways to classify businesses. Firstly, there is the type of production that the business is engaged in. In other words, what kinds of goods or services does it produce? Secondly, we can look at the type of business ownership. That means we need to see who owns it, how many owners there are, and so on.

Introduction 2
OK, today I'd like to follow on from last week's discussion by looking in a bit more detail at business ownership. In particular, I want to compare sole traders and partnerships. What are their advantages and disadvantages? Is it better to be your own boss or is it better to have a partner?

Introduction 3
Good morning, everyone. There are many people who are interested in businesses, both inside and outside the businesses themselves. The different types of people who have an interest in businesses and their activities are called the stakeholders. So who are these stakeholders? What is their interest in a business? In what ways do businesses and stakeholders interact? We will have a look at each group of stakeholders in turn.

Introduction 4
In today's lecture I'm going to look at the history of management. The study of business management is a relatively new subject, compared with, say, mathematics or philosophy – it is often said to have begun in the late 18th century or early 19th century. But it may surprise you to know that the roots of many of today's management ideas can be found in practices and activities that took place a very long time ago, as early as 3000 BCE.

Introduction 5
This week I want to examine some of the effects of the external environment on businesses. Businesses need to keep an eye on what is happening outside the walls of their factories and offices. Why?

Because they will have to adapt to changes which are outside their control. I'm going to look at four types of external influence. Then I'll talk about the effects on business of one type of external influence.

Introduction 6
As we all know, money makes the world go round. In today's talk I want to consider the importance of the role of money by first tracing its development from ancient times to the present day. Then we'll look at the flow of money through a business.

Methodology note
Spiral bound or stitched/stapled notebooks are not the best way to keep lecture notes. It is impossible to reorganize or add extra information at a later date, or make a clean copy of notes after a lecture. Encourage students, therefore, to use a loose leaf file, but make sure that they organize it in a sensible way, with file dividers, and keep it tidy. Tell students to use a separate piece of paper for each outline in this lecture.

Exercise C
Set for pair or group work. Feed back, but do not confirm or correct. Students should be able to predict reasonably well the kind of information which will fit into their outline.

🎧 Exercise D
Before you play the next part of each lecture, refer students to their outline notes again. Tell them to orally reconstruct the introduction from their notes. They don't have to be able to say the exact words, but they should be able to give the gist.

Remind students that they are only going to hear the next part of each lecture once. Play each extract in turn, pausing if necessary to allow students to make notes but not replaying any section. Tell students to choose an appropriate type of notes for this part of the lecture – it could be a continuation of the type they chose for the introduction, or it could be a different type.

Transcript 🎧 1.6
Lecture 1
OK. Of course, businesses produce different types of goods. And this is one way in which we can classify business activity – that is, according to the type of production. Here there are three main production types: primary, secondary and tertiary. First there are the industries which exploit the Earth's natural resources. This may be taking raw

materials from the Earth, such as metals, oil, coal, and so on. Or it may involve the production of food through farming and fishing. These types of activity are called primary production. Secondary production involves the transformation of raw materials into goods. All manufacturing is secondary production, as are building and construction – of things like ships, houses, offices, and so on. Finally, tertiary production refers to the service industries. Tourism, entertainment, health care are some examples of services; I'm sure you can think of others.

The type of ownership is the second important way to distinguish between different businesses. It's concerned with whether companies have limited liability or not. In a limited company, the liability for debts is limited to the company. This means that if the business owes money, the owners themselves are not liable for the debts. In other words, they don't have to pay the debts with their own money. A limited company therefore has a separate legal identity from its owners.

In a business with unlimited liability, the owners are liable for the business's debts. This means that they must pay all the debts, even if it means that they have to lose everything they own – including their house. If a business that is not limited is owned and run by one person, they are called a sole trader. If there are two or more people, the business is called a partnership. Most sole traders can be found in tertiary production – in other words, the service industries. For example, they may be hairdressers, accountants or shop owners.

🎧 1.7

Lecture 2

Let's start with sole traders. As we know, a sole trader is a one-person business. In the UK, this is by far the most common form of business ownership. Many people like this way of operating because they have total control of everything. They can make all the decisions quickly and easily. In fact, a common reason for people starting their own business is for exactly this reason. They want to be their own boss.

Secondly, sole traders get to know their customers well, which means they can quickly tell when markets change. And because they are small, they can adapt easily to changing market conditions and so they can remain competitive.

Another point is that, although a sole trader may employ one or two people, since they own the business, they get all the profits – which is of course a major benefit.

However, there are some disadvantages of running your own business. The first thing is that because you are working on your own, you may have to work very long hours. And you may not be able to take a holiday. Also, you have no one to talk to about problems with the business. And finally – possibly the worst problem – the amount of money you can raise to invest in your business is going to be quite small.

One answer to these problems, of course, is to find one or more partners. This is what many people do when they want to expand their business. If you take on a partner for your business, you will obviously gain additional skills because everyone has different skills and abilities. So if you have people with different skills from your own, you can develop new activities and thus strengthen the business.

Bringing in more people also means that there is more money to invest, of course – which is a very important point. And finally, there are more people to do the work, so things may become easier.

However, having a partner does not solve all the sole trader's problems. With one or more partners, the sole trader is no longer able to make all the decisions but has to make sure everyone agrees. Also, of course, the sole trader no longer gets all the profits but has to share them with the partners.

🎧 1.8

Lecture 3

First of all, obviously, there are the owners. The owners of a limited company invest capital in the company, and this capital is divided into shares. Each owner has a number of shares and is called a shareholder. Shareholders expect to receive some financial return, or dividend, for their investment. In the case of public limited companies, their shares can be bought and sold on the Stock Exchange. Public limited companies may have many thousands of shareholders, who are members of the public. Shareholders can vote on some matters of company policy, such as, for example, the appointment of a new director.

An important group of people are those who work for the company – in other words, its employees. Employers hire employees to do what is necessary for the business to operate. All employees are paid a wage or a salary by the business in return for their work. Some companies encourage their employees to take part in company decision-making – though some do not.

Who are the stakeholders that are outside the business? First, there are the other businesses which supply goods and raw materials to enable the business to function – in other words, suppliers. A business must have a good relationship with its suppliers, because, for example, it may need suppliers to respond quickly to requests for raw materials. Equally, suppliers are themselves businesses, and so they need to be paid in good time.

Another group of external stakeholders is the customers. In a way, this group is perhaps the most important of all, for without customers, no business can survive. Businesses must have a very good idea of what their customers want to buy. If they make a mistake about this, it can be disastrous. For example, when Coca-Cola decided to launch a new type of cola with a slightly different taste, customers didn't like it and the company lost a lot of money.

Then there is the community in which the business operates. Businesses provide work for people in the community, which of course can benefit the community. Businesses may also help their communities through raising money for local charities. At the same time, what a business does may affect the community in a negative way, for example through noise or pollution or increased road traffic. As a result, people may complain about what the business does and try to control its activity.

Finally, governments also have an interest in businesses. They want businesses to be successful because this generates work and wealth for the country. So they may support businesses through their economic or tax policies. At the same time, governments need to control the activity of businesses in order to protect society. For example, there are laws about how many hours people can work, about working in safe conditions, and so on.

🎧 1.9

Lecture 4

Let's look at some examples. With the development of writing around 3000 BCE in Sumeria in Asia, the Sumerians started to use record-keeping systems – very important in business, obviously.

Later, from around 2000 BCE, in terms of people management, the Egyptians were using large teams of workers in the enormous projects to build pyramids. They also tried a kind of participatory management in which workers could 'get things off their chests'.

The Greeks had some sophisticated people management techniques in the 4th century BCE. These included job rotation, working to music, and division of labour. They also, like the Egyptians, had some worker participation in management.

In the Middle Ages, there were some important developments. For example, in the 15th century, the Venetians, who were expert shipbuilders, used assembly-line techniques for building their ships. They also established wine breaks several times a day for their workers – but I don't think this technique should be used today!

Also in Italy, in 1494, the first book on double-entry bookkeeping was published. The simple practice of recording sums of money in columns so that they could be added up easily was a key development in financial management.

🎧 1.10

Lecture 5

In order to analyse external influences on business it is helpful to use a technique known as 'PEST' analysis. PEST is an acronym – that means each letter stands for a word. The first letter, P, stands for the political factors which can affect businesses. E stands for economic factors. There are a great many of these, and the economic environment is very important for businesses. S means social factors, or trends and activities taking place in society at large. Finally, T is for technological factors. Developments in technology have always been responsible for changes in the world of work.

So how might social factors cause businesses to change what they do? Well, one area of change is in the products themselves. If society changes, then businesses have to change the products that they offer. For example, in some countries there is a falling birth rate and a big rise in the number of older people. So companies need to think about increasing the types of products they have which are designed for older people. Society may also change its attitudes, or the way it thinks about certain things: for example, many people now believe that certain types of foods, such as French fries, burgers, and so on, are bad for health. As a result, McDonald's, the fast food chain, now sells low fat 'healthy' meals alongside its cheeseburgers.

🎧 1.11

Lecture 6

Well, what is money? Money is anything that is used to pay for goods. Without money, we have to barter – that is, we exchange one type of good for another. But bartering has certain problems, such as: How do you compare the values of different goods? How do you give change?

In the ancient world, some goods were especially valuable and so they began to be used for payment. One of the oldest types of money, used as early as 9000 BCE, was cattle. In China around 1200 BCE, shells were used as money – and shells have continued to be used in primitive societies even to the present day.

The first known use of coins was in Asia Minor – at around 630 BCE. From Asia, the use of coins spread quickly to Greece, where they were used from 600 BCE. By around 270 BCE coins were in use throughout the Roman empire.

As time went on, the value of coins was fixed according to the amount of gold or silver that they contained. This type of money – where the money is itself valuable – is called *commodity money*. One problem with commodity money is that people often 'debased' it. That is, they mixed a cheap metal with the gold or silver.

An important development in the history of money came with 'representative' or 'credit' money – that is, with something which represented money but was not actually the valuable thing itself. Paper notes were used in China as early as 806 CE, but in England it wasn't until 1660 that people realized that notes could perform the same function as coins. By the early 20th century most countries were using banknotes linked to a 'gold standard'. However, in 1931 Britain left the gold standard and the US dollar abandoned it in 1971. Nowadays, the world's currencies are 'fiat' money – that is, money which can't be changed into something valuable. Instead, the value of the currency is decided by market demand and by governments.

Money is, of course, one of the key factors of production. Businesses raise money to finance their activities, often through borrowing from banks or shareholders. Money has to be paid out to cover the production costs, such as wages and cost of raw materials. Then, when the goods are sold, money flows back into the business. So manufacturers must spend money on the input and transformation processes, but expect to receive back more than they spend, in order to make a profit.

Exercise E

Allow students to uncover the opposite page or open their books. Give them plenty of time to compare their answers with the model notes. Feed back on the final question.

Exercise F

1 Ask students to work in pairs. Assign a set of notes to each pair. They must try to reconstruct the lecture orally – including the introduction – from the notes.

2 Put the pairs together in groups of four, with different topics. Each pair should give their lecture to the other pair.

Closure

1 Work on any problems you noticed during the pairwork (Exercise F).

2 Refer back to the pictures at the top of the Course Book page. Students should now be able to name them with confidence.

Extra activities

1 Work through the *Vocabulary bank* and *Skills bank* if you have not already done so, or as a revision of previous study.

2 Use the *Activity bank* (Teacher's Book additional resources section, Resource 1A).

A Set the crossword for individual work (including homework) or pairwork.

Answers

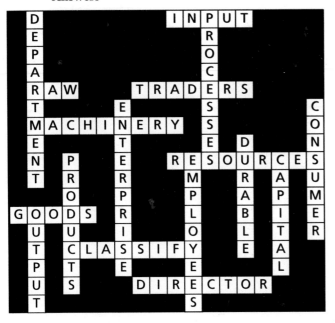

B Play noughts and crosses in pairs. There are two boards. The first contains words with affixes, the second contains business concepts.

Teach students how to play noughts and crosses if they don't know – they take it in turns to choose a word and try to use the word/phrase in context or explain it means. If they succeed, they can put their symbol – a nought **0** or a cross **X** – in that box. If a person gets three of their own symbols in a line, they win.

First board: Tell students to remove the affixes to find the basic word in each case. Make sure they can tell you the meaning of the basic word (e.g., *limit* for *unlimited*) but don't elicit the meaning of the affixed word at this stage. Put students in pairs to play the game. Monitor and adjudicate.

Second board: Put students in different pairs to play the second game. Clearly, this time they have to actually remember the facts from the lectures. Don't let them look back at notes.

3 Each of the mini lectures from Lesson 4 can lead on to a great deal more work. Tell students to research one of the following, according to which group they ended in. Explain that they must come back and report to the rest of the class in the next lesson/next week.

Lecture	Research
1	Another way in which businesses can be classified with examples of each type (i.e., public versus private sector)
2	The process of becoming a limited company and the rules which must be followed by limited companies
3	The difference between private and public limited companies and the advantages and disadvantages of each
4	Writers on business in the 18th and early 19th centuries, e.g., Adam Smith, Robert Owen, Charles Babbage. What books did they publish and when? What were some of their ideas?
5	Ways in which political, economic and technological factors can cause businesses to have to change
6	(i) More information on bartering: when and where was it used? What are the problems with it? (ii) Why did Britain and other countries leave the gold standard?

4 Brainstorm note-taking techniques. For example:
- use spacing between points
- use abbreviations
- use symbols
- underline headings
- use capital letters
- use indenting
- make ordered points
- use different colours
- use key words only

2 THE ORGANIZATION OF WORK

Unit 2 looks at different organizational structures within organizations, from large, traditional hierarchies to flatter 'delayered' structures. The first reading text discusses possible advantages and disadvantages of these different structures. The second reading text looks at what makes a successful business leader, and identifies different types of manager and leadership style.

Note that students will need dictionaries for some exercises in this unit.

Skills focus

Reading

- using research questions to focus on relevant information in a text
- using topic sentences to get an overview of the text

Writing

- writing topic sentences
- summarizing a text

Vocabulary focus

- English–English dictionaries:
  headwords
  definitions
  parts of speech
  phonemes
  stress markers
  countable/uncountable
  transitive/intransitive

Key vocabulary

administrator	labour (n)	procedure
boardroom	layer	professional (n and adj)
CEO (chief executive officer)	leadership	resource (n)
communication	manage	responsibility
complex (adj)	management	rigid
delayered	manager	role
delegate (v)	managerial	routine
hierarchy	managing director	skill
informal	market (n and v)	skilled
initiative	marketable	structure (n)
job description	marketer	task
	marketing	team

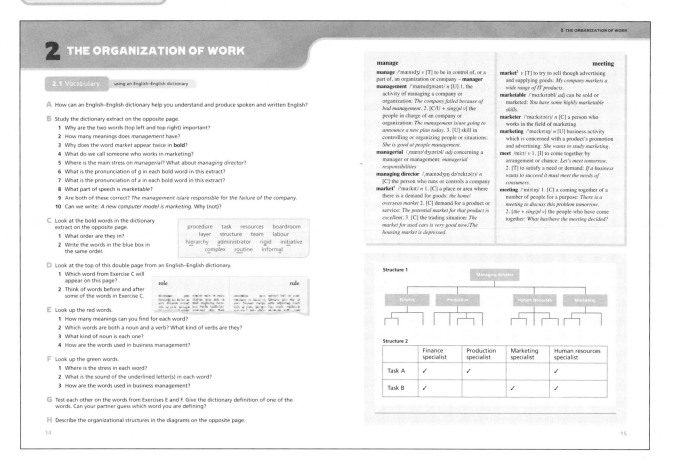

General note

Take in a set of English–English dictionaries.

Read the *Vocabulary bank* at the end of the Course Book unit. Decide when, if at all, to refer students to it. The best time is probably at the very end of the lesson or the beginning of the next lesson, as a summary/revision.

Lesson aims

- learn how to make full use of an English–English dictionary
- gain fluency in the target vocabulary

Introduction

1 Revise the vocabulary from the last unit. Check:
   - meaning
   - pronunciation
   - spelling
2 Ask students whether they use a translation (bilingual) dictionary or an English–English (monolingual) dictionary. Elicit the advantages and disadvantages of a translation dictionary.

Answers

Possible answers:

+	–
good when you know the word in your own language and need a translation into English	not good when there is more than one possible translation of a word – which is the correct one?
when you look up an English word, the translation into your language is easy to understand	English–English dictionaries often have more examples and precise definitions of each word

Methodology note

Recent research has shown that, despite the insistence of generations of language teachers on the use of English–English dictionaries in class, nearly 90 per cent of students use a translation dictionary when studying on their own.

Exercise A

Ask the question as a general discussion. Confirm but do not explain anything. Point out that the next exercise will make the value of this kind of dictionary clear.

Answers

Model answers:

The following information is useful for spoken English:

- stress
- pronunciation of individual phonemes – particularly when a phoneme has multiple pronunciations

The following information is useful for written English:

- information about the type of word – C/U; T/I
- the spelling – students might make the point that if you don't know the spelling, you can't find the word in the first place, but point out that you can often guess the possible spelling – for example, *management* could be *managment*, but if you don't find it there, you can try it with an *e* in the middle
- examples of the word in use to memorize
- some synonyms for lexical cohesion – this is a very important point, although you may not want to get into this now

Exercise B

Set for individual work and pairwork checking. Feed back, ideally using an OHT or other visual display of the dictionary extract to highlight points. You might suggest that students annotate the dictionary extract in their books, highlighting symbols, etc., and writing notes on the meaning and value.

Answers

Model answers:

1 They tell you the first and last words on the pages to help you locate the word you want.
2 Three.
3 Because the same word can be a noun or a verb.
4 A *marketer*.
5 *Managerial* – on the third syllable; *managing director* – on the second syllable of *director*.
6 /dʒ/ (e.g., *manage*); /ŋ/ (e.g., *marketing*). Ask what other pronunciation *g* can have and elicit examples such as *gas*, *go*, *get*. As a guide, *g* is more usually 'hard'. The soft pronunciation /dʒ/ occurs before *e*, *i* or *y* – usually in words of French or Latin origin. The digraph *ng* /ŋ/ occurs at the end of words in present participles or gerunds
7 Four pronunciations: /æ/ or /ɑː/ in stressed syllables; /ɪ/ or /ə/ in unstressed syllables.

8 Adjective – *able* marks an adjective.
9 Both are correct, but once you have chosen to use one form, you should not use the other in the same text.
10 Usually *no* – because *to market* is transitive, so it must have an object. In this example, we would expect a *new computer model* to be the object, i.e., the action is done to it, as in *The company is marketing a new computer model*. Alternatively, we could find a passive sentence: *A new computer model is being marketed* (*by the company*). However, in business, people often use words in unusual ways, so it might not be impossible to find examples of the use of *market* as an intransitive verb.

Exercise C

Note: If students are from a Roman alphabet background, you may want to omit this exercise.

1 Students should quickly be able to identify alphabetical order.
2 Set for individual work and pairwork checking. Feed back, getting the words on the board in the correct order. Don't worry about stress and individual phonemes at this point – students will check this later with their dictionaries.

Language note

It may seem self-evident that words in a dictionary are in alphabetical order. But students from certain languages may not automatically recognize this. In the famous Hans Wehr dictionary of written Arabic, for example, you must first convert a given word to its root and look that up, then find the derived form. So *aflaaj* (the plural of *fallaj* = irrigation channel) will not be found under A but under F since the root is *f-l-j*.

Exercise D

1 Set for pairwork. Feed back orally, explaining the principle if necessary.
2 Set for pairwork. Ask each pair to choose five words to work on. Ask them to find words connected with business management if they can. Feed back orally.

Answers

1 *Routine* will appear on the double page spread.
2 Answers depend on which words students choose.

Exercise E

Give out the dictionaries, if you have not already done so.

Remind students that dictionaries number multiple meanings of the same part of speech and multiple parts of speech. Remind them also of the countable/uncountable and transitive/intransitive markers. (Note that different dictionaries may use different methods for indicating these things. The *Oxford Advanced Learner's Dictionary*, for example, uses [V] for intransitive verbs and [Vn] for transitive verbs.)

Write the headings of the table in the Answers section on the board, and work through the first word as an example.

Set for pairwork. Feed back, building up the table in the Answers section on the board. (Students' answers will vary – accept any appropriate meanings and definitions.)

Answers

Model answers:

Word	Part of speech	Type	Main meaning in business	Main meaning(s) in general English
procedure	n	C	a set of rules for how a business activity should be carried out or managed (e.g., sending out invoices; dealing with a problem worker)	a set of actions necessary to do something (e.g., how to apply for a driving licence)
task	n	C	a piece of work that must be done	the same
resources	n	C, usually plural	used with *human* it means the department which deals with the people in an organization; it can also be used with *financial* to mean *money*	qualities or possessions that are to be used; often used in relation to a country (e.g., natural resources such as coal, oil)
boardroom	n	C	the room where the directors of a company have their meetings	
layer	n	C	a level of management	a thickness of a material (e.g., layers of different types of rock)
	v	T		cut hair or arrange clothes in layers
structure	n	C	when used with *organizational*, a type of organization	something that has been made or constructed
	n	U*	when used with *organizational*, the concept of structure in organizations	how the parts of something make a whole (e.g., brain structure)
	v	T		arrange parts into a whole
team	n	C	a group of people who work on a task together	a group of people who play together in a game (e.g., football team)
labour	n	U	1. workers, considered as a group, e.g., organized labour; 2. work	1. work; 2. giving birth; 3. (Labour) UK political party
	v	I	work	the same

*words are often U when they mean a concept or idea and C when a specific example or type, as in *All organizations have structure* versus *This company has a hierarchical structure*

Exercise F

Remind students how stress and the pronunciation of individual phonemes are shown in a dictionary. Refer them to the key to symbols in the dictionary if necessary. Write the headings of the table in the Answers section on the board, and work through the first word as an example.

Set for pairwork. Feed back, building up the table in the Answers section on the board.

Answers

Model answers:

Word/stress	Sound	Part of speech	Type	Main meaning in business
'hierarchy	/aɪ/	n	C/U	a pyramid-shaped organizational structure. In a business hierarchy, the CEO or MD is at the top, with several layers below, each person having responsibility for a number of people below him/her
ad'ministrator	/ə/	n	C	a person whose job is to organize
'rigid	/dʒ/	adj		a rigid hierarchy is one where there are strict definitions of jobs and many layers of management
i'nitiative	/ʃ/	n	U/C	(U) being able to do things at work without having to be told to first; (C) a new plan or scheme
'complex	/ɒ/	adj		not easy or simple. A complex production process has many stages; a complex organization has many different parts
rou'tine	/uː/	n	C	a regular way of working
		adj		1. something that always happens (e.g., a *routine* inspection); 2. boring (e.g., a *routine* job)
in'formal	/ə/	adj		not following fixed rules

Exercise G

Demonstrate how to do the exercise by giving a few definitions and getting students to tell you the word (without reading from the board or their books, if possible). Stick to business/management usage rather than general English and encourage students to do the same. Point out that dictionaries often use a small set of words that help to define, e.g., *place, set, method, kind, type, principle, person*. Give definitions using these words and ask students to identify what you are defining, e.g., *It's a place where the directors meet; It's a person who organizes*; etc.

Exercise H

Set for pairwork. Students should first say what types of organizational structure the diagrams illustrate. Then they should try to describe the diagrams, saying how people might work differently in the two types of organization.

Answers

Model answers:

Structure 1 – hierarchical (or pyramid) structure in which several people are managed by one person above them.

Structure 2 – task (or matrix) structure in which people work together as a team.

Closure

1 Remind students that you can identify the part of speech of an unknown word by looking at the words before or after the word, i.e.,

- nouns often come before and after verbs, so if you know that X is a verb, the next content word before or after is probably a noun
- nouns often come immediately after articles
- verbs often come after names and pronouns
- adjectives come before nouns or after the verb *be*

Come back to this point when you are giving feedback on the reading texts in this unit.

2 Ask students if they have experienced the organizational structures illustrated. Or can they think of examples? Can they imagine any other kinds of organizational structure?

2.2 Reading

General note

Take in an English–English dictionary.

Read the *Skills bank* section on doing reading research at the end of the Course Book unit. Decide when, if at all, to refer students to it. The best time is probably at the very end of the lesson or the beginning of the next lesson, as a summary/ revision. Alternatively, you could refer students to the *Skills bank* after Exercise C.

Lesson aims

● prepare for reading research
● use research questions to structure reading research

Introduction

1 Hold up an English–English dictionary and say a word from Lesson 1. Ask students where approximately they will find it in the dictionary – i.e., beginning, middle, two-thirds of the way through, etc. Follow their advice and read the word at the top left. Ask students if the target word will be before or after. Continue until you get to the right page. Repeat with several more words from Lesson 1.

2 Give definitions of some of the words from Lesson 1 for students to identify.

Exercise A

Set the question for pairwork. Feed back ideas to the whole class.

Exercise B

Refer students to the photographs. Discuss answers for the first question with the whole class. Set the remaining questions for pairwork. General discussion to check answers.

Answers

Possible answers:
See table on next page.

Type of work	Team work?	Skilled?	Hierarchy
1 individual employees working on a production line	no – in a production line each person completes their own stage of a process. This is called 'division of labour'	no	these people are probably unskilled manual workers – usually at the bottom of the hierarchy in a manufacturing production process
2 a group of people working together on a task – in this case, medical staff during an operation	yes	yes	these people are higher in a hierarchy than the worker in the picture above
3 a secretary is carrying out her boss's instructions	no	the secretary is skilled; bosses are usually skilled and educated – though it is possible that they are not (depending on the company and the role)!	this is a typical hierarchical situation: the boss tells the secretary what to do
4 a potter making a pot	no – this is an example of a 'craft' production process in which one person working on their own makes (most of) the complete object. Not many objects at a time can be made on this basis	yes – this worker is highly skilled and may take a long time to learn his trade	he may be employed, and fairly low in the hierarchy; or he may work for himself (self-employed)

Exercise C

Students may or may not be able to articulate preparation for reading. Elicit ideas. One thing they must identify – reading for a purpose. Point out that they should always be clear about the purpose of their reading. A series of questions to answer, or **research questions**, is one of the best purposes.

Refer students to the *Skills bank* at this stage if you wish.

Exercise D

1 Set for pairwork. Elicit some ideas, but do not confirm or correct.

2 Refer students to the Hadford University research questions at the bottom of the page. Check comprehension. If students have come up with better research questions, write them on the board for consideration during the actual reading.

Exercise E

Remind students about topic sentences if they haven't mentioned them already in Exercise C. Give them time to read the topic sentences in this exercise. Point out that the topic sentences are in order, so they give a rough overview of the whole text. Some topic sentences clearly announce what the paragraph will be about. Others may only give a hint of how it will develop.

1 Set for group discussion.

2 Remind students of the research questions. Look at the first research question as an example, then set for pairwork. Point out that they may match a research question to more than one topic sentence, and that some topic sentences may not relate to the research questions (i.e., they don't have to write a number for each topic sentence).

3 Explain that here students look at the topic sentences they *didn't* number in question 2, and try to work out the likely content of each paragraph. Do the first as an example, then set for pairwork. Feed back, eliciting and checking that they are reasonable possibilities, based on the topic sentence. You can accept multiple ideas for the same paragraph provided they are all possible.

Answers

Possible answers:

1 Large, traditional hierarchies; flatter hierarchies; plus other types, of which two are mentioned here: task structure and person structure.

2 The following is probably the best prediction:

In the first half of the 20ᵗʰ century, organizations tended to be controlled in rigid hierarchies.	1
However, there are a number of problems with large, traditional hierarchies.	
As a result, some companies have moved towards flatter hierarchies, …	2
However, different types of company may need different types of organizations.	3
There are other possible ways in which organizations can be structured.	
In the 'task' structure, several people work together as a team, using their different skills.	3
Finally, a 'person' structure can be found where there is a group of people who are experts in their field.	3
Of course, in real life, organizations rarely have just one structure.	

3 Answers depend on the students. Discuss.

Exercise F

Point out, if students have not already said this, that the topic sentences are normally the first sentences of each paragraph. Tell students to compare the contents of each paragraph with their predictions. Encourage them to take notes as they read.

If necessary, the reading can be set for homework.

Closure

1 Unless you have set the reading for homework, do some extra work on oral summarizing as a comprehension check after reading (See *Skills bank – Using topic sentences to summarize*). Students work in pairs. One student says a topic sentence and the other student summarizes the paragraph from memory in his/her own words, or if necessary reads the paragraph again and then summarizes it without looking.

You may also want to redo the text as a jigsaw – the text is reproduced in the additional resources section (Resource 2B) to facilitate this.

2 As a further activity after reading, remind students of the note-taking skills practised in Unit 1. Discuss appropriate note-taking forms for this text. They can then write notes on the text. Tell them to keep their notes, as they will be useful for the summary exercise in Lesson 3.

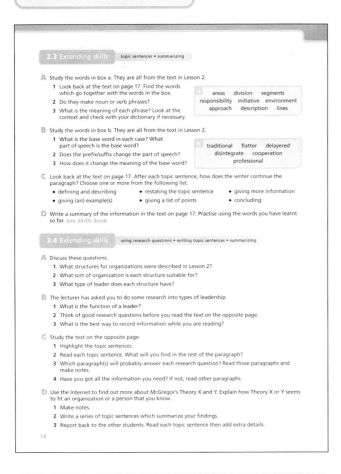

General note

Take in a set of English–English dictionaries.

Lesson aims

- identify paragraph structure
- produce good topic sentences and a summary text

Further practice in:

- vocabulary from Lesson 2

Introduction

Test students on the factual information in the text, e.g., *Who told companies to get rid of some of the layers in their organizations? When did he do this?* If a student says, accurately: *I didn't read about that. It wasn't relevant to my research*, accept it and praise the student.

Exercise A

Set for pairwork. Feed back orally, asking students for the location of the phrase.

Methodology note

Don't help students to find words in a text. It's a key reading skill to be able to pattern match, i.e., get a word in your mind's eye and then find it on the page.

Answers

Possible answers:

Phrase	Noun or verb phrase?	Meaning
functional areas	noun phrase	parts of a business concerned with a particular function, e.g., marketing
division of labour	noun phrase	dividing the work so that each person has one small job to do. Based on a system of 'scientific analysis' of work devised by F.W. Taylor at the beginning of the 20th century (in *The Principles of Scientific Management* 1911)
clearly defined segments	noun phrase	the bits of work which go to make up the whole job. They have a very clear beginning and end, and clear instructions
take responsibility (for their work)	verb phrase	work without being told how to or what to do. The worker feels capable and trusted to do the work
use their initiative	verb phrase	contribute or use their own ideas in their work
(a changing) business environment	noun phrase	the business world outside the company which changes according to many social, political and other factors
a team approach	noun phrase	a way of working, using teams
a (precise) job description	noun phrase	a document stating exactly what an employee should do in his/her job
(clear) lines of management	noun phrase	an organizational structure which makes it clear who is in charge of who/what
communication lines	noun phrase	who communicates with who

Exercise B

Set for individual work and pairwork checking. Students can check these points in a dictionary. Feed back, taking apart the words and showing how the affixes can change the meaning.

Answers

Model answers:

Word	Base word	Affix and meaning
traditional	tradition (n)	*al* = noun ? adjective
flatter	flat (adj)	*er* = comparative form; note that *t* doubles
delayered	layer (n)	*de* = negate, reverse (a process) *ed* = verb ? adjective
disintegrate	integrate (v)	*dis* = negate, reverse (a process)
cooperation	operate (v)	*co* = together, with *(t)ion* = verb ? noun
professional	profession (n)	*al* = noun ? adjective – but in this case, the adjective form is used as a noun, meaning the person

Exercise C

Do the first paragraph first, then set the rest for individual work followed by pairwork checking.

Feed back with the whole class. Ask students to locate the discourse markers used which help to identify the way in which the paragraph is continued. Build the table in the Answers section below on the board (or on an OHT or PowerPoint slide).

An alternative procedure would be to look at each topic sentence in turn and feed back before moving on to the next topic sentence.

Discourse note

In academic writing, topic sentences often consist of a general point. The sentences that follow then support the general statement in various ways, such as:

- giving a definition and/or a description
- giving examples
- giving lists of points (e.g., arguments or reasons)
- restating the topic sentence in a different way to help clarify it
- giving more information and detail on the topic sentence to clarify it

Often – but not always – the type of sentence is shown by a 'discourse marker' – e.g., *for example, first of all,* etc. This helps to signal to the reader how the writer sees the link between the sentences and is therefore a good clue as to purpose of the sentences following the topic sentence.

Answers

Possible answers:

Topic sentence	Followed by	Discourse markers
In the first half of the 20th century, organizations tended to be controlled in rigid hierarchies.	defining and describing (hierarchical structure)	none – but note the way in which the link is made: *In this type of structure …*
However, there are a number of problems with large, traditional hierarchies.	a list of points (problems)	First of all, … Secondly, … Finally, …
As a result, some companies have moved towards flatter hierarchies, as recommended by Tom Peters in his book *Thriving on Chaos* (1987).	restating the topic sentence (clarifying the change in hierarchy)	In other words, …
	giving more information (about team approaches)	In addition, …
However, different types of company may need different types of organizations.	giving an example	For example, …
There are other possible ways in which organizations can be structured.	giving an example	For instance, …
	defining and describing	
In the 'task' structure, several people work together as a team, using their different skills.	defining and describing	
Finally, a 'person' structure can be found where there is a group of people who are experts in their field.	defining and describing	
Of course, in real life, organizations rarely have just one structure.	restating the topic sentence	In fact, …

Exercise D

Students can work individually (for homework) or in pairs (in class). Ask them to write a summary in about 150 words. They should use their own words as far as possible, but they should also try to incorporate the vocabulary they have practised so far. Refer students to the *Skills bank – Using topic sentences to summarize*.

Methodology note

There are two reasons for students to use their own words in written work (except when quoting and acknowledging sources):

1 The work involved in rewording information and ideas helps us to mentally process them and to retain them in memory.

2 Copying whole sentences from the work of other writers is plagiarism (unless the quotation is acknowledged). Universities disapprove of plagiarism and may mark down students who plagiarize. In the commercial world an accusation of plagiarism can cause legal problems, and in the academic world it can severely damage a teacher's reputation and career.

Closure

Tell students to define some of the business organization terms from the text on page 17. Alternatively, give definitions of some of the words and tell students to identify the words.

2.4 Extending skills

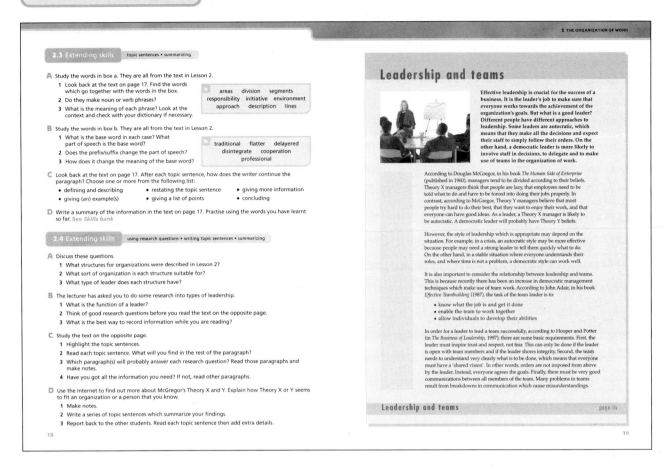

Lesson aims

- use research questions to structure reading research
- write topic sentences for a short research report/summary

Introduction

Give some verbs from the text in Lesson 2 which are followed by a preposition plus noun. Ask students to try to complete the phrase with the correct preposition, and noun if they can manage it. Alternatively, write the whole phrase on the board, leaving a space for the preposition.

Suggestions:

to divide into (functional areas)

to take responsibility for (their work/the quality of their work)

to adapt to (a changing business environment)

to work together on (a task)

to react to (change)

to work together as (a team)

to have control over (the professionals)

Exercise A

Group discussion. Build up a table on the board, students' books closed. Students can contribute their own ideas on suitability of the structure for different types of organization.

Answers

Model answers:

Structure	Suitable for	Type of leader
hierarchy	big organizations	one person at the top (e.g., the managing director or CEO)
club structure	small organizations	one person – like a spider in a web (the other people have the same beliefs and values)
task structure	problem-solving organizations	the leader can change depending on the task
person structure	groups of professionals	may have no clear leader

Exercise B

1 This question relates to the reading text on page 19 and acts as a pre-question. Set for pairwork. Feed back orally.

2 Remind students of the importance of research questions – reading for a purpose. Set for pairwork. Feed back, writing up suitable questions on the board.

3 Elicit the different kinds of notes you can use – see Unit 1 *Skills bank*. Remind students to think about the best kind of notes before and while they are reading.

Methodology note

It is good for students to get into the habit of thinking about the form of their notes before they read a text in detail. If they don't do this, they will tend to be drawn into narrative notes rather than notes which are specifically designed to help them answer their research questions.

Answers

Possible answers:

1 The simplest (and most common) view is that a leader tells a group of other people what to do. However, there are other (more sophisticated) views – some of which are given in the text.

2 Questions such as: *How many types of leaders are there? What type of leader is best for what purpose or organization? What sort of people become leaders?* etc.

3 See Unit 1 *Skills bank*.

Exercise C

1/2 Remind students of the importance of topic sentences. Set for individual work and pairwork checking. Encourage students not to read ahead. Perhaps you should ask students to cover the text and only reveal each topic sentence in turn, then discuss possible contents of the paragraph. Remind them that this is technique for previewing a text and at this point they do not need to read every part of the text. This will come later. If you have an OHP or other visual display, you can tell students to close their books and just display the topic sentences (additional resources section, Resource 2C), or you can give them out on a handout.

3 Set the choice of paragraphs for pairwork. Students then read individually, make notes and compare them. Monitor and assist.

4 Give students time to read other paragraphs if they need to.

Answers

Possible answers:

2

Topic sentence	Possible paragraph content
Effective leadership is crucial for the success of a business.	what is effective leadership, and why it is crucial for the success of a business
According to Douglas McGregor, in his book *The Human Side of Enterprise* (published in 1960), managers tend to be divided according to their beliefs.	different beliefs of managers about leadership
However, the style of leadership which is appropriate may depend on the situation.	different types of situation/organization
It is also important to consider the relationship between leadership and teams.	the relationship between leadership and teams; how teams are managed
In order for a leader to lead a team successfully, according to Hooper and Potter (in *The Business of Leadership*, 1997), there are some basic requirements.	list of requirements for successful team leadership (e.g., vision, trust)

3 The appropriate paragraphs to read depend on the research questions from Exercise B.

Discourse note

It is as well to be aware (though you may not feel it is appropriate to discuss with students at this point) that in real academic texts, the topic sentence may not be as obvious as in the texts in this unit. Sometimes there is not an explicit topic sentence, so that the overall topic of the paragraph must be inferred. Or the actual topic sentence for the paragraph can be near rather than at the beginning of the paragraph. Sometimes, also, the first sentence of a paragraph acts as a topic statement for a succession of paragraphs. An example of this can be seen in text 1 in the fifth paragraph, which begins: *There are other possible ways in which organizations can be structured.* The two paragraphs which follow continue the 'possible ways' of structuring an organization.

Exercise D

Set the task for homework and feed back next lesson. Encourage students to make notes on the points as given, i.e.,

1 Theory X beliefs

2 Theory Y beliefs

3 an example of a person or organization that they know

Make sure students realize that they only have to write the topic sentences. They can add the details orally.

An Internet search on Douglas McGregor will throw up a lot of references. However, a good place to start is www.bized.co.uk/. This is a UK website for further and higher education students.

Closure

1 Focus on some of the vocabulary from the text, including:

appropriate
autocratic
basic
breakdown (in communication)
crisis
crucial
delegate (v)
democratic
effective
impose
inspire
integrity
misunderstanding
open (= honest, frank)
order (n)
requirement
respect (n)
'shared vision'
stable
trust (n)

2 You may also want to redo the text as a jigsaw, as before – the text is reproduced in the additional resources section (Resource 2D) to facilitate this.

1 Work through the *Vocabulary bank* and *Skills bank* if you have not already done so, or as a revision of previous study.

2 Use the *Activity bank* (Teacher's Book additional resources section, Resource 2A).

   A Set the wordsearch for individual work (including homework) or pairwork.

   Answers

   B Do the quiz as a whole class, or in teams, or set for homework – students can re-read the texts to get the answers if necessary.

   Answers

   1 a A team.
      b An expert.
      c Delayering.
   2 a Autocratic.
      b Democratic.
   3 Figure A – club structure.
      Figure B – person structure.
   4 a Finance, marketing, human resources, production, sales.
      b Must inspire trust/respect; must be open; must have integrity.

3 Ask students to work in small groups to research the qualities needed for leadership. They should:

   • find an example of a successful leader in business and say what the leader's methods and/or personal qualities are

   • find an example of a successful leader from another domain (e.g., sport, the army, politics, history, etc.). Again, they should identify the personal qualities and/or methods

In addition, they could consider whether leaders and managers are the same thing.

If students are going to do research on the Internet, a good place to start (at the time of writing) is www.bized.co.uk/educators/16-19/business/hrm/index.htm.

Alternatively, you can do this research before the lesson and print off some pages for students to work from. Remind students that they can't possibly read everything they find, so they must use the topic sentences to decide if a paragraph is worth reading.

4 You can get students to practise their reading aloud – a skill which is not vital but is sometimes useful – by following this approach.

Photocopy and cut up one of the jigsaw texts (Resources 2B and 2D). Give topic sentences to Student A and the corresponding paragraph to Student B.

Student A reads out a topic sentence.

Student B finds the corresponding paragraph and reads it out.

An alternative is to give Student A the topic sentences and Student B a set of sentences chosen from each paragraph (one sentence per paragraph). Student A reads out the topic sentences one by one. Student B decides which of his/her sentences is likely to appear in the same paragraph as the topic sentence. Both students have to agree that the paragraph sentence matches the topic sentence.

5 Have a competition to practise finding words in a monolingual dictionary. Requirements:

   • English–English dictionary for each student (or pair of students if necessary)

   • Unit 2 key vocabulary list

Put students in teams with their dictionaries closed. Select a word from the vocabulary list and instruct students to open their dictionaries and find the word. The first student to find the word is awarded a point for their team. Additional points can be awarded if the student can give the correct pronunciation and meaning.

3 GETTING THE WORK DONE

Unit 3 looks at productivity in the workplace, and how this can be affected by factors such as automation, working environment and employee motivation. The first lecture examines the theories of motivation put forward by two American psychologists, Abraham Maslow and Frederick Herzberg, and suggests how these theories might relate to the business world. The second lecture looks at an approach to management which takes account of motivation factors: Management by Objectives.

Skills focus

🎧 Listening
- preparing for a lecture
- predicting lecture content
- making lecture notes
- using different information sources

Speaking
- reporting research findings
- formulating questions

Vocabulary focus
- stress patterns in multi-syllable words
- prefixes

Key vocabulary

appraisal	factor (n)	repetitive
automation	impose	responsibility
capability	measurable	reward (n and v)
challenge (n and v)	mission statement	self-actualization
colleague	motivation	self-employed
culture	multidisciplinary	self-esteem
demotivated	multinational (n and adj)	socialize
disadvantage	objective (n)	supervision
dissatisfaction	overtime	target (n)
efficiency	prioritize	unique
enrich	productivity	
environment		

3.1 Vocabulary

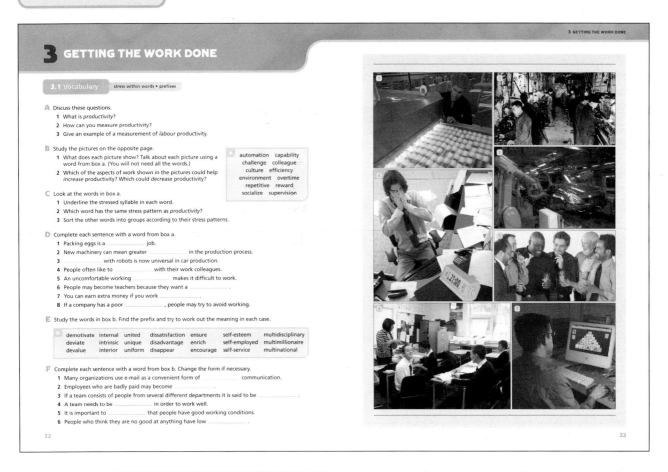

General note

Read the *Vocabulary bank* at the end of the Course Book unit. Decide when, if at all, to refer your students to it. The best time is probably at the very end of the lesson or the beginning of the next lesson, as a summary/revision.

Dictionaries will be useful in this lesson.

Lesson aims

- gain a greater understanding of the importance of stress within words and some of the common patterns
- extend knowledge of words which contain prefixes
- gain fluency in the target vocabulary

Introduction

1 Revise the vocabulary from the first two units. Check:
  - meaning
  - pronunciation
  - spelling

2 Revise the business model from Unit 1. Ask students for the three key words: *input – transformation – output*. Write these on the board. Ask students to say what activities are associated with inputs and outputs.

Exercise A

Tell students that the answers to these questions should involve the words on the board. Put students in pairs to discuss the questions. Feed back orally.

Answers

Possible answers:

1 Productivity is a way of measuring a firm's efficiency. (Note: *productive* = making lots of things, therefore *productivity* = how much you make.)

2 We can measure productivity by comparing inputs and outputs.

3 One measure of productivity is *output per employee*, i.e., how much each employee makes in a particular time period.

Exercise B

1 Refer students to the pictures on the opposite page. Ask what students can see in the first picture. Elicit *It's a production line*. Ask which word from the box could be used to say something more about the picture. Accept any suggestions which use the word *repetitive*, e.g., *The work is repetitive*.

Set the remaining pictures for pairwork. Students should make two statements: first what they can see and then a further comment about each picture using at least one word from the box. If necessary, they should check the meanings of the words in their dictionaries. Not all the words are relevant. Feed back with the whole class. Accept any reasonable suggestions. Check/correct pronunciation, especially the stress patterns.

2 Set for pairwork. Students should consider how the words they have used in question 1 can affect productivity. (For example, if a job is repetitive, is this likely to increase or decrease productivity?) Feed back orally, but do not confirm or correct at this stage.

Answers

Possible answers:

1 1 It's a production line. The employee is packing eggs. It's a **re'petitive** job.

  2 This is a very old factory. There is probably not much **e'fficiency** in the production process. The working **en'vironment** is poor.

  3 These are robots in a car factory. This is an example of **auto'mation**.

  4 This person is working **'overtime**. You can earn extra money like this.

  5 This is an office party. People from a workplace often **'socialize** with their **'colleagues**.

  6 This person is a teacher. Teaching is not an easy job. It's a **'challenge**.

  7 This employee is playing a computer game at work. This is an example of poor company **'culture**.

2 Accept all reasonable suggestions.

Methodology note

From now on, whenever you present a group of words in a box, as here, ask students for the part of speech of each word. This is good practice and also good preparation for changing the form of the word if a different part of speech is required in the associated exercise(s).

Exercise C

Write *productivity* on the board. Ask students to say how many syllables there are in the word (there are five). Draw vertical lines to divide the syllables. Then ask students to say where the main stress is and draw a line under the syllable:

| pro | duc | <u>tiv</u> | it | y |

Point out the importance of stressed syllables in words – see *Language note* below. Although you can mark stress with a straight stress marker (') or diacritic, it may be easier for students to use an underline. Another possibility is to use capital letters for the stressed syllable: *producTIVity*.

1 Set for pairwork. Tell students to identify the syllables first, then to underline the strongest stress. Feed back.

2 Ask students to find the word which has the same stress pattern as *productivity*. Write it on the board like this:

| pro | duc | <u>tiv</u> | it | y |
| ca | pa | <u>bil</u> | i | ty |

3 Set for pairwork. Students should match words with the same number of syllables and with main stresses in the same place.

Language note

In English, speakers emphasize the stressed syllable in a multi-syllable word. Sometimes listeners may not even hear the unstressed syllables. Vowels, in any case, often change to schwa or a reduced form in unstressed syllables. Therefore it is essential that students can recognize key words from the stressed syllable alone when they hear them in context. Multi-syllable words may seem to have more than one stressed syllable. This is a secondary stress, e.g., *‚produc'tivity*. For the present purposes, students should identify only the primary, or strongest, stress in the word.

Stress sometimes moves to fit common patterns when you add a suffix, e.g., *'capable, capa'bility*. Other suffixes, such as *~ment* or *~al*, don't affect the stress of the root word, e.g., *em'ploy, em'ployment; 'person, 'personal*.

Sometimes it is difficult to be sure how exactly a word should be divided into syllables. Use vowel sounds as a guide to the number of syllables. If in doubt, consult a dictionary.

Answers

1 auto<u>ma</u>tion
  capa<u>bili</u>ty
  <u>cha</u>llenge
  <u>co</u>lleague
  <u>cul</u>ture
  e<u>ffi</u>ciency
  en<u>vir</u>onment
  <u>o</u>vertime
  re<u>pe</u>titive
  re<u>ward</u>
  <u>so</u>cialize
  super<u>vis</u>ion
3 <u>co</u>lleague, <u>cha</u>llenge, <u>cul</u>ture
  <u>o</u>vertime, <u>so</u>cialize
  re<u>ward</u>
  e<u>ffi</u>ciency, en<u>vir</u>onment, re<u>pe</u>titive
  auto<u>ma</u>tion, super<u>vis</u>ion

Exercise D

Set for individual work and pairwork checking. Not all the words are needed.

Answers

1 Packing eggs is a <u>repetitive</u> job.
2 New machinery can mean greater <u>efficiency</u> in the production process.
3 <u>Automation</u> with robots is now universal in car production.
4 People often like to <u>socialize</u> with their work colleagues.
5 An uncomfortable working <u>environment</u> makes it difficult to work.
6 People may become teachers because they want a <u>challenge</u>.
7 You can earn extra money if you work <u>overtime</u>.
8 If a company has a poor <u>culture</u>, people may try to avoid working.

Exercise E

Set for pairwork. Students should look at all three words in each column to find and then deduce the meaning of the prefix. Encourage them to use a phrase as a definition rather than a single-word translation. They need to develop a sense of the broader meaning of the prefix. Feed back, getting the meanings on the board.

Answers

Model answers:

de = to remove from, to decrease, to change in the opposite direction
in = inside*
uni = one, all the same as
dis = to show the opposite or negative
en = to make or cause to become
self = through or by means of itself or oneself
multi = many
*this prefix also means *not* in some cases, e.g., *invalid, inaccurate, indecisive*

Methodology note

With some of these words it is difficult to work out the base word, e.g., *trinsic*. However, you can point out that you can sometimes understand roughly what a word means if you understand the prefix, e.g., *intrinsic* must be something to do with being in something, so context will help you to guess the rough meaning.

Exercise F

This is further practice in using words with prefixes. If students are struggling, point out that all the missing words are from the top row. Feed back, checking pronunciation and stress patterns.

Answers

Model answers:

1 Many organizations use e-mail as a convenient form of <u>internal</u> communication.
2 Employees who are badly paid may become <u>demotivated</u>.
3 If a team consists of people from several different departments it is said to be <u>multidisciplinary</u>.
4 A team needs to be <u>united</u> in order to work well.
5 It is important to <u>ensure</u> that people have good working conditions.
6 People who think they are no good at anything have low <u>self-esteem</u>.

Closure

1 Ask students to decide whether the sentences in Exercise F are facts or opinions. Discuss ideas with the whole class.

2 If you have not already done so, refer students to the *Vocabulary bank* at the end of Unit 3. Work through some or all of the stress patterns.

Language note

The patterns shown in the *Vocabulary bank* in Unit 3 are productive, i.e., they enable you to make more words or apply the rules accurately to other words. The words with unusual patterns tend to be the more common ones, so if students come across a new multi-syllable word at this level, it is likely to conform to the patterns shown. Native speakers recognize the patterns and will naturally apply them to unusual words, e.g., proper nouns. How, for example, would you pronounce these nonsense words?

felacom

bornessity

shimafy

emtonology

scolobility

nemponary

cagoral

andimakinise

ortepanimation

3.2 Listening

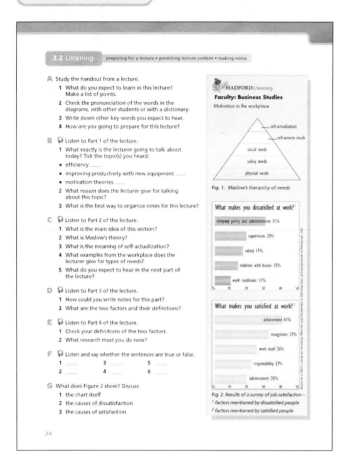

Lesson aims

Further practice in:

- planning and preparing for a lecture
- predicting lecture content
- choosing the best form of notes
- making notes

Introduction

Review key vocabulary by:

- using flashcards
- playing the alphabet game in the extra activities section at the end of this unit

Exercise A

Refer students to the handout with Figures 1 and 2. Write the title *Motivation in the workplace* on the board.

1 Set for individual work and pairwork checking. Feed back, eliciting some ideas.

2 Set for pairwork.

3 Brainstorm to elicit key words. Allow the class to decide whether a word should be included.

4 Elicit some points – the four Ps (Plan, Prepare, Predict, Produce). If necessary, refer students to Unit 1 *Skills bank* to review the preparation for a lecture. One way to help the students to make provisional notes is to:

- brainstorm what they would include
- organize their topics into a logical sequence

Answers

Answers depend on the students.

🎧 Exercise B

1 Tell students they are only going to hear the introduction to the lecture. Ask what information they expect to get from the introduction (i.e., the outline of the lecture).

Give students time to read the choices of topics. Check that they understand the meaning and relevance. Remind them they will only hear the introduction once, as in a lecture. Play Part 1. Allow them to compare answers.

Feed back. Ask them to justify their choice by saying what they heard related to it. Confirm the correct answer.

2 Elicit ideas. Confirm or correct.

3 Elicit ideas.

Answers

Model answers:

1 Motivation theories.

2 Motivation can affect productivity.

3 Since these are theories which try to explain motivation – i.e., highlight causes and effects – a flowchart (or spidergram) could be used. For example:

Theory 1

Equally, headings and bullet points:

Theory 2

- . . .
- . . .

Transcript 🎧 1.12

Part 1

Good morning, everybody. A key issue in the area of productivity is motivation. The reason for this is that motivation can affect productivity, both positively and negatively. As we know, a measurement of the productivity of a company is in fact a measurement of its efficiency, or in other words the size of its output in relation to its input. Of course a company can improve its efficiency by investing in more modern equipment. But that's not my concern today. A company's most valuable resource is its employees, and so in the next two lectures I want to consider how the management and behaviour of employees can impact on productivity. One way to achieve productivity gains in a company is by somehow getting people to work harder, or in better, more efficient ways. So, today we'll consider two different theories which try to explain how people are motivated at work.

🎧 Exercise C

Before playing Part 2, refer students to Figure 1. Ask students what they expect to hear. Give them time to read questions 1–4. Tell them to write only brief notes. The main task is to absorb the meaning.

Play Part 2. Give them time to answer questions 1–4. Allow them to compare their answers. Feed back.

When they thoroughly understand the concepts in Maslow's hierarchy of needs, ask them what they expect in the next part of the lecture (question 5). Elicit ideas but do not confirm or correct.

Answers

Model answers:

1 Main idea = *Maslow's hierarchy of needs*. People are motivated to do things because they have needs.

2 There are different types of needs. There are basic needs at the bottom of the hierarchy. Once these are satisfied, the person can think about satisfying needs which are higher up the hierarchy.

3 Self-actualization: becoming the best person you can possibly be; achieving everything you are capable of.

4 Physical needs: pay, work environment. Safety needs: job security, job description, clear structures. Social needs: working with other people, socializing. Self-esteem: recognition, power, being trusted. Self-actualization: new skills, new challenges, developing capabilities.

5 Answers depend on the students.

Transcript 🎧 1.13

Part 2

What makes somebody do something? What drives people to work to the best of their ability? Do you work because you enjoy it? Or because you will get some benefit from doing it – perhaps, for example, you will get some money, or someone will admire you?

Abraham Maslow, a famous American psychologist, believed that we do things because we have needs, and that these needs drive our behaviour. What are our most basic needs? The things we need before anything else? Clearly, our most basic needs are physical – that is, we need food, warmth and shelter. Maslow pointed out that we generally try to satisfy these needs first, before we consider doing anything else. In the 1950s, Maslow developed a hierarchical model of motivation, in which physical needs are at the bottom of the hierarchy. You can see this model in Figure 1. Once we have enough food, shelter, etc., we can start to think about ensuring our 'safety' needs. Safety here means being in a safe and secure environment, with no worries or anxieties. If we feel safe and secure, then our attention shifts to our social needs. People are social beings and they want to be able to socialize and communicate with other people, to have friends and a sense of belonging. In addition to this, people need a strong sense of self-esteem, which means that things like confidence, status and recognition for their achievements are important. Finally, at the top of the hierarchy of needs comes 'self-actualization'. By this is meant achieving your full potential, developing and learning, so that you become as skilled and as capable as you can be.

How do these ideas work in business? Well, physical needs are met by the pay received for work and the actual working environment. Pay is turned into accommodation and food, for example. Safety needs can be seen as things like having job security, having a clear job description, having a clear structure of accountability. In other words, safety here does not mean safety just for now, but for the future, too. Social needs are satisfied in the workplace by aspects such as communication, working with others in multidisciplinary teams, socializing after work. Self-esteem can be achieved in the workplace through recognition for achievements, through having power over others or being trusted by others. Finally, self-actualization occurs when people develop new skills or take on new challenges, thereby increasing and developing their capabilities.

🎧 Exercise D

Play the first two sentences of Part 3. Ask the first question. Set the second question for individual work and pairwork checking. Play the rest of the recording. Tell students to take notes. Allow students to compare their definitions. Don't, at this stage, confirm the answers.

Answers

Model answers:

1 A table is good for definitions.
2 See Exercise E.

Transcript 🎧 1.14

Part 3

In the 1950s, an American psychologist called Frederick Herzberg carried out some research into job satisfaction, and he came up with a two-factor theory of motivation at work. First, there are the aspects of work which contribute to job satisfaction. These are: achievement, recognition for achievement, interesting work, responsibility and advancement – the last one means not just promotion but a sense of progressing. It is important to note that these things are about the job itself, not the material rewards for the job. These job satisfaction elements Herzberg said were 'motivators', because they improve people's motivation at work. However, some aspects of work can make people unhappy. Herzberg called these the 'hygiene' factors. These are basically concerned with the working environment and consist of the following: company rules and policies, supervision, pay, interpersonal relations and working conditions. The hygiene factors don't motivate people but they can cause dissatisfaction and have a negative impact on motivation. For example, low pay makes people angry and frustrated. On the other hand, what really gets people to perform better is not so much better pay (which people quickly get used to) but job enrichment. To motivate people you need to give them interesting work, or responsibilities which challenge them. People need to be allowed to feel in control of their work.

🎧 Exercise E

Part 4 summarizes the definition of motivation and Herzberg's two factors. Tell students that this is the last part of the lecture. What do they expect to hear? Confirm that it is a summary. Play Part 4.

1 Students should check their definitions as they listen. After the summary has finished, they should correct their definitions and complete their notes. Guide them to the correct answer: that is, the correct meaning, not necessarily the words given here.

2 Elicit ideas. Then set the research for students to work on in pairs or individually. They will need to report back in Lesson 3.

Answers

Model answers:

1

Factors	Definition
motivators	aspects of work which increase motivation/encourage people to work more productively
hygiene factors/dissatisfiers	aspects of work which make people unhappy/demotivated

2 Students should research management systems which can help to improve people's performance, such as *Management by Objectives*.

Transcript 🎧 1.15

Part 4

So let's summarize Herzberg's ideas, then. There are two factors which managers need to bear in mind. Firstly, there are *motivators*, which actually encourage people to achieve more. Secondly, there are *dissatisfiers*, which are those aspects of work that cause people to become demotivated. Herzberg called these *hygiene factors*, because he saw them as aspects which have to be 'cleaned up' before we can expect people to be motivated. They are not motivators in themselves. Nobody would say 'I love my job because I get a lot of holidays,' but they may well complain if they don't get much holiday.

That's enough for now. Next time, we'll have a look at the way in which management systems can improve people's performance – in particular I want to talk about a concept known as *Management by Objectives*. So don't forget to do some research on this topic before you come.

🎧 Exercise F

These are sentences about the ideas in the lecture.

Set for pairwork. Say or play the sentences. Give time for students to discuss and then respond. Students must justify their answers.

Answers

1	false	Productivity is also affected by how efficient the workplace is, old/new machinery, etc.
2	true	Food is one of the things at the bottom of the hierarchy of needs (physical needs).
3	true	People need to feel safe before they can have a social life.
4	false	According to Herzberg, improving the work environment doesn't motivate people, but a poor working environment can demotivate people.
5	false	However, people may not work as hard if they don't feel they are adequately paid.
6	true	This is another of Herzberg's 'hygiene factors'.

Transcript 🎧 1.16

1 Productivity is only about how hard people work.

2 According to Maslow, one of the first things that people need is food.

3 People need to feel safe before they can have a social life.

4 According to Herzberg, improving the work environment motivates people.

5 People will work harder if they are paid more.

6 Bad relations with other people at work can make people feel demotivated.

Exercise G

This exercise practises making questions and describing information in a table.

Ask students to think of three questions they could ask about the chart using *Wh~* question words such as *What …? Where …? When …? Who …? How many …? What proportion/percentage …?* etc. Elicit some examples. Write these on the board:

1 *What does the chart show?*

2 *What is the most/least important satisfier/dissatisfier?*

3 *When did the survey take place?*

4 *Who took part in it?*

5 *What proportion/percentage of people thought that X was a cause of dissatisfaction/satisfaction?*

Put students in pairs to ask each other their questions, making sure they include the questions above. Check.

Answers

Possible answers:

1 The chart shows the factors which made people

satisfied and dissatisfied at work. The bars represent the percentage of people who mentioned each factor. The survey of engineers and accountants was conducted in the 1950s in the US.

2 Most important satisfier: achievement; least important satisfier: advancement.

3 Most important dissatisfier (or hygiene factor): company policy and administration; least important dissatisfier: work conditions.

Closure

Ask students to:

● give a definition of motivation. One possibility is: *It's the reason why people do things. One view is that people do things because they want to satisfy their needs.*

● discuss whether they think Maslow's hierarchy of needs and Herzberg's two-factor theory have anything in common. See if students can identify that the items at the bottom of Maslow's hierarchy tend to be Herzberg's dissatisfiers while the ones at the top are the motivators

Note: Students will need their lecture notes from Lesson 2 in the next lesson.

3.3 Extending skills

3.3 Extending skills   stress within words • using information sources • reporting research findings

A Listen to some stressed syllables. Identify the word below in each case. Number each word.
Example:
You hear: *1 mu /mju:/* You write:

achievement	esteem	negative
automation	factor	objective
behaviour	hygiene	physical
communicate *1*	interpersonal	responsibility
demotivated	issue	secure
employee	multidisciplinary	status

B Where is the main stress in each multi-syllable word in Exercise A?
1 Mark the main stress.
2 Practise saying each word.

C Work in pairs or groups. Define one of the words in Exercise A. The other student(s) must find and say the correct word.

D Look at the spidergram on the right.
1 For each method of communication, state the medium used.
2 Say why each method might be used.
3 What other methods of communication are there?

Method	Medium	Why?
telephone	speaking (not face to face)	quick responses; internal (to other employees in the building); external (e.g., to suppliers)

E Before you attend a lecture you should do some research.
1 How could you research the lecture topics on the right?
2 What information should you record?
3 How could you record the information?

F You are going to do some research on a particular lecture topic. You must find:
1 a dictionary definition
2 an encyclopedia explanation
3 a useful Internet site

HADFORD *University*

Faculty: Business Studies

1 Increasing productivity: motivating staff
2 What is the future for IT in business communication?
3 Appraisal and reward systems: a brief history
4 Intrinsic and extrinsic motivation

Student A
• Do some research on **intrinsic and extrinsic motivation**.
• Tell your partner about your findings.

Student B
• Do some research on **appraisal and reward systems**.
• Tell your partner about your findings.

25

General note

Read the *Skills bank* at the end of the Course Book unit. Decide when, if at all, to refer students to it. The best time is probably at the beginning of the lesson or the end of the next lesson, as a summary/revision.

Lesson aim

This lesson is the first in a series about writing an assignment or giving a presentation based on research. The principal objective of this lesson is to introduce students to sources of information.

Introduction

1 Tell students to ask you questions about the information in the lecture in Lesson 2 as if you were the lecturer. Refer them to the *Skills bank* for typical language if you wish.

2 Put students in pairs. Student A must ask Student B about the information in the lecture in Lesson 2 to help him/her complete the notes from the lecture. Then they reverse roles. Go round, helping students to identify gaps in their notes and to think of good questions to get the missing information. Refer them to the *Skills bank* if you wish for language they can use in the pairwork.

Pairs then compare notes and decide what other information would be useful and where they could get it from. For example, more technical definitions of the words in the motivation models might be useful, from a specialist dictionary or an encyclopedia. In the feedback, write a list of research sources on the board, at least including dictionaries, encyclopedias, specialist reference books (about management: people in business; psychology: motivation) and the Internet.

Point out that dictionaries are good for definitions, although you may need to go to a specialist dictionary for a technical word. Otherwise, try an encyclopedia, because technical words are often defined in articles when they are first used. You could also try Google's 'define' feature, i.e., type *define: self-actualization*. But remember you will get definitions from other disciplines, not just your own, so you need to scan to check the relevant one. (*Self-actualization* is a psychological term.)

When doing an Internet search it is also useful to try both American and British English spellings. British spelling: *actualization or actualisation*; US: *actualization*.

Exercise A

In this exercise, students will hear each word with the stressed syllable emphasized, and the rest of the syllables underspoken.

Play the recording, pausing after the first few to check that students understand the task. Feed back, perhaps playing the recording again for each word before checking. Ideally, mark up an OHT of the words.

Language note

In English, speakers emphasize the stressed syllable in a multi-syllable word. Sometimes listeners may not even hear the unstressed syllables. Vowels, in any case, often change to schwa or a reduced form in unstressed syllables. Therefore it is essential that students can recognize key words from the stressed syllable alone when they hear them in context.

Answers

achievement	3
automation	4
behaviour	7
communicate	1
demotivated	8
employee	14
esteem	10
factor	17
hygiene	2
interpersonal	13
issue	6
multidisciplinary	18
negative	9
objective	5
physical	11
responsibility	16
secure	12
status	15

Transcript 🎧 1.17

1 co'mmunicate
2 'hygiene
3 a'chievement
4 auto'mation
5 ob'jective
6 'issue
7 be'haviour
8 de'motivated
9 'negative
10 e'steem
11 'physical
12 se'cure
13 inter'personal
14 em'ployee
15 'status
16 responsi'bility
17 'factor
18 multidisci'plinary

Exercise B

Erase the words or turn off the OHP. Ask students to guess or remember where the stressed syllable is on each word. Tell them to mark their idea with a light vertical stroke in pencil. Elicit and drill. Refer students to the *Vocabulary bank* at this stage if you wish.

Answers

See transcript for Exercise A.

Exercise C

Set for pair or group work. Go round and assist/correct.

Exercise D

1/2 Refer students to the spidergram and the table. Elicit question forms for this discussion such as:
What is the medium of communication for … ?
Why do you think … is used?
Why do people use … ?
What do people use … for?
Put students in small groups or pairs to discuss the questions.

Feed back, building up the table in the Answers section on the board. The more reasons students can give, the better.

3 Discuss with the whole class. Accept any reasonable suggestions.

Answers

Model answers:

1/2

Method	Medium	Why?
telephone	speaking, not face to face	quick response; internal (to other employees in the building); external (e.g., to suppliers)
e-mail	writing	quicker than a letter but not as quick as a phone call; useful for messages which are not urgent. Usually informal and sometimes confidential. Useful for communicating between countries as well as within an organization – not good for difficult discussions
memo	writing	internally in an organization between departments or levels of management; usually giving information or instructions
team briefing/ meeting	speaking, face to face	necessary when clear and full communication is needed, such as for complex instructions or discussions
annual report	writing	give shareholders and other external stakeholders annual information about the company plans, achievements and financial performance

Exercise E

Remind students again about the four Ps. Refer students to the lecture topics and the questions. Work through as a whole class if you wish.

Answers

Model answers:

1 Look up key words in a dictionary/encyclopedia/on the Internet. Check pronunciation so you will recognize the words in the lecture.

2 Lecture 1: meanings of these key words; examples

Lecture 2: predictions on future uses and developments in computers and information technology

Lecture 3: key dates and famous people if any; different systems of appraisal and reward; key uses for both

Lecture 4: key principles for intrinsic and extrinsic motivation; names of key thinkers

3 Perhaps do a spidergram so that it is easier to brainstorm with fellow students and cover all the possible areas that the lecturer might focus on.

Exercise F

Set for pairwork, giving each member of the pair a different research task. If students have access in class to reference material, allow them to at least start the activity in class. Otherwise, set the task for homework. Before the feed back to partner stage, refer students to the *Skills bank – Reporting information to other people*.

Closure

Dictate sentences with words from Exercise A in context for students to identify the words again.

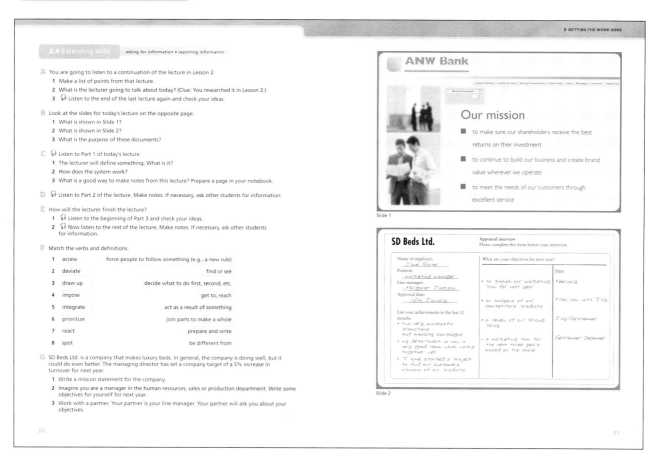

Lesson aims

- ask for information to complete notes

Further practice in:

- choosing the best form of notes
- making notes
- reporting information

Introduction

Elicit some information from the lecture in Lesson 2. If necessary, prompt students by reading parts of the transcript and pausing for students to complete in their own words. Don't spend too long on this, however.

🎧 Exercise A

Remind students of the language involved in asking for information about a lecture from other people – see *Skills bank*. Drill some of the sentences if you wish.

1/2 Set for pairwork.

3 Play Part 4 of the lecture from Lesson 2 to enable students to check their answers.

Feed back. Elicit information from the students' research. Do not confirm or correct at this stage except for pronunciation mistakes on key words.

Answers

Model answers:

1 Motivation is the reason why people do things.

Maslow's hierarchy of needs is one way to understand motivation. People do things because they have needs. There are basic needs, such as physical needs. And there are other needs such as self-esteem and self-actualization.

Herzberg's two-factor theory suggests that at work there are motivators and dissatisfiers. Motivators can encourage people to work better, whereas dissatisfiers make people demotivated.

2/3 Management by Objectives.

Transcript 🎧 1.15

Part 4

So let's summarize Herzberg's ideas, then. There are two factors which managers need to bear in mind. Firstly, there are *motivators*, which actually encourage people to achieve more. Secondly, there are *dissatisfiers*, which are those aspects of work that cause people to become demotivated. Herzberg called these *hygiene factors*, because he saw them as aspects which have to be 'cleaned up' before we can expect people to be motivated. They are not motivators in themselves. Nobody would say 'I love my job because I get a lot of holidays,' but they may well complain if they don't get much holiday.

That's enough for now. Next time, we'll have a look at the way in which management systems can improve people's performance – in particular I want to talk about a concept known as *Management by Objectives*. So don't forget to do some research on this topic before you come.

Exercise B

Refer students to the lecture slides. Set for pairwork discussion. Feed back.

Answers

Model answers:

1 A company mission statement.

2 An appraisal interview document for an individual employee.

3 Answer depends on the students. Suggestions could be: to help motivate employees; to develop a company culture; to enable individuals to decide their objectives; etc.

🎧 Exercise C

Set for individual work, then pair or group discussion. Play Part 1 of the lecture.

> ### Methodology note
>
> Don't tell students words they can't remember. It would be quite normal in a lecture that they can't write all of them down. If they don't remember them all this time, they should at least put the key words they remember in order. They can then listen for the other key words as the text develops.

Answers

Model answers:

1 Objectives.

2 The MBO system works by setting objectives. These work with a mission statement and objectives involving the whole company, departments/teams, and individual employees.

3 The definition of objectives could be a spidergram.

The key words relating to how the system works could be written on the left of the page in a column.

The advantages and disadvantages could be a table with + and − at the top.

(See answers to Exercises D and E in this lesson.)

Transcript 🎧 1.18

Part 1

In the last lecture, we talked about two theories of motivation. Today we will look at an approach to management which takes account of motivation factors. The system is called *Management by Objectives*, and it was developed in 1954 by Peter Drucker, one of the most important thinkers in management of the last century. MBO – as it is known – is a system for ensuring that everybody in the company is working in the same direction; in other words, that all the activities are coordinated. This is done through setting objectives – or targets – at each level in the organization. So in this talk I will first define what is meant by 'objectives'. Then I'll explain how the system works through a mission statement and objectives at the level of the whole company, the department or team, and the individual employee. Finally, I'll consider some of the advantages and disadvantages of MBO.

🎧 Exercise D

Play Part 2 of the lecture. Students should recognize the rhetorical structure – see Answers section – and complete in effect a spidergram and a table. When students have done their best individually, put them in pairs or small groups to complete their notes by asking for information from the other student(s).

In the feedback, allow the correct meaning, not just these words.

Answers

Model answers:

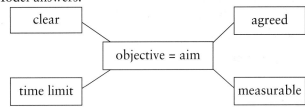

Type of objective	Purpose	Example
mission statement	to give general aim for company	Google: provide fast, accurate, easy-to-use search service
company objectives	to give specific aims for company	increase profits by 20% in next 5 years
department/ team objectives	to give specific aims for department	marketing dept: increase sales by 5% each year for next 5 years
individual objectives	to set targets for each employee; help motivation	none given

Transcript 🎧 1.19

Part 2

An objective is an aim or a goal – that is, it's a statement about what you intend to do. Another word for objective is *target*. An objective must have four important qualities. First, it must be agreed by everyone involved. Second, it must be very clear. Third, it must be something that you can measure, such as a percentage increase. And finally, an objective must have a time limit. It's no good having an objective which goes on for ever!

As I've said, the purpose of MBO is to make sure everyone is working together for the same things. So how does the system work? First the company draws up a *mission statement*. This is a written document which says in a simple, general way what the company's aims are. For example, Google, the Internet search engine, aims to 'provide a fast, accurate and easy-to-use search service that can be accessed from anywhere'. Slide 1 shows another example of a mission statement, this time from a bank.

In order to make things clear so that everyone knows exactly how to try to achieve these aims and what must be planned, the mission statement is turned into *specific objectives*. So a director might set a target for the company such as 'to increase profits by 20% in the next five years'.

As well as whole company targets, each functional department or team should have targets which are agreed between the head of the department and the CEO. For example, the marketing department might have a target of a 5% increase in sales each year for the next five years. Therefore, they will need to plan activities which they will put in place to reach this target. For example, they may decide to increase their special promotions.

Finally, each person in the company also has targets which they agree with their manager or supervisor. The individuals themselves often draw up their own targets before discussing them with their boss. This is because for the objectives to be effective as motivators, they must be agreed by the individuals, not imposed from above.

🎧 Exercise E

Ask the initial question and elicit ideas, but do not confirm or correct at this stage.

1 Play the first two sentences of Part 3. Feed back.

2 Play the rest of Part 3. Give students time to do their own work, then set for pair or group completion.

Answers

Model answers:

1 Advantages and disadvantages of MBO.

2

+	–
everyone knows what to do	too much time discussing targets
motivating	targets can be unrealistic
performance can be measured	targets become out of date
everyone is united	targets can prevent quick reactions to change

Transcript 🎧 1.20

Part 3

So how good is this system? Does it have any disadvantages? Well, firstly, if MBO works well there are several advantages. For example, everyone knows exactly what they should do and how they should prioritize their work. Secondly, the system acts as a motivator since people are given responsibility to decide their own targets. Also for individuals and at company level, performance can be measured against the agreed targets. If a department's or an individual's performance deviates from the target, this can be spotted easily. Finally, an integrated system of targets ensures that everyone is united as a team, working harmoniously and in the same direction.

On the other hand, MBO doesn't always work well in practice. Firstly, sometimes people spend too much time on discussing the targets rather than doing the job. Secondly, sometimes targets can be unrealistic, and just by setting a target it does not mean that it will be achieved. Also, circumstances change very quickly so that targets can quickly become out of date. Finally, if targets are too specific they can prevent people from reacting quickly to changing situations.

Exercise F

Set for pairwork. Monitor and assist. Feed back, writing the words on the board as the students correctly identify them. Check pronunciation and stress patterns.

Answers

1	access	get to, reach
2	deviate	be different from
3	draw up	prepare and write
4	impose	force people to follow something (e.g., a new rule)
5	integrate	join parts to make a whole
6	prioritize	decide what to do first, second, etc.
7	react	act as a result of something
8	spot	find or see

Exercise G

Refer students to Slide 1, which provides a model mission statement. Check that students understand *do well* in this context.

1 Set for individual work or pairwork. Students should write two or three sentences beginning *To ...* . They should use their own ideas. Feed back. Accept any reasonable suggestions. Write a few on the board.

2 Elicit a couple of suitable objectives as examples. Then set for pairwork. For a model, refer students to the part of the sample appraisal form in which objectives are listed. Objectives can begin *To ...* or they could be just a noun phrase. They should include a date or time period as in the sample appraisal form. They should also be concrete (that is, result in a visible product such as a document) or measurable, such as: 'increase sales by 10%'.

3 Put students in different pairs to do the role-play. Remind students of the ways of asking politely for information (refer to *Skills bank* if necessary).

Answers

Answers depend on the students.

Closure

Ask students to list ways of ensuring that everyone works effectively in an organization. Suggestions are: good communications; effective leadership; good teams; good working conditions; good pay; etc.

Extra activities

1 Work through the *Vocabulary bank* and *Skills bank* if you have not already done so, or as a revision of previous study.

2 Use the *Activity bank* (Teacher's Book additional resources section, Resource 3A).

   A Set the coded crossword for individual work (including homework). They can also copy the words into their notebooks and check the definitions of any words they can't remember.

   Answers

   B This game practises pronunciation and meaning recognition. It can only be played in groups in class.

   Students must think of one word for each of the categories on the bingo card. Allow them to use any of the vocabulary from this unit. They should write their words on card 1, or copy the bingo grid into their notebooks.

   Each student says one of their own words at random once only, concentrating on the pronunciation. The others must identify the category and cross it out on card 2.

   The winner is the first student to identify the correct category for all the words. If the teacher keeps a record of which words have been said, he/she can say when a successful card could have been completed.

3 Students can play an alphabet game by themselves or as a group/class. The aim is to think of a word related to business for each letter of the alphabet. For example:

Student A: **a**utomation

Student B: automation, **b**oss

Student C: automation, boss, **c**olleague

Each student adds something for the next letter of the alphabet. They should try to use words from the unit if possible. A student misses a turn if he/she can't remember the items, or add another letter.

4 Tell students to do some Internet research on one or both of these topics:

   a What these early writers said about the work environment, motivation and productivity:

   Frederick Taylor

   Henry Gantt

   Frank and Lillian Gilbreth

   Elton Mayo

   Useful websites (at the time of writing):
   www.bized.co.uk
   www.accel-team.com/motivation/intro.html

   b The Investors in People scheme in the UK (www.investorsinpeople.co.uk)

Note that a lot of the information will be in very complex English, but students should be able to record the basic details and report back in the next lesson.

4 THE WORLD OF TECHNOLOGY

In this unit, one type of external influence on business is covered: technology. Lesson 2 looks at how technology impacts on business, e.g., in manufacturing, strategy and communication. At the same time, the use of computers in education is covered: Lessons 1, 3 and 4 guide students to a more efficient use of the Internet and computers in research.

Note that students will need access to a computer with an Internet connection for some exercises in this unit. Check that all students have used the Internet. If any haven't, sit them beside someone who has, to guide them.

Skills focus

Reading
- identifying topic development within a paragraph
- using the Internet effectively
- evaluating Internet search results

Writing
- reporting research findings

Vocabulary focus

- computer jargon
- abbreviations and acronyms
- discourse and stance markers
- verb and noun suffixes

Key vocabulary

access (n and v)	exit (v)	password
browse	hyperlink	register
data	Intranet	search (n and v)
database	keyword	search engine
default (adj)	log in/log on	search results
digital	log off	software
digitize	login (n)	technology
document	media	username/ID
electronic	menu	web page

Abbreviations and acronyms

The *Computer Jargon Buster* on page 31 of the Course Book lists the meanings of most of these.

CAD	HTTP	PPT
CAL	ISP	ROM
CAM	IT	URL
CIM	LCD	USB
FAQs	PDF	WAN
HTML	PIN	WWW

4.1 Vocabulary

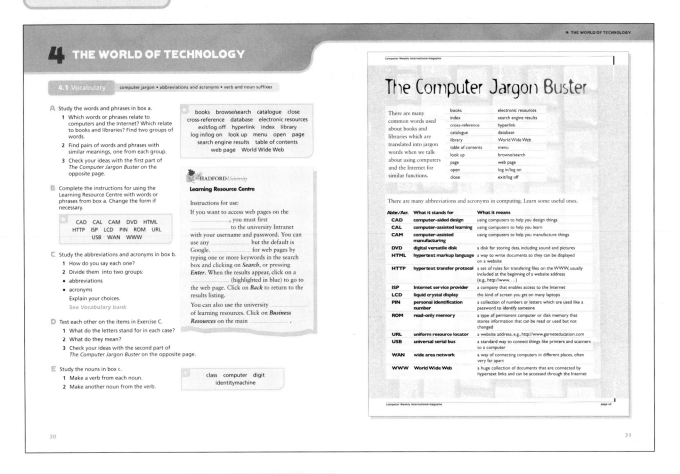

General note

If possible, hold this lesson in a room where there is a computer, or bring in a computer.

Read the *Vocabulary bank* at the end of the Course Book unit. Decide when, if at all, to refer your students to it. The best time is probably at the very end of the lesson or the beginning of the next lesson, as a summary/revision.

Lesson aims

- gain fluency in the meaning, pronunciation and spelling of key computing terms, acronyms and abbreviations

- understand how verbs can be formed from nouns, and nouns from verbs, through the addition of suffixes

Introduction

Familiarize students with computer terminology using some or all of the following activities.

1 Using a computer or a picture of a computer as a starting point, elicit some or all of the following terms:

PC	laptop	database
monitor	screen	hand-held computer
icon	keyboard	desktop
mouse	CPU (central	keys
hard disk	processing unit)	program
slot	floppy disk	DVD
USB port	CD	printer
scanner	accessory	Internet
e-mail	CD burner	the Web

2 Ask students to suggest verbs used in computing. Elicit some or all of the following. A good way to do this is to open a program such as Word (in English) and look at the words and symbols on the toolbars.

switch on	start up	shut down
log on/log off	click	double-click
hold	press	open
close	exit	save
select	copy	paste
enter	delete	insert
highlight	undo	

3 Ask students whether they normally use the library or the Internet to find information. Elicit the advantages and disadvantages of both. (There is so much emphasis on using computers nowadays, students often forget that there is a lot of information readily to hand in the library.)

Answers

Possible answers:

Library

+	–
easy to look things up in a dictionary or an encyclopedia	books can be out of date
you can find information in your own language	the book may not be in the library when you want it
information is usually correct	most books can't be accessed from home (though this is now starting to change)

Internet

+	–
a lot of information from different sources	difficult to find the right keywords
information is usually more up-to-date than books	difficult to know which results are the best
can be accessed from home	information is often not correct
you can quickly and easily get copies of books or journal articles not in your library	you may have to pay for the books/articles/information

Exercise A

Ask students to study the words in the box and elicit that they all relate to research.

Set for pairwork. Tell students to decide *and justify* the pairs they choose. If necessary, give an example: *index, search engine results.*

To help students understand what a database is, refer to ones they are familiar with in your college, e.g., student records, exam results, library catalogues, etc.

Students may argue that some terms are not exact equivalents, e.g., *catalogue/database*. Discuss any objections as they arise.

Answers

Model answers:

Common word or phrase for books and libraries	Word or phrase for Internet and electronic information
books	electronic resources
index	search engine results
cross-reference	hyperlink
catalogue	database
library	World Wide Web
table of contents	menu
look up	browse/search
page	web page
open	log in/log on
close	exit/log off

Language note

Log in and *log on*: these two verbs are used a little differently. *Log in* is used when accessing a closed system such as a college Intranet. *Log on* is used for open systems such as the Internet in general, as in *You can log on to the Internet with a hand-held computer*. Note also that the related noun has now become one word *(login)*. The opposite of *log in* is *log out*, while the opposite of *log on* is *log off*.

Exercise B

Set for individual work and pairwork checking. Ensure that students read *all* the text and have a general understanding of it before they insert the missing words.

Feed back by reading the paragraph or by using an OHT or other visual display of the text. Discuss alternative ideas and decide whether they are acceptable. Verify whether errors are due to using new words or to misunderstanding the text.

Answers

Model answers:

If you want to access web pages on the World Wide Web, you must first log in to the university Intranet with your username and password. You can use any search engine but the default is Google. Browse/Search for web pages by typing one or more keywords in the search box and clicking on *Search*, or pressing *Enter*. When the results appear, click on a hyperlink (highlighted in blue) to go to the web page. Click on *Back* to return to the results listing.

You can also use the university database of learning resources. Click on *Business Resources* on the main menu.

Exercise C

Set for pairwork. Feed back, eliciting ideas on pronunciation and confirming or correcting. Build up the two lists on the board. Establish that one group are acronyms, i.e., they can be pronounced as words: PIN = /pɪn/. The other group are abbreviations, i.e., they are pronounced as letters: HTTP = H-T-T-P. Drill all the abbreviations and acronyms. Make sure students can say letter names and vowel sounds correctly.

Elicit that words with normal consonant/vowel patterns are *normally* pronounced as a word and those with unusual patterns are *normally* pronounced with single letters. Refer to the *Vocabulary bank* at this stage if you wish.

Methodology note

Don't discuss the meaning at this point. This is covered in the next activity.

Answers

Acronyms: CAD /kæd/, CAL /kæl/, CAM /kæm/, PIN /pɪn/, ROM /rɒm/, WAN /wæn/.

Abbreviations: DVD, HTML, HTTP, ISP, LCD, URL (not pronounced /ɜːl/), USB, WWW.

Exercise D

1 Introduce the verb *stand for*. Elicit examples of common abbreviations and ask what they stand for. Set for pairwork. Tell students to pick out the ones they already know first. Next, they pick out the ones they are familiar with but don't know what they stand for – and guess.

2 Elicit the meanings without reference to the *Jargon Buster* if possible.

3 Refer students to the *Jargon Buster* to verify their answers. As a follow-up, elicit other common abbreviations from IT or business.

Language note

If students do not use acronyms or initial abbreviations in their language, a discussion about the reasons for using them is useful. They will then know how to find the meaning of new ones when they meet them. You might point out that abbreviations can sometimes be longer than the thing they abbreviate! For example, World Wide Web is three syllables, whereas WWW is six. It evolved because it is quicker to write, but it is longer, and harder, to say. It is also possible to mix acronyms with abbreviations, for example: JPEG – J /peg/. Point out the field of ICT is developing at an incredible speed and new acronyms and abbreviations are constantly being created.

Exercise E

Set for individual work and pairwork checking. Feed back, highlighting the changes from noun form to verb in the case of *identity/identify* and *machine/mechanize*.

Answers

Model answers:

Noun 1	Verb	Noun 2
class	classify	classification
computer	computerize	computerization
digit	digitize	digitization
identity	identify	identification
machine	mechanize	mechanization

Closure

Ask students whether they agree with the following statements.

1 Every college student must have a computer.
2 The college library uses a computer to help students find information.
3 College departments use computers to store research data.
4 Students can't do research without a computer.
5 College computers can access research data from other colleges and universities.
6 College computers can access research data from businesses and the media.
7 A personal computer can store information students think is important.
8 Computers can help us to talk with students from other colleges and universities.
9 Computers can help students access data from anywhere in the world.
10 A computer we can carry in our pocket can access worldwide data.

4.2 Reading

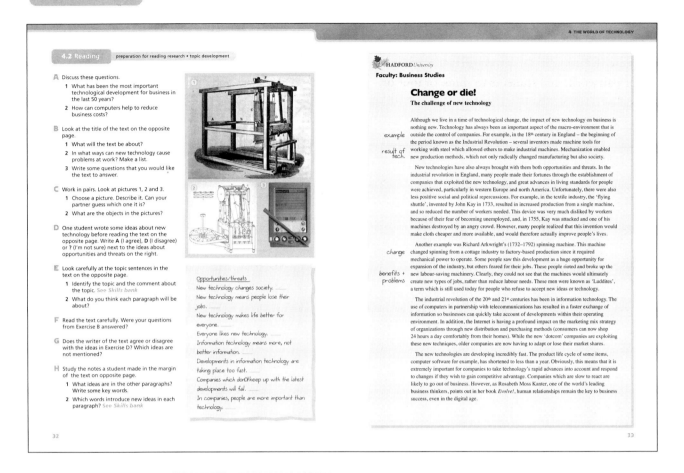

General note

Read the *Skills bank – Developing ideas in a paragraph* at the end of the Course Book unit. Decide when, if at all, to refer students to it. The best time is probably Exercise E, or at the very end of the lesson or the beginning of the next lesson, as a summary/revision.

Lesson aims

- prepare to read a text by looking at the title and topic sentences
- understand the purpose of discourse markers and stance markers in the development of a topic

Introduction

Ask students how, where and why they use computers. They should answer in some detail with examples. Encourage them to use the vocabulary, abbreviations and acronyms from Lesson 1.

Exercise A

Set for general discussion. Allow students to debate differences of opinion. Encourage them to give examples if they can.

Answers

Possible answers:

1 Probably information technology, i.e., the use of computers in all aspects of businesses and services. For example: keeping records, controlling production and distribution processes, assisting in design and planning, monitoring quality and cash flow, storing data, communicating with customers and the workforce.

2 Business costs include labour, time and materials. A computer can reduce the number of workers needed. It can make the production process quicker and more efficient; it can reduce wastage of materials.

Exercise B

1 Write the title of the reading text on the board. Discuss with the whole class, eliciting suggestions.

2 Set for pairwork and whole class feedback. Tell students to think of four or five possible problem areas. Do not confirm or correct at this point.

3 Set for pairwork. Tell students to think of four or five questions with different *Wh~* question words:

What ...?

Where ...?

When ...?

Why ...?

How ...?

If you want, you could choose some questions to write on one side of the board.

Answers

Possible answers:

1 If a business does not take advantage of new technology it will lose competitive edge and it will not survive.

2 Possible problems associated with introduction of new technology:

- cost: it may be expensive to introduce
- labour relations: people may resist new technology if it threatens their jobs
- skills: people may need to learn new skills
- reliability: the new technology may not work well
- motivation: staff may not like the new machines
- managing the introduction of the technology: it may be difficult to decide when to introduce it because of the speed of new developments
- unemployment: this may be the result of increased automation

3 Possible questions:

What are the current challenges of new technology?

What were the results of new technology in the past?

Where has there been the most change from new technology?

When has there been the most change from new technology?

Why does new technology mean change?

etc.

Exercise C

1 Set for pairwork.

2 Set for pairwork and whole class feedback. Write the answers on the board.

Answers

Model answers:

1 The 'flying shuttle': an invention for weaving, i.e., making cloth.

2 A spinning machine for making thread.

3 A hand-held computer or 'palm pilot'.

Exercise D

Set for individual work and pairwork checking. Feed back, trying to get consensus on each point, but do not actually confirm or correct. Preface your remarks with phrases like: *So most of you think ... You all agree/disagree that ...*

Point out that the statements are very strong. Draw students' attention to words like *everyone*. Point out also that the use of plurals with countable nouns when making a generalizing statement implies *all*, e.g., *companies* means *all companies*. The truth may actually be better expressed with a limiting word, e.g., *most/some/many*, or with words which express possibility such as *may* or *seem*, or adverbs such as *sometimes, usually, often*.

Remind students to look back at these predictions while they are reading the text (Exercise F).

Exercise E

Review paragraph structure – i.e., paragraphs usually begin with a topic sentence which makes a statement that is then expanded in the following sentences. Thus, topic sentences give an indication of the contents of the paragraph. You may wish to refer students to the *Skills bank* at this point.

1 Write the topic sentences from the text on an OHT, or use Resource 4B from the additional resources section. Take the first sentence and identify the subject of the main clause with a box. This is the topic. For example:

Although we live in a time of technological change, *the impact of new technology on business is nothing new.*

What is the sentence saying about *the impact of new technology on business*? The answer is: *it is nothing new.* Underline these words. These words constitute the comment which the sentence is making about the topic. Note that the subordinate clause simply provides more information about the topic: it is not the focus of the sentence. The focus of the sentence is on the **comment** being made. Thus a topic sentence consists of both a topic and a comment about the topic which is explained and expanded on in the rest of the paragraph.

Set the remaining sentences for individual work and pairwork checking.

2 Set for pairwork. Tell students that their analysis of the topic sentences may help them. Feed back with the whole class. Point out any language features which led them to draw their conclusions.

Answers

Possible answers:

1

	Topic	Comment
Para 1	the impact of new technology on business	is nothing new.
Para 2	New technologies	have also always brought with them both opportunities and threats.
Para 3	Another example	was Richard Arkwright's (1732–1792) spinning machine.
Para 4	The industrial revolution of the 20th and 21st centuries	has been in information technology.
Para 5	The new technologies	are developing incredibly fast.

2

	Predicted content	Notes
Para 1	a historical view of technology and business	the words *nothing new* point to the idea of a historical perspective
Para 2	a historical view of opportunities and threats of technology	the use of the present perfect and *always* point to the historical view
Para 3	how another machine brought benefits and problems	the word *another* links this paragraph with the previous one in which opportunities and threats are discussed
Para 4	information technology in the 20th and 21st centuries	
Para 5	the speed of technological development and its effects	the focus of the sentence is on speed, not technological development as such; this is because speed is part of the comment

Exercise F

Set the reading. Tell students to read for good understanding. When everyone has read the text, discuss any vocabulary items that may have caused difficulties.

If you have previously written questions on the board, ask students to say which were answered. Then tell the same pairs as in Exercise B to discuss which of their questions were answered. Feed back with the whole class, asking a few pairs to say which of their questions were answered and which were not.

Exercise G

Set for individual work and pairwork checking. Feed back with the whole class, asking students to say which parts of the text discuss the ideas. Ask students to say how some of the sentences in Exercise D could be better worded so they are not so strong.

Answers

Possible answers:
See table on next page.

Exercise H

The purpose of this exercise is for students to try to identify the information structure of each paragraph and to see how a new step in the progression of ideas may be signalled by a rhetorical marker or phrase. Direct students' attention to the handwritten notes in the left margin of the text. Explain that the notes are key words which summarize (in the reader's own words) the ideas in the text. The notes are written next to the relevant parts of the text. A good idea is to make a OHT of the text and use a highlighter to indicate which are the relevant parts of the text. Point out that often (but not always) a new step in the development of ideas is shown by a rhetorical marker or a phrase. The development may be more information: in paragraph 1 we have *for example*. Or the development may be a contrast: in paragraph 2 we have *however*.

1 Set for pairwork. Tell students to decide on some similar key words for the ideas in the remaining three paragraphs and to write these words next to the appropriate part of the text. Feed back with the whole class, eliciting suitable key words for the left margin and the phrases or sentences in the text which correspond to the key words. For reference, the text is reproduced in the additional resources section (Resource 4C) with suggested annotations.

2 Set for individual work and pairwork checking. Feed back with the whole class, identifying the markers as shown.

Answers

Possible answers:
See next page.

Answers

Possible answers for Exercise G:

Idea	Agree/disagree/no mention	Possible rewording
New technology changes society.	agree – para 1, last sentence	New technology *can* change society.
New technology means people lose their jobs.	agree – para 2, sentence 4 disagree – para 3, sentence 5	New technology *can* mean that *some* people lose their jobs.
New technology makes life better for everyone.	agree – para 2, sentence 2 and last sentence	New technology tends to make life better for *most people*.
Everyone likes new technology.	disagree – para 3, last sentence	There are *usually/often some people* who dislike new technology.
Information technology means more, not better information.	not mentioned	
Developments in information technology are taking place too fast.	not mentioned/disagree – the text says only that 'the new technologies' are developing very fast	
Companies which don't keep up with the latest developments will fail.	agree – para 5, sentence 4	Companies which don't keep up with the latest developments *are likely to* fail.
In companies, people are more important than technology.	agree – para 5, last sentence	

Answers

Possible answers for Exercise H:

1 See Resource 4C in the additional resources section.

2 Para 1 for example

Para 2 unfortunately, for example, however

Para 3 but, clearly

Para 4 in addition

Para 5 obviously, however

Language note

The relation of one sentence to the previous sentence is not always made explicit by rhetorical markers or phrases. In fact, overuse of markers is to be avoided.

If there is no marker or phrase, the relationship can usually be deduced by the position of the sentence in the paragraph, or by the meaning. For example, in the first and last paragraphs, the second sentences expand on the first sentences.

Closure

1 Divide the class into groups. Write the five topic sentences on strips, or photocopy them from the additional resources section (Resource 4B). Make a copy for each group. Students must put them into the correct order.

Alternatively, divide the class into two teams. One team chooses a topic sentence and reads it aloud. The other team must give the information triggered by that topic sentence. Accept a prediction or the actual paragraph content. However, ask students which it is – prediction or actual.

Language note

There is no universal logic to the structuring of information in a text. The order of information is language-specific. For example, oriental languages tend to have a topic sentence or paragraph summary at the end, not the beginning, of the paragraph. Or students whose first language is Arabic might structure a particular type of discourse in a different way from native English speakers. So it is important for students to see what a native speaker writer would consider to be a 'logical' ordering.

2 Refer students back to the sentences in Exercise D. Students should find it easier to comment on these now that they have read the text.

3 Focus on some of the vocabulary from the text, e.g., *competitive advantage, market share, product life cycle.*

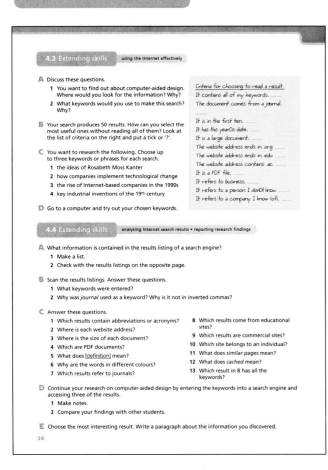

Put students in groups and ask them to compare how they normally use a computer to find information. Ask each group to produce a set of advice for using the Internet. Then, as a class, produce an accepted set of advice.

Key words to elicit: *search engine, keyword, website, web page, website address, search result, subject directory*

Note: Where the subject is a new one or a fairly general topic, it is a good idea to start first with a **subject directory** which evaluates sites related to the topic and collects them in one place. Some examples are:

● Academic Info

● BUBL LINK

● INFOMINE

● The WWW Virtual Library

A useful website for guidance on searching the Internet (at the time of writing) is http://library.albany.edu/internet/.

Exercise A

Write *computer-aided design* on the board.

1 Set for class discussion. Make sure students give reasons for their answers. Accept their answers at this stage.

2 Remind students that words in English often have more than one meaning, so care must be taken to get the desired result.

Answers

Possible answers:

1 In a current technical journal – very useful, as recent articles give the latest information.

On the Internet – good if the correct keywords are used and a careful selection of results is made. Since it is a general topic, it would benefit from a search with a subject directory such as The World Wide Web Virtual Library on http://vlib.org/.

In a textbook – useful if there is an up-to-date one, but books take time to publish, so even the latest may be out of date in these technologically fast-moving times.

General note

Students will need access to a computer with an Internet connection. If computers are not available during the lesson, part of the lesson can be set for private study.

Lesson aim

● learn or practise how to use the Internet effectively for research

Introduction

Brainstorm the uses of the Internet. Then brainstorm what the important factors are when using the Internet. These should include:

● the search engines students use and why. Note that there is now a large number of search engines to suit different purposes. It is not necessarily a good idea to use Google exclusively.

● how to choose *and write* keywords in their preferred search engine

● how they extract the information they want from the results

2 In this list of possible keywords, the first three are obvious starting points; others are also possible.

computer
aided ⎤ – very specific to the task
design ⎦

journal — journals give the latest information

this year ⎤
(the year's date) ⎬ – the time factor
current state ⎪
nowadays ⎦

business ⎤
latest ⎪
technology ⎬ relevant to the general
computerization/isation ⎪ topic area
manufacturing ⎪
production ⎦

Exercise B

Set for pairwork. Remind students of the research topic.

Feed back, encouraging students to give reasons for their decisions. Emphasize that we only know what *might* be useful at this stage.

Establish that the company sites often end in '.com'.

Answers

Model answers:

? It contains all of my keywords. (*but check that the meaning is the same*)

? The document comes from a journal. (*current information*)

? It is in the first ten. (*a web page can have codes attached to put it high in the list*)

? It has this year's date. (*current information*)

? It is a large document. (*size is no indication of quality*)

? The website address ends in .org (*because it is a non-profit organization*)

? The website address ends in .edu (*because it is an educational establishment*)

? The website address contains .ac (*because it is an educational establishment*)

? It is a PDF file. (*file type is no indication of quality*)

? It refers to business. (*may not be relevant*)

? It refers to a person I don't know. (*may not be reliable*)

? It refers to a company I know (of). (*reliable*)

Language note

PDF stands for *portable document format*. PDF documents can be viewed and printed on most computers, without the need for each computer to have the same software, fonts, etc. They are created with Adobe Acrobat software.

Exercise C

Set for individual work and pairwork checking. Ask students to compare their choice of keywords with their partner, and justify their choice.

Answers

Possible answers:

The following combinations will produce results provided the words in bold are included.

1 **Kanter** business thinker / Kanter how to lead / Kanter global information age

2 **technological business** strategy / **managing e-business** / managing technological change

3 **1990s dotcom** bubble / new economy / dotcom boom bust

4 **19th century inventors** / most important 19th century **inventions** / 19th century industrial **pioneers**

Exercise D

Students should try out different combinations to discover for themselves which gives the best results.

Closure

Tell students to think of their own question for research, as in Exercise C, and find the best web page for the data by entering appropriate keywords.

Ask students to write their question on a piece of paper and sign it. Put all the questions in a box. Students pick out one of the questions at random and go online to find the best page of search results. From those results they can find the most useful web page. They should ask the questioner for verification.

4.4 Extending skills

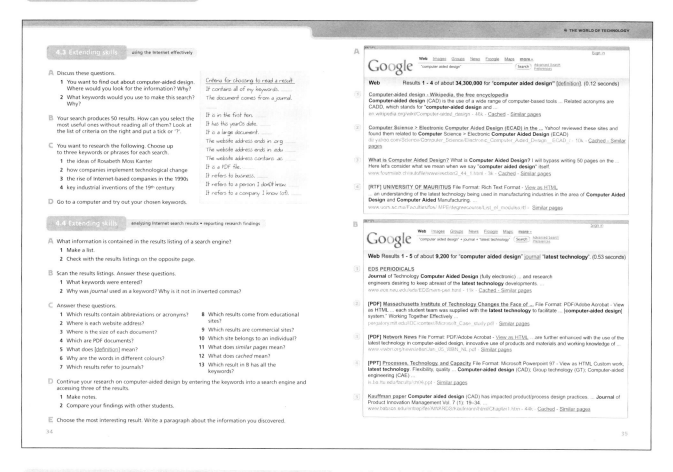

General note

Students will need access to a computer with an Internet connection. If computers are not available during the lesson, part of the lesson can be set for private study.

Lesson aims

- examine a page of Internet search results critically
- report Internet search findings in a short written summary

Introduction

Ask students what problems they had, what lessons they have learnt and what advice they can give from their Internet search experience in the previous lesson. Brainstorm the important factors when searching for information on the Internet and put them in order of importance.

Exercise A

Set for pairwork. Students should first make a list of information they expect to find in search engine results.

(They should do this before they look at the search engine results on the right-hand page.) They should then look at the page of results and identify any other information that is there.

Answers

Possible answers:

number of results
keywords used
time taken
title of document
type of document
quotations from the text with keywords highlighted
date
web address/URL

Exercise B

This is further reinforcement on keywords. Set for pairwork or whole class discussion.

Answers

Model answers:

1 A: "computer aided design"

B: "computer aided design" journal "latest technology"

2 Because journals give the most current information. Inverted commas are put round a phrase to indicate that it is all one meaningful lexical item. In Google, *journal* does not need them as it is one word.

Exercise C

This detailed examination of the results should make students aware of the content, so that they can make an educated selection of a web page with useful information. Set for pairwork.

Make sure in feedback that students are aware of what the following abbreviations stand for: PDF (portable document format), PPT (PowerPoint), RTF (rich text format).

Answers

Model answers:

1 Acronyms/abbreviations:

   Result A1: CAD, CADD

   Result A2: ECAD

   Result A3: html

   Result A4: RTF, HTML

   Result B2: PDF, HTML

   Result B3: PDF, HTML

   Result B4: PPT, HTML, CAD, GT, CAE

   Result B5: CAD, Vol.

Note: Students may identify further abbreviations, e.g., in the website addresses.

2 At the end.

3 At the end (if it is given), e.g., 46k.

4 Results B2 and B3 (portable document format = viewed as a real text page).

5 If you click on the word, a definition will be provided.

6 Blue = titles and viewing information; green = website address; black = keywords.

7 Results B1 and B5.

8 In the heading: results A4, B2; in the web address: results B1, 2, 4, 5.

9 Results A2 (notice that this is the Yahoo subject directory site), B3.

10 Result A3.

11 There were other very similar results, so the search engine ignored them. They are available if you click on the words.

12 It is a more efficient way of storing information. (It means that you can go to a copy of the page stored by Google, in case the actual website happens to be down at the time of the search; of course, it could be a little out of date.)

13 Result B1.

Exercise D

1 Set for individual work. Students should input the keywords again. They will not get exactly the same results page as here, but the results should be comparable. Tell them to take notes.

2 Set for pairwork. Feed back, getting students to tell the rest of the class about their most interesting findings. Encourage other students to ask questions.

Exercise E

Set for individual work. Students can complete it in class or for homework.

Closure

1 Focus on some of the vocabulary connected with using the Internet, including:

   website
   web address/URL
   search engine
   search results
   input
   keyword
   log in/log on
   login (n)
   username
   password
   access

2 The importance of the care needed when selecting keywords can be demonstrated by a simple classroom activity. Tell the class you are thinking of a particular student who you want to stand up. Say (for example):

   It's a man. (all the men stand up and remain standing)
   He has dark hair. (only those with dark hair remain standing)
   He has a beard.
   He has glasses.
   He's tall.
   His name begins with A.
   And so on.

   When only one student remains, ask the class to list the minimum number of keywords necessary to identify only that student. Make sure they discard unnecessary ones. For example, if all students have dark hair, that is unnecessary.

3 Finding the keywords for familiar topics is another activity, done in groups. For example, they could:

   ? find their own college record (name, ID number or date of entry)

   ? find their last exam results (name, class, subject, date)

   ? find a book about robots used in manufacturing in the library (robot, manufacture, factory, etc.)

Extra activities

1 Work through the *Vocabulary bank* and *Skills bank* if you have not already done so, or as a revision of previous study.

2 Use the *Activity bank* (Teacher's Book additional resources section, Resource 4A).

A Set the wordsearch for individual work (including homework) or pairwork.

Answers

Verb	Noun
construct	construction
cooperate	cooperation
coordinate	coordination
create	creation
define	definition
divide	division
expand	expansion
exploit	exploitation
innovate	innovation
integrate	integration
interact	interaction
miscalculate	miscalculation
motivate	motivation
operate	operation
promote	promotion
protect	protection
satisfy	satisfaction
select	selection
separate	separation
transform	transformation

B Teach students how to play noughts and crosses if they don't know – they take it in turns to say the abbreviation or acronym, and what it stands for. If they succeed, they can put their symbol – a nought 0 or a cross X – in that box. If a person gets three of their own symbols in a line, they win.

3 Write the acronyms and abbreviations from the unit on cards, or photocopy them from the additional resources section (Resource 4D). Divide the class into two teams. A student selects a card and reads it correctly. (Speed is of the essence.) Alternatively, one team picks a card and the other team gives the actual words.

You can follow this up by eliciting other acronyms and abbreviations from the students – in particular, useful ones from the field of business.

4 Have a class debate: 'If a company does not have the latest technology, it cannot possibly compete successfully.' Ask two students to prepare an opening argument for and against.

Remind students of the points in Lesson 2 Exercises A and B2. If new technology seems so great, why doesn't every company use it? Although new businesses may be able to set up with the latest technology, established companies already have facilities in place which may not be compatible. For them, the introduction of new technology can only occur when the budget allows. There is also the question of workers losing their jobs, or lack of people with appropriate skills. It is possible to make gradual changes which may be highly productive (as in some of the Japanese management approaches such as 'kaizen') without spending large sums of money on the latest equipment.

5 Ask students to work in small groups to research and feed back to the group on some other commercially successful inventions of the 20th century. Three research questions could be:
1 *What problem did people face in this area?*
2 *How did they solve the problem?*
3 *How did the solution change business or life?*

If students are going to do research on the Internet, suggest that they type in *History* then their topic to get some potential texts. Alternatively, you can do this research before the lesson and print off some pages for students to work from. Remind students that they can't possibly read everything they find, so they must use the topic sentences to decide if a paragraph is worth reading.

5 PEOPLE AND MARKETS

Marketing is covered in this unit and in Unit 6. In Unit 5, the focus is on the nature of marketing, types of markets, market segmentation and market research. The first listening extract, from a lecture, looks at what marketing is and why it is important, and gives an overview of some key marketing concepts. The second listening extract is from a seminar about market mapping. This leads into work on the four types of market research: primary, secondary, qualitative and quantitative.

Skills focus

🎧 Listening

- understanding 'signpost language' in lectures
- using symbols and abbreviations in note-taking

Speaking

- making effective contributions to a seminar

Vocabulary focus

- word sets: synonyms, antonyms, etc.
- the language of trends
- common lecture language

Key vocabulary

Marketing	Market segmentation and target markets	Statistical/market trends	Research methods
advertising	category	decline (n and v)	analyse
brand (n)	gender	decrease (n and v)	data analysis
consumer	manual	drop (n and v)	focus group
mailing	mass market	gradual	interview
make (n)	niche market	growth	market research
market leader	professional	increase (n and v)	primary research
market share	skilled	outperform	qualitative research
marketing mix (n)	socio-economic status	rise (n and v)	quantitative research
product	unskilled	steady (adj)	questionnaire
promotion			reliable
satisfy (demand)			response rate
special offer			sample (n and v)
sponsorship			secondary research
strategy			statistical
target (n and v)			statistics
			survey (n and v)

5.1 Vocabulary

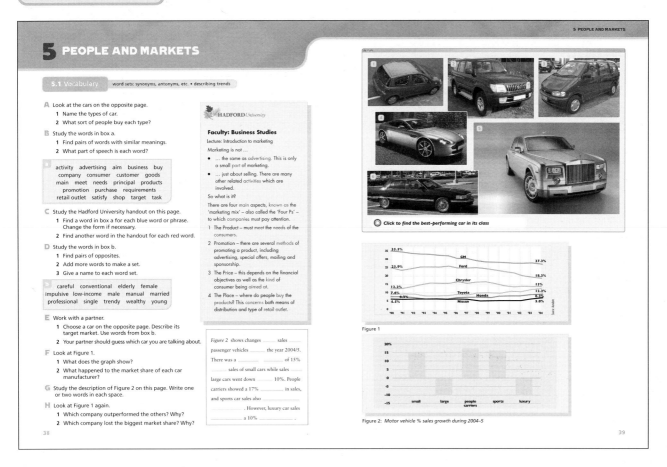

General note

Read the *Vocabulary bank – Vocabulary sets* and *Describing trends* at the end of the Course Book unit. Decide when, if at all, to refer your students to it. The best time is probably at the very end of the lesson or the beginning of the next lesson, as a summary/revision.

Lesson aims

● gain an understanding of lexical cohesion in texts through building word sets, synonyms and opposites/converses

● use appropriate language for describing trends

Introduction

Do some vocabulary revision from the previous units. For example:

1 Choose some words with different meanings in general and business English (see Units 1 and 2). Ask students to say or write two sentences using each word with a different meaning. Some examples are: *layer, resources, board, structure, rigid, flexible, section, labour, enterprise, head*, etc. If necessary, students can work with their dictionaries.

2 Choose some prefixes and suffixes (see Units 1 and 4). Write them on the board. Ask students to give the meaning of the affix and an example of a word.

3 Dictate some of the key vocabulary from Unit 3. Ask students to check their spellings (with a dictionary) and group the words according to their stress patterns.

Exercise A

Set both questions for pairwork discussion and whole class feedback. Do not comment or correct at this point. Students don't need to be able to identify the make/brand (although some may be able to do this) – just the type of car.

Elicit the general word *vehicle* and write it on the board. Ask for some other examples of vehicles and write these on the board under *vehicle* (e.g., *truck, lorry, train, bus*). Point out that the general word can be used instead of the more specific word to avoid repetition in a text – this happens to some extent in conversation and is also particularly useful in written texts. For each type of vehicle there are also different *makes* (= usually the name of the company that makes the vehicle) with *models* (= usually a vehicle with a particular design or set of specifications) to suit different customers.

Language note

General words like *vehicle* are called hypernyms or superordinate terms. Words like *bus* and *car* are called hyponyms or class members.

Answers

Model answers:

1. 1 A small car (a Toyota Yaris).
   2 A sports utility vehicle or SUV (a Toyota Landcruiser).
   3 A people carrier (a Nissan Serena).
   4 A luxury sports car (an Aston Martin V8 Vantage made by Ford).
   5 A luxury car (a Rolls-Royce Phantom made by BMW).
   6 A large car (a Cadillac).
2. Accept all reasonable answers.

Exercise B

The purpose of this exercise is to build sets of synonyms. This not only helps in understanding textual cohesion, but is useful for paraphrasing.

Set both questions for pairwork. Students should look for pairs of words/items. Tell them to use their dictionaries if necessary to check the grammatical information, and to note if they find other words with similar meanings.

Feed back with the whole class, building up a table on the board, and eliciting other words which can be used with the same meaning.

Answers

Model answers:

Word 1/ part of speech		Word 2/ part of speech		Words with similar meanings/ notes
activity	n (C)	task n	(C)	job
advertising	n (U)	promotion	n (C/U)	a special promotion = a special offer to promote a product
aim	n (C) v (T)	target	n (C) v (T)	objective, goal if *aim* is a transitive verb it is followed by *at*
business	n (C/U)	company	n (C)	firm, organization business U = the activity
buy	v (T)	purchase	v (T)	get, acquire
consumer	n (C)	customer	n (C)	client (for services); shopper (for shops)
goods	pl n	products	pl n	can also use *items* meaning things
main	adj	principal	adj	major, chief, key
meet	v (T/I)	satisfy	v (T)	use with *needs* or *requirements*
needs	pl n	requirements	pl n	
retail outlet	n (C)	shop	n (C)	*shop* can also be a verb

Language note

The synonyms given here are those which can replace the words in Exercise C. There may well be other words with similar meanings, but they will not necessarily fit into the *Introduction to marketing* text. For example, *multinational* is another word for *company/organization* but it would not work in this context. *Meet* and *satisfy* are synonymous when used with *needs/ requirements*, but not in other contexts.

Exercise C

1. Set for individual work and pairwork checking.
2. Set for pairwork. Students may need to change the part of speech.

   Feed back with the whole class by reading the paragraph or by using an OHT of the text. The text is reproduced in the additional resources section (Resource 5B) for this purpose. Discuss alternative ideas and decide whether they are acceptable. Check the meaning of any unknown words in the text (e.g., *mailing, sponsorship*). Note that the blue words are business words whereas the red words are general purpose words frequent in academic contexts.

Answers

Model answers:

1

Marketing is not …

- … the same as (*advertising*) promotion. This is only a small part of marketing.
- … just about selling. There are many other related (*activities*) tasks which are involved.

So what is it?

There are four (*main*) principal aspects, known as the 'marketing mix' – also called the 'Four Ps' – to which (*companies*) businesses must pay attention.

1 The **Product** – must (*meet*) satisfy the (*needs*) requirements of the (*consumers*) customers.

2 **Promotion** – there are several methods of promoting a product, including advertising, special offers, mailing and sponsorship.

3 The **Price** – this depends on the financial objectives as well as the kind of consumer being (*aimed at*) targeted.

4 The **Place** – where do people (*buy*) purchase the (*products*) goods? This concerns both means of distribution and type of (*retail outlet*) shop.

2

part	aspect
known as	called
methods	means
kind	type
concern(s)	involve(d)

Exercise D

1 Set for pairwork. Feed back. Start the first column of the table as shown in the Answers section.

2 Do the first pair of words with the whole class as an example. Set the remainder for pairwork. Feed back, completing the second column of the table on the board.

3 Discuss with the whole class. Elicit a word or phrase which describes the whole set of words and add this to the table in the next column.

Answers

Model/possible answers:

Opposites	Other words	Word for set
careful, impulsive	cautious, risk-taker	personality
conventional, trendy	traditional, fashionable	style/lifestyle
elderly, young	old, middle aged, teenage, in his/her 20s etc., child, adult	age
female, male	woman, man	gender/sex
low-income, wealthy	high/middle/average income, poor, rich, well-off	income
manual, professional	managerial, clerical, skilled/unskilled/semi-skilled, casual, part time, blue collar/white collar, unemployed, higher/lower professional/managerial, middle manager, housewife, retired	occupation/type of job/socio-economic status
married, single	divorced, widowed, with/without children, parent	marital or family status

Language note

There are clearly a very large number of words which can be used to describe lifestyle or personality. The above words are just a small selection.

Exercise E

Introduce the terms *market segmentation* and *target market*. Elicit or give definitions, e.g., *Market segmentation is the division of a market for a product into groups of customers who have similar needs or characteristics. Each of the groups is likely to want different types of the product. Each market 'segment' can thus be a* **target market**.

Point out that the names for the word sets in Exercise D are actually the categories that are used to segment markets. Choose one of the cars yourself and give a description of its target market (see table in Answers section, asking students to identify which car you are talking about). Set the remainder for pairwork, telling students to use several of the categories in Exercise D for each car, adding other words or ideas if they need to.

Feed back as a class discussion, building the table in the Answers section if you wish. Note that the suggestions here may not fit certain countries or cultures. While the segmentation categories should apply universally, the descriptors can be changed to suit students' culture.

Answers

Possible answers:

Type of car	Gender/age	Marital status	Occupation	Income/ lifestyle	Personality
1 small car (Toyota Yaris 2-door)	female – any age male – either elderly or young (e.g., student just passed driving test)	single, or elderly with no family	retired, housewife, student	middle to low income	careful, conventional
2 sports utility vehicle (Toyota Landcruiser)	male or female middle aged (30s, 40s)	married couple with children	white collar, professional, managerial	middle to high income	cautious driver but fashionable/ trendy
3 people carrier (Nissan Serena)	male or female middle aged (30s, 40s)	married couple with children	any profession	middle income	fairly careful; not as fashionable as SUV owners
4 luxury sports car (Aston Martin V8 Vantage)	male or female 20s, 30s	single	white collar, higher professional, managerial, footballer	very rich	risk-taker, fashionable, impulsive
5 luxury car (Rolls-Royce Phantom)	male or female middle aged, elderly	probably single, or couple with no children	higher managerial, company director, rich widow	extremely wealthy	traditional, conventional
6 large car (Cadillac)	male or female middle-aged, elderly	may have family	higher managerial (e.g., successful businessperson, company director)	rich	not practical; doesn't care about environment

Exercise F

Introduce *market share*. Elicit or give a definition, e.g., *Market share is a company's sales of a product as a percentage of the total sales in the market.*

1 With the whole class, discuss what Figure 1 shows. Elicit some of the verbs and adverbs which students will need in order to discuss question 2. For example:

Go up	No change	Go down	Adverbs
rise	stay the same	fall	sightly
increase	remain at …	decrease	gradually
grow	doesn't change	decline	steadily
improve	is unchanged	worsen	significantly
		drop	sharply
			dramatically

Note: These verbs are generally used in an intransitive sense when describing trends.

2 Set for pairwork. Students should write or say a sentence about each company. Feed back, eliciting sentences from the students. Write correct sentences on the board, or display the model answers on an OHT. Make sure that students notice the prepositions used with the numbers and dates.

Answers

Model answers:

1 The graph shows changes in the US market share for six important car manufacturers between 1990 and 2004.

2 GM's market share <u>fell</u> <u>steadily</u> from 35.5% in 1990 to 27.3% in 2004.

Ford's market share <u>increased</u> between 1990 and 1995 and then <u>fell</u> <u>sharply</u> to 18.3% in 2004.

Chrysler's market share <u>rose</u> until 1998. Then it <u>fell</u> <u>significantly</u> from about 16% to 13% in 2004.

Toyota's market share <u>increased</u> <u>steadily</u> from 7.6% in 1990 to 12.2% in 2004.

Honda's market share <u>dropped</u> between 1990 and 1995. Then it <u>increased</u> <u>gradually</u> to 8.2% in 2004.

Nissan's market share <u>increased</u> <u>slightly</u> between 1990 and 2004.

Underline the verbs and adverbs. Ask students to make nouns from the verbs and adjectives from the adverbs. Alternatively, you could reproduce the table on the next page (minus the noun and adjective forms) on the board, on an OHT or on a handout. The incomplete table is reproduced in the additional resources section (Resource 5C) to facilitate this.

Verbs	Nouns	Adverbs	Adjectives
rise	a rise	gradually	gradual
increase	an increase	sharply	sharp
grow	growth*	slightly	slight
improve	improvement	markedly	marked
fall	a fall	significantly	significant
decrease	a decrease	rapidly	rapid
drop	a drop	steeply	steep
decline	a decline	steadily	steady

*usually (but not always) uncountable in this sense

Return to the original answer sentences and ask students to make sentences with the same meaning, using the nouns and adjectives in place of the verbs and adverbs. Note that when using the noun + adjective, sentences can be made using *There was ...* or *showed*. Do one or two examples orally, then ask students to write the remaining sentences. Feed back.

Answers

Model answers:

GM's market share <u>fell steadily</u> from 35.5% in 1990 to 27.3% in 2004.	There <u>was</u> a <u>steady fall</u> in GM's market share from 35.5% in 1990 to 27.3% in 2004.
Ford's market share <u>increased</u> between 1990 and 1995 and then <u>fell sharply</u> to 18.3% in 2004.	There <u>was</u> <u>an increase</u> in Ford's market share between 1990 and 1995 and then a <u>sharp fall</u> to 18.3% in 2004.
Chrysler's market share <u>rose</u> until 1998. Then it <u>fell significantly</u> from about 16% to 13% in 2004.	There <u>was</u> a <u>rise</u> in Chrysler's market share until 1998, and then <u>a significant fall</u> from about 16% to 13% in 2004.
Toyota's market share <u>increased steadily</u> from 7.6% in 1990 to 12.2% in 2004.	Toyota's market share <u>showed</u> a <u>steady increase</u> from 7.6% in 1990 to 12.2% in 2004.
Honda's market share <u>dropped</u> between 1990 and 1995. Then it <u>increased gradually</u> to 8.2% in 2004.	Honda's market share <u>showed</u> a <u>drop</u> between 1990 and 1995, and then a <u>gradual increase</u> to 8.2% in 2004.
Nissan's market share <u>increased slightly</u> between 1990 and 2004.	Nissan's market share <u>showed</u> a <u>slight increase</u> between 1990 and 2004.

Exercise G

First ask students to look at Figure 2 and discuss in pairs the information it shows. Feed back. Elicit two types of sentence using a verb and a noun to express the changes. For example:

There was <u>a rise of</u> *15% in sales of small cars.*

Sales of small cars <u>rose by</u> *15%.*

Again, make sure that students notice the prepositions, especially the use of *by* to show the size of the increase.

Set the text completion for individual work and pairwork checking.

Answers

Model answers:

Figure 2 shows changes <u>in</u> sales <u>of</u> passenger vehicles <u>for/in</u> the year 2004/5. There was a <u>sharp rise</u> of 15% <u>in</u> sales of small cars while sales <u>of</u> large cars went down <u>by</u> 10%. People carriers showed a 17% <u>improvement/growth/rise/increase</u> in sales, and sports car sales also <u>rose/went up/increased/grew/improved</u> dramatically. However, luxury car sales <u>showed</u> a 10% <u>drop/fall/decrease/decline</u>.

Exercise H

Check the meaning of *outperformed*. Tell students to look at all the information on the right-hand page, i.e., the pictures of the cars as well as Figure 2. They should be able to see *possible* reasons for the trends.

Set for pairwork. Feed back with the whole class. You could take the discussion further by asking why students think these increases and decreases took place. (Among the reasons are probably that large cars are generally less popular for environmental reasons.)

Answers

Model answers:

1 Toyota increased its market share by 4.6%, possibly because sales of small cars and SUVs increased.

2 GM lost 8.2% of its market share, possibly because sales of large cars decreased.

Closure

In the box below are some important features of cars which affect how well they sell. Ask students to work in small groups or pairs to:

● rank the features from most to least important when buying a car

● discuss how Japanese and US cars compare in these areas

● discuss which of these features might be the chief reasons for the Japanese car manufacturers' increasing share of the US car market and the corresponding decrease for US car manufacturers

> price
> quality
> durability
> design and style
> fuel efficiency
> environmental standards for fuel emissions

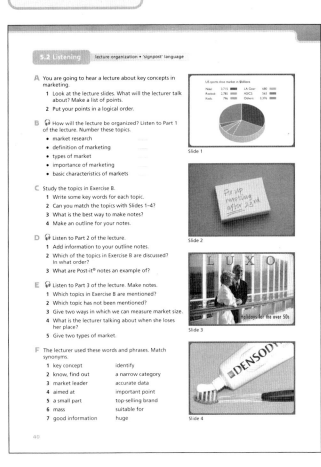

General note

Read the *Skills bank – Signpost language in a lecture* at the end of the Course Book unit. Decide when, if at all, to refer students to it. The best time is probably at the very end of the lesson or the beginning of the next lesson, as a summary/revision.

Lesson aims

- improve comprehension through understanding of signposts and lexical cohesion
- deal with disorganization in lectures/fractured text

Further practice in:

- predicting content from own background knowledge and from the lecture introduction
- using the introduction to decide the best form of notes to use

Introduction

Review key vocabulary by writing a selection of words from Lesson 1 on the board and asking students to put the words in groups, giving reasons for their decisions.

Exercise A

Remind students about preparing for a lecture. If you wish, review Unit 1 *Skills bank – Making the most of lectures.*

Remind students that when lecturers begin their talks, they usually provide their listeners with an outline.

Sequencing words		Verbs
To start with, Firstly,	I'll	begin/start by …ing
Secondly, Then … After that,		discuss examine consider mention talk about look at define give a(n) outline/overview/ definition/summary of … end/finish/conclude by …ing
Finally,		

Remind/tell students about the *signpost language* which speakers use at the beginning to list the areas they will cover. On the board, build the table above, eliciting suggestions from the students. Alternatively (or in addition), you could refer to the *Skills bank* at this point.

Language note

Speakers will usually avoid repeating words. So they would be unlikely to say *To start with, I'll start by … .*

Refer students to the lecture slides. Set the exercise for pairwork.

Ask students to feed back their possible lecture ideas to the whole class using the signpost language on the board to order their points. Accept any reasonable ideas. One possibility is given below.

Answer

Possible answer:

To start with, the lecturer will examine the US shoe market. After that he/she will talk about the market for Post-its. Then he/she will discuss holidays for the over 50s. He/she will finish by looking at the toothpaste market.

Methodology note

If students are new to the subject of marketing, they may only be able to make simple points about the slides, as in the model answer above. If they already know something about the subject they may realize that the slides illustrate the concepts which the lecturer will discuss, i.e., Slide 1: market size, market share and market leaders; Slide 2: creating new markets; Slides 3 and 4: niche and mass markets. These words will appear in the exercises that follow.

🎧 Exercise B

Tell students they are only going to hear the introduction to the lecture. Give students time to read the topics. Check that they understand the meaning. Remind them they will only hear the introduction once, as in a lecture. Tell them to listen out for the signpost language on the board. While they listen, they should number the topics from 1–5 in the order in which the lecturer will talk about them.

Play Part 1. Allow students to compare answers. Feed back. Ask students to say what signpost language they heard related to each topic. Confirm the correct answer.

Answers

market research – 3 (After that I'll talk about …)

definition of marketing – 1 (to start with, we need to consider …)

types of market – 5 (I'll finish by mentioning …)

importance of marketing – 2 (And secondly, …)

basic characteristics of markets – 4 (So then I'll discuss …)

Transcript 🎧 1.21

Part 1

Good morning, everyone. This morning we're going to begin the topic of marketing. In this first talk I'm just going to give you an overview of a few key concepts, and then other aspects will be dealt with in the next few lectures. Also, in your seminars and assignments you'll be able to cover all the important points in more detail. So … er … let's see – yes – to start with, we need to consider firstly what marketing is. In other words, why do businesses engage in marketing? And secondly, why is marketing so important? After that I'll talk about market research, because businesses need good information on which to base their marketing strategy. Part of this involves analysing markets. So then I'll discuss some basic characteristics of markets, and I'll finish by mentioning some different types of markets.

Exercise C

1 Set for pairwork. Divide the topics up among the pairs so that each pair concentrates on one topic. Feed back. Accept any reasonable suggestions.

2 Refer students to the lecture slides. Students should try to guess which of the topics each slide could refer to. Set for individual work and pairwork checking. Feed back but do not confirm or correct yet.

3 Elicit suggestions from the whole class. If you wish, refer to students to Unit 1 *Skills bank*.

4 Set for individual work. Students should prepare an outline on a sheet of paper preferably using either numbered points (with enough space between the points to allow for notes to be added) or a mind map/spidergram (see example below).

Answers

Possible answers:

1 Some key words are:

market research – *survey, focus group, interview, qualitative, quantitative*

definition of marketing – *promotion, satisfy customer needs*

types of market: any words from Lesson 1 concerned with market segmentation; also *niche* and *mass* (to be mentioned in the lecture)

importance of marketing – *ensure company profits, help meet company objectives*

basic characteristics of markets – *size, trends, growth, share, leader, brand, value, volume of sales, analysis*

2 Accept any reasonable answers with good justifications.

3/4 Example of spidergram:

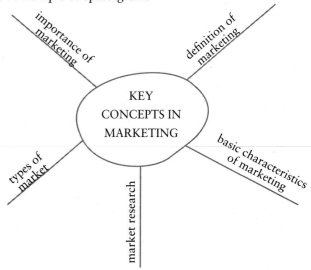

🎧 Exercise D

Tell students to use their outline from Exercise C to take notes. Which topics do they expect to hear in this section?

Play Part 2. Put students in pairs to compare their notes and discuss the questions.

Feed back. When it becomes clear that the lecturer did not actually stick to the plan in the introduction, say that this happens very often in lectures. Lecturers are human! Although it is a good idea to prepare outline notes, students need to be ready to alter and amend these. Discuss how best to do this. One obvious way is to use a non-linear approach such as a mind map or spidergram, where new topics can easily be added.

After checking answers to questions 2 and 3, build a complete set of notes on the board as a spidergram, as in the example in the Answers section.

Answers

Possible answers:

1 Example notes: see spidergram below.
2 Discussed first: importance of marketing; second: definition of marketing.
3 Creating new markets.

Transcript 🎧 1.22

Part 2

Actually, marketing is arguably *the* most important aspect of management. You can manage your staff and your production processes well, but if nobody buys your products, your business will fail. So, it follows that a business has to satisfy customers' needs if it is going to make a profit. So that's what marketing is all about – it's not just advertising. Marketing is all the processes involved in supplying customers with the right products at the right time and at the right price. But what *are* the needs of customers? Of course, there are many products that people will always need, but really successful companies identify gaps in markets and create new markets with new products. What I mean is, they anticipate consumers' requirements. A good example of this is those little packets of sticky notes – they're called Post-it notes. They were invented by the 3M Company in 1977 and are now extremely popular, which is not surprising because they're incredibly useful. We never knew we needed them until 3M came up with them.

🎧 Exercise E

Ask students what they expect to hear about in the next part. Refer students to their outline again. Give them time to read the questions. Note that the final part of the lecture will be heard in Lesson 3, but there is no need to tell them this at this point. Play Part 3. Set the questions for pairwork. Students should use their notes to help them answer the questions.

Feed back. Note that there is no need to build a set of notes on the board at this point – this will be done in Lesson 3. Ask students if they can remember exactly what the lecturer said to indicate that she had lost her place.

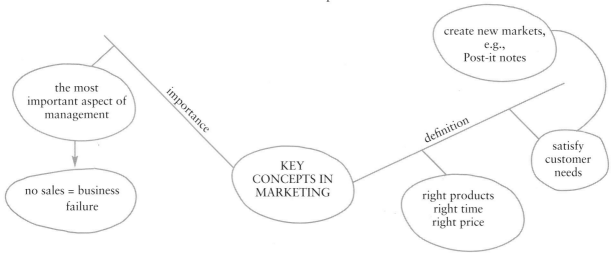

Answers

Model answers:

1 Basic characteristics of markets; types of market.

2 Market research (although students may argue that this is implicit from the first sentences of Part 3).

3 By what it is worth (value) and by number (volume) of sales.

4 The different types of running shoes. *(Er ... Where was I? Oh, yes.)*

5 Mass market; niche market.

Transcript 🎧 1.23

Part 3

Anyway, er ... to return to the main point – fundamentally, successful marketing is about having accurate data so that customers' needs can be met. So what is it that marketers need to know? Well, first they must begin by analysing the market. For example, it's essential to identify basic characteristics of the market such as its size, and which companies are the market leaders; that is to say, we need to look at the share of the market which each company has. Naturally, it's the aim of all companies to become the market leader – or to have the top-selling brand in a particular field. If we take the sports shoe market in the US as an example – you can see the size statistics on this slide. As you can see, in 2006 this market was worth nearly $12 billion per year. In terms of sales, it had annual sales of more than 370 million pairs of sports shoes. And what's more, it seems to be getting bigger, too. Before the 1970s, buying a pair of running shoes was a simple matter. But these days, there's a huge variety. There are different running shoes for men and women, light and heavy people, different sports, different foot shapes, and so on ... Er ... Where was I? Oh, yes. We also need to be clear about the type of market. One way to categorize the type of market is to think about whether the product is aimed at a mass market, like toothpaste, for example, which everyone needs. Or is it more suitable for a niche market – by that I mean a small part of a larger market. For example, vacations for people over 50 is a niche market inside the huge vacation market. In other words, is the product aimed at one narrow category of customer?

Exercise F

This gives further practice in identifying words and phrases used synonymously in a particular context. Set for individual work and pairwork checking.

Answers

1	key concept	important point
2	know, find out	identify
3	market leader	top-selling brand
4	aimed at	suitable for
5	a small part	a narrow category
6	mass	huge
7	good information	accurate data

Closure

1 Do a survey to find out the market leaders for products in the class. Set students to work in groups of 6–8, and make pairs within the groups. Ask each pair to choose a mass-market product which they are interested in. If necessary, give them some examples, such as sports shoes, pens, mobile phones, jeans, soft drinks, fast food, laptop computers, etc. They should list several brands in a table such as the one in Resource 5D in the additional resources section and then ask different students which brands they use. They can include their own responses. The results can be presented orally, using phrases such as:

The market leader for ... in our group is ...
The second most popular brand is ...
The least popular brand is ...

Alternatively, the results could be put into graphic form and written up.

2 Check that students understand some of the concepts and vocabulary in the unit so far, including:

make (of car)
brand
market characteristics
market share
market leader
market segment
target market
market segmentation
volume of sales
market size
market trends
gap in the market
anticipate (consumers' needs)
socio-economic status
marital status

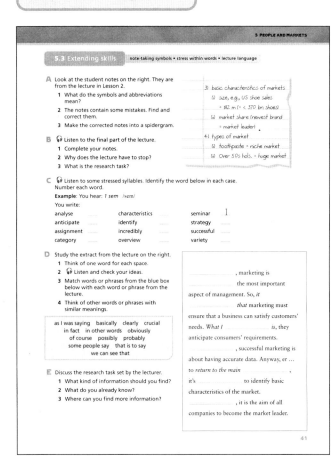

Lesson aims

- use symbols in note-taking
- understand and use lecture language such as stance adverbials (*obviously, arguably*), restatement (*in other words*) and other commentary-type phrases

Further practice in:

- stress within words
- asking for information
- formulating polite questions

Introduction

1 As in Unit 3, encourage students to ask you questions about the information in the lecture in Lesson 2 as if you were the lecturer. Remind them about asking for information politely. If they can't remember how to do this, you could tell them to revise the *Skills bank* for Unit 3.

2 Put students in pairs. Student A must ask Student B about the information in the lecture in Lesson 2 to help him/her complete the notes from the lecture. Then they reverse roles. Again, they can revise language for this in the *Skills bank* for Unit 3.

Exercise A

1 Revise/introduce the idea of using symbols and abbreviations when making notes. Ask students to look at the example notes and find the symbols and abbreviated forms. Do they know what these mean? If not, they should try to guess.

If you wish, expand the table in the Answers section below with more symbols and abbreviations that will be useful for the students. There is also a list at the back of the Course Book for students' reference.

2 Ask students to tell you what kind of notes these are (linear and numbered). Set the question for pairwork. Students will need to agree what the notes are saying and then make the corrections.

3 Set for individual work. Feed back with the whole class and build the spidergram in the Answers section on the board.

Answers

Model answers:

1

Symbol/abbreviation	Meaning
e.g.	(for) example
US	United States
=	equals, the same as, is
$	US dollar
m	million
<	less than/smaller than
bn	billion
over 50s	people over 50
hols.	holidays

2 Suggested corrections:

3) basic characteristics of markets

(i) size, e.g., US <u>sports</u> shoe sales = $12 <u>bn</u>

(= ≥ 370 <u>m</u> <u>pairs of</u> shoes)

(ii) market share (<u>top</u> brand = market leader)

4) types of market

(i) <u>mass</u> market, <u>e.g.,</u> toothpaste

(ii) <u>niche</u> market, <u>e.g.,</u> over 50s hols.

3

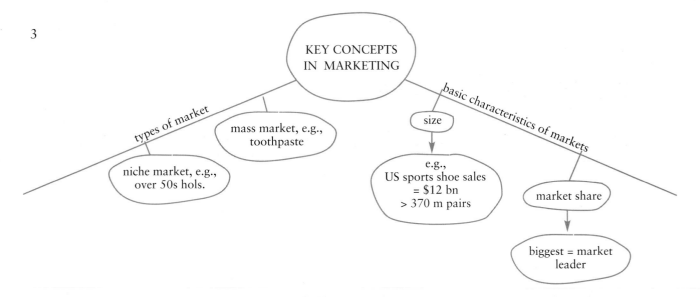

Language note

Some abbreviations are universal and some are personal. People often develop their own personal system of symbols and abbreviations. For example, *bn* for billion is used by many people, but *hols* is an example of a longer word abbreviated by the individual who wrote these notes.

🎧 Exercise B

Tell students they will hear the final part of the lecture. Give them time to read the questions. They should complete the final leg of the spidergram.

Play Part 4. Put students in pairs to compare their notes and discuss the questions. Feed back. For question 2 ask students if they can remember the exact words used by the lecturer (*oh, dear … sadly, I see that we've run out of time.*).

Answers

Model answers:

1

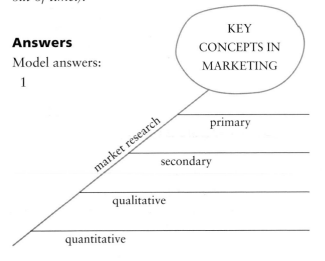

2 Because there is no more time.

3 The research task is to find out about the four different types of market research: *primary, secondary, qualitative* and *quantitative research.*

Transcript 🎧 1.24

Part 4

So how does the marketer get the necessary information? By research, obviously. There are several ways to categorize market research. Let me see … one way is to distinguish between primary and secondary research. Another important distinction is between qualitative and quantitative research. However … oh, dear … sadly, I see that we've run out of time. This means that I'll have to ask *you* to do some research. I'd like you to find out what is meant by the four types of research I've just mentioned, that is, primary and secondary research, and qualitative and quantitative research. We'll discuss what you've found out next time I see you.

🎧 Exercise C

Remind students of the importance of stressed syllables in words (see teaching notes fot Unit 3, Lesson 3, Exercise A). Play the recording, pausing after the first few to check that students understand the task.

Feed back, perhaps playing the recording again for each word before checking. Ideally, mark up an OHT of the words.

Answers

analyse	8
anticipate	7
assignment	3
category	11
characteristics	5
identify	10
incredibly	9
overview	2
seminar	1
strategy	4
successful	6
variety	12

Transcript 🎧 1.25

1 'seminar
2 'overview
3 a'ssignment
4 'strategy
5 character'istics
6 suc'cessful
7 an'ticipate
8 'analyse
9 in'credibly
10 i'dentify
11 'category
12 va'riety

🎧 Exercise D

This exercise gives students a chance to focus on some typical lecture language.

1 Set for pairwork. Students should try to think of a word for each of the blank spaces. Note that they should *not* try to use the words from the box for this. Do not feed back at this point.

2 Tell students they will hear the sentences from the lecture and should fill in the missing words as they listen. There will be pauses at the end of each sentence but you will play the recording straight through without stopping (as a kind of dictation).

Feed back with the whole class, playing the sentences again if necessary. Check the meanings and functions of the words and phrases. Point out the fixed phrases (in italics in the text) and encourage students to learn these. Ask students to repeat the sentences for pronunciation practice, making sure that the stress and intonation is copied from the model.

3 Set for individual work and pairwork checking. Students should check in their dictionaries for meanings or pronunciations of words from the box that they don't know. Feed back, building the first two columns of the table in the Answers section on the board.

4 Elicit suggestions from the whole class for a third column: *Other similar words.*

If you wish, students can practise saying the sentences in question 2 but this time with words from questions 3 and 4.

After completing Exercise D, students can be referred to the *Vocabulary bank – Stance* and the *Skills bank – Signpost language in a lecture* for consolidation.

Answers

Model answers:

1/2 <u>Actually</u>, marketing is <u>arguably</u> the most important aspect of management. So, *it follows that* marketing must ensure that a business can satisfy customers' needs. *What I mean is*, they anticipate consumers' requirements. <u>Fundamentally</u>, successful marketing is about having accurate data. Anyway, er ... *to return to the main point*, it's <u>essential</u> to identify basic characteristics of the market. <u>Naturally</u>, it is the aim of all companies to become the market leader.

3/4

Word/phrase from the lecture	Words/phrases from the box	Other similar words/phrases
Actually	in fact	in reality
arguably	probably, possibly, some people say	perhaps
it follows that	we can see that	logically
What I mean is	that is to say, in other words	or, by that I mean, to put it another way
Fundamentally	basically	in essence, really
to return to the main point	as I was saying	
essential	crucial	important
Naturally	of course, obviously, clearly	certainly

Transcript 🎧 1.26

Actually, marketing is arguably the most important aspect of management.

So, it follows that marketing must ensure that a business can satisfy customers' needs …

What I mean is, they anticipate consumers' requirements.

Fundamentally, successful marketing is about having accurate data.

Anyway, er … to return to the main point, …

It's essential to identify basic characteristics of the market …

Naturally, it is the aim of all companies to become the market leader …

Language note

There are three main categories of language here:

1 Stance markers. These are words or phrases that speakers use to show what they feel or think about what they are saying. Adverbs used like this are generally (though not always) positioned at the beginning of the sentence.

2 Phrases used to indicate a restatement. It is very important for students both to understand and to be able to use these, since speakers frequently need to repeat and explain their points.

3 Phrases used to show that the speaker has deviated from the main point and is now about to return to it. Again, this type of phrase is very common in lectures and discussions.

Exercise E

Remind students of the task set by the lecturer at the end of Part 4. Set the questions for pairwork discussion. Students should first list the sort of information they will need to find, then discuss and make notes on what they already know. Then they should compile a list of possible sources of information.

Feed back on all three tasks with the whole class. Do not discuss further at this point, as the topic will be taken up in the next lesson.

If you wish, you can tell students to focus on only *one* of the types of market research in preparation for Exercise G in Lesson 4, and to follow up one of their references, not forgetting to record the necessary bibliographical details. Since this will act as preparation for Exercise G in Lesson 4, you need to make sure that there are equal numbers of students investigating each type of market research.

Answers

Possible answers:

1 Definitions, methods and anything else that is relevant.

2 Answers depend on the students.

3 Internet, library, subject textbooks, encyclopedias, etc.

Closure

Play a version of the game 'Just a minute'. Put students in groups of four. Give them an envelope in which some topics are written on slips of paper. Students take turns to take a slip of paper from the envelope and then talk for one minute on the topic. Encourage them to use as many of the words and phrases from Exercises C and D as they can. Each person should talk for up to a minute without stopping. If they can talk for one minute they get a point. If they deviate from their topic or can't think of anything more to say, they have to stop. The person who has the most points is the winner.

Suggestions for topics follow. Or if you prefer, you can use other topics unrelated to business.

car sales
target markets
market leaders
holidays
socio-economic status
toothpaste
customers' needs
types of markets
what is marketing?
the 'four Ps'
office equipment
the shoe market
advertising
market segmentation

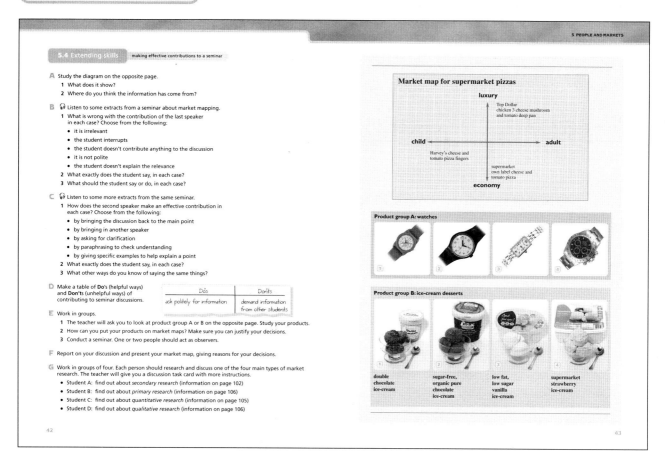

5.4 Extending skills

making effective contributions to a seminar

A Study the diagram on the opposite page.
  1 What does it show?
  2 Where do you think the information has come from?

B Listen to some extracts from a seminar about market mapping.
  1 What is wrong with the contribution of the last speaker in each case? Choose from the following:
    • it is irrelevant
    • the student interrupts
    • the student doesn't contribute anything to the discussion
    • it is not polite
    • the student doesn't explain the relevance
  2 What exactly does the student say, in each case?
  3 What should the student say or do, in each case?

C Listen to some more extracts from the same seminar.
  1 How does the second speaker make an effective contribution in each case? Choose from the following:
    • by bringing the discussion back to the main point
    • by bringing in another speaker
    • by asking for clarification
    • by paraphrasing to check understanding
    • by giving specific examples to help explain a point
  2 What exactly does the student say, in each case?
  3 What other ways do you know of saying the same things?

D Make a table of **Do's** (helpful ways) and **Don'ts** (unhelpful ways) of contributing to seminar discussions.

Do's	Don'ts
ask politely for information	demand information from other students

E Work in groups.
  1 The teacher will ask you to look at product group A or B on the opposite page. Study your products.
  2 How can you put your products on market maps? Make sure you can justify your decisions.
  3 Conduct a seminar. One or two people should act as observers.

F Report on your discussion and present your market map, giving reasons for your decisions.

G Work in groups of four. Each person should research and discuss one of the four main types of market research. The teacher will give you a discussion task card with more instructions.
    • Student A: find out about *secondary research* (information on page 102)
    • Student B: find out about *primary research* (information on page 106)
    • Student C: find out about *quantitative research* (information on page 105)
    • Student D: find out about *qualitative research* (information on page 106)

42

Market map for supermarket pizzas

luxury

Top Dollar chicken 3 cheese mushroom and tomato deep pan

child —————————— adult

Harvey's cheese and tomato pizza fingers

supermarket own label cheese and tomato pizza

economy

Product group A: watches

Product group B: ice-cream desserts

double chocolate ice-cream

sugar-free, organic pure chocolate ice-cream

low fat, low sugar vanilla ice-cream

supermarket strawberry ice-cream

43

Lesson aims

• make effective and appropriate contributions to a seminar

Further practice in:

• speaking from notes
• reporting information

Introduction

Revise stance words and restatement/deviation phrases from the previous lesson. Give a word or phrase and ask students to give one with a similar meaning. Alternatively, give a sentence or phrase from the lecture in Lessons 2 and 3 and ask students to tell you the accompanying stance word or restatement/deviation phrase.

Exercise A

1 Tell students to look at the market map. Set for pairwork discussion.

2 Ask students to use what they know about marketing to speculate on the answer. Feed back, accepting any reasonable suggestions.

Answers

Possible answers:

1 It shows how the pizza market is segmented according to two variables, and where each brand is positioned according to the variables.

2 The information has probably come from some form of market research, for example by asking people, by reading or by observing.

Subject and methodology note

Market mapping is a technique based on surveys of customers' attitudes and profiles. Two main variables are identified which enable products in a particular market to be distinguished from each other, and then the brands are plotted on the map. Companies can use the technique to help spot gaps in a market. They can also see if their target market is being reached or if they need to reposition their brand with a new advertising campaign and a different image.

In this lesson, students will be asked to make market maps based on their own ideas rather than by using statistics from a survey.

🎧 Exercise B

In this exercise, students will hear examples of how *not* to contribute to a group discussion.

1/2 Allow students time to read the questions. Tell students they will hear five extracts. They should choose a different answer for each one. Set for individual work and pairwork checking. Play all the extracts through once.

Play the extracts a second time, pausing after each one. Students should write down the actual words, as in a dictation, then check in pairs. When students have completed questions 1 and 2, feed back with the whole class, maybe building up columns 1 and 2 of the table in the Answers section on the board.

3 Set for pairwork discussion. Feed back, adding a third column to the table on the board.

Answers

Model answers:
See table below.

Transcript 🎧 1.27

Extract 1

LECTURER: Right, Leila and Majed, what did you find out about the segmentation of the pizza market?

LEILA: Well, first of all, we looked in the local supermarket to see what pizzas there were.

MAJED: I had pizza last night.

Extract 2

LECTURER: And what else did you do?

LEILA: We talked to the manager. She was quite helpful.

MAJED: That's rubbish. She obviously didn't want to talk to us.

Extract 3

LECTURER: Leila, can you give us an explanation of your market map?

LEILA: Well, yes, it has a vertical and a horizontal axis: children versus adults, and economy versus luxury. And as you can see, we've put some different pizza brands on it.

LECTURER: What do the rest of you make of this? Evie, what about you?

EVIE: Well, erm ... I'm not sure really.

Extract 4

LECTURER: Majed, can you explain how you decided where to place the different pizzas on your map?

MAJED: Well, yes, it's based on what the supermarket told us.

JACK: So it's secondary.

Extract 5

LECTURER: What do you mean by 'secondary', Jack?

JACK: I mean it's an example of secondary research. They did two things – they asked someone for information and ...

EVIE: (interrupting) Actually, that's primary.

	Contribution is poor because	Exact words	How to improve
Extract 1	it is irrelevant	Majed: I had pizza last night.	say something relevant: for example, something about the pizzas they found
Extract 2	it is not polite	Majed: That's rubbish. She obviously didn't want to talk to us.	use polite (tentative) language when disagreeing, e.g., *Actually, that's not that's not quite right. I don't think she really wanted to talk to us.*
Extract 3	the student doesn't contribute anything to the discussion	Evie: Well, erm ... I'm not sure really.	be ready to contribute something when brought into the discussion by the lecturer or other students
Extract 4	the student doesn't explain the relevance	Jack: So it's secondary.	the comment is relevant to the topic but he doesn't explain why. He should say, for example, what he said later after the lecturer asked him to explain (i.e., it's an example of secondary research)
Extract 5	the student interrupts	Evie: (interrupting) Actually, that's primary.	she should wait until the speaker has finished

Exercise C

1/2 This time students will hear good ways of contributing to a discussion. Follow the same procedure as for 1 and 2 in Exercise B above.

Again when students have completed 1 and 2, feed back with the whole class, maybe building up a table on the board. If you wish, students can look at the transcript in the Course Book.

3 Ask the whole class for other words or phrases that can be used for the strategy and add a third column to the table on the board.

Answers

Model answers:
See table below.

Transcript 🎧 1.28

Extract 6

LECTURER: Let's go back to this diagram for the moment to see how it can help with segmentation. First of all, tell us about the dimensions you chose.

LEILA: Well, the supermarket used price and age group as the main ways to distinguish the pizzas. Didn't they, Majed?

MAJED: Absolutely. Those were really the only criteria they used. So that's why we chose them.

Extract 7

MAJED: They put the children's pizzas in one display cabinet, with cheap ones at the bottom and expensive ones in the middle and top. And the same with the adult pizzas.

JACK: Sorry, I don't follow. Could you possibly explain why that's important?

MAJED: Well, basically they arrange the pizzas according to their target markets.

Extract 8

EVIE: I don't understand how the retailers know exactly which pizzas are suitable for which market.

LEILA: Well, the manager said that the manufacturers give very specific information about their target markets. For example, they say that pizza fingers are for children.

Extract 9

MAJED: Yes, manufacturers tell retailers exactly how and where to arrange their goods in the shops to achieve maximum sales.

JACK: If I understand you correctly, you're saying that manufacturers supply their retailers with information about how to market their products.

MAJED: Yes, that's right.

Extract 10

LECTURER: This is all very interesting, isn't it?

EVIE: Yes, but if we just go back to the market map, the pizza fingers are for children so they go on the left, and they're in the cheap to middle price range, so they go around the middle on the vertical axis.

LEILA: Correct!

	Helpful strategy	Exact words	Other ways to say it
Extract 6	bringing in another speaker	Leila: Didn't they, Majed?	What do you think, Majed?/What do you make of this, Majed?
Extract 7	asking for clarification	Jack: Sorry, I don't follow. Could you possibly explain …?	I don't quite understand. Could you say a bit more about …?
Extract 8	giving specific examples to help explain a point	Leila: Well, the manager said that … For example, they say that …	For instance …
Extract 9	paraphrasing to check understanding	Jack: If I understand you correctly, you're saying that manufacturers …	So what you are saying is …
Extract 10	making clear how the point is relevant	Evie: Yes, but if we just go back to the market map, the pizza fingers …	Thinking about …/If we can go back to … for a moment, …

Exercise D

Set for group work. Tell students to brainstorm suggestions for more good and bad seminar strategies. They should think about what helps a seminar discussion to be successful. It may help to think about having seminar discussions in their own language, but they should also think about what is involved in having a seminar discussion in English. Aspects to consider include language, how to contribute to discussions and how to behave.

Feed back, making a list on the board.

Answers

Possible answers:

Do's	Don'ts
ask politely for information	demand information from other students
try to use correct language	
speak clearly	mumble, whisper or shout
say when you agree with someone	get angry if someone disagrees with you
contribute to the discussion	sit quietly and say nothing
link correctly with previous speakers	
build on points made by other speakers	
be constructive	be negative
explain your point clearly	
listen carefully to what others say	start a side conversation
allow others to speak	dominate the discussion

Exercise E

Set students to work in groups of five or six. Give the groups a letter: A or B. Group As should look at the watches, and Group Bs should look at the ice-cream.

In each group there should be one ore two observers and three or four discussing. Groups should also appoint one person to take notes on the discussion, since they will have to present their solution to another group. During the discussion, they will need to identify two key variables (consisting of a pair of antonyms) for the market map. They will then need to decide where to place each product on the map and be able to justify their decisions. If you wish, give each group a large sheet of paper on which to draw their market map. While students are talking, you can listen in and note where students may need help with language, and where particularly good examples of language are used.

The students acting as observers for the discussion should use a checklist of things to watch for. One observer can concentrate on poor contributions and the other on good contributions. Sample checklists are provided in the additional resources section (Resource 5E) – students simply mark in each cell whenever the behaviour occurs.

Exercise F

For this exercise, an A and a B group can join together to make one larger group. Alternatively, if the groups are already large, divide each group in half and send one half plus one observer to another group, so that the new groups consist of 50% As and 50% Bs.

Before the groups report on their discussion, remind them about speaking from notes (see Unit 1 *Skills bank*).

First, the observers should give an overview of how the seminar discussion went and should highlight especially good practice. They can also report on poor contributions, but this needs to be done carefully and constructively (possibly without mentioning names), so that individuals are not embarrassed or upset.

Then the person who took notes should present the decisions of their group to the other group.

Finally, feed back to the whole class on what you heard as you listened in to the groups. Suggest improvements for words and phrases, and highlight good practice.

Exercise G

With the whole class, revise asking for information, opinions and clarification, and agreeing or disagreeing in a seminar. Remind students of the questions used by the lecturer in Lesson 3, Exercise B. If necessary, play the seminar extracts again or refer students to the *Skills bank*. Remind students also about reporting information to people (see Unit 3 *Skills bank*).

For this discussion exercise, students will make use of the information they have already found on the four research types, as set in Lesson 3. Ideally, each student should have found out information about one type of research (primary, secondary, qualitative, quantitative) and be able to give the source reference for their information.

Set students to work in groups of four. If students have done the research task in Lesson 3, each group should consist of students who have each found out about a different type of market research. The easiest way to manage this is to give students a letter: all the people who have researched primary research are As, secondary research are Bs, qualitative are Cs and quantitative are Ds. Make groups with one of each. Give each student the appropriate *discussion task card* from the additional resources section (Resource 5F).

In their groups, students should do some more research individually on definitions, methods, advantages and disadvantages of the four categories of market research. They should work as follows:

As (who have already looked at primary research) can find out about secondary research

Bs (who have already looked at secondary research) can find out about primary research

Cs (who have already looked at qualitative research) can find out about quantitative research

Ds (who have already looked at quantitative research) can find out about qualitative research

Refer each student to the notes on market research at the back of the Course Book.

Then each student should feed back to the group the information they have found (as instructed on the discussion task card).

Alternatively, the research activity can be done as a 'wall dictation' as follows. Make large copies of the research notes (Resource 5G), one type of research per page, and pin the sheets on the classroom walls. Each student should leave his/her seat and go to the wall to find the information he/she needs. Students should not write anything down: instead they should read and try to remember the information. Then they return to their group and tell them the information. If they forget something they can go back to the wall to have another look. (Alternatively, you can ask students to read the information, remember it and then fold up the paper – it's important that they do not simply read out the information but use it to inform their speaking.)

It is best to discuss each type of research in turn. For example, first, Student A goes to the wall to find out about secondary research and returns with the information. After hearing what A has to say, the other students can ask the student who has already researched the definition of secondary research (i.e., Student B): *Do you agree with X's view on Y?* Student B should give their definition and also the source reference for the information.

If students have *not* previously researched these topics, do *not* use the discussion task cards. Instead, use the wall dictation method or refer each student to the appropriate notes on market research at the back of the Course Book.

When the discussion on secondary research has finished, Student B should go to find the information on primary research, repeating the process described, and so on until all four types of research have been discussed.

While students are discussing, 'eavesdrop' the conversations, noting where students are having difficulty with language and where things are going well. When everyone has finished, feed back with the class on points you have noticed while listening in to the discussions.

Closure

1 If you wish, refer students to the *Skills bank – Seminar language* for consolidation.

2 Focus on some of the vocabulary connected with research from Lessons 2 and 4. For example:

analyse (v)	*methods*
analysis	*observation*
attitudes	*overview*
axis	*psychology*
beliefs	*qualitative*
category	*quantitative*
concept	*questionnaire*
data	*reliable*
define	*response rate*
definition	*sample*
dimension	*sources*
examine	*statistical*
factual	*statistics*
focus group	*survey*
generalize	*trend*
horizontal	*verbal*
identify	*vertical*
market reseach	

Extra activities

1 Work through the *Vocabulary bank* and *Skills bank* if you have not already done so, or as a revision of previous study.

2 Use the *Activity bank* (Teacher's Book additional resources section, Resource 5A).

A Set the crossword for individual work (including homework) or pairwork.

Answers

B Students should select any six words from the box (listed in *Students' words* column). Call out words at random from the *Teacher's words* column, not forgetting to note which words you have called. When someone has crossed out all the words on his/her bingo card, he/she should call out *Bingo!* Check to see if all the words are correctly crossed out. The first person to correctly cross out all the words on his/her bingo card is the winner.

An alternative is to put students in groups to play the game, with one student acting as the teacher. In this case, you will need to prepare a list of teacher's words for each group.

Students' words	Teacher's words
careful	impulsive
child	adult
easy	difficult
elderly	young
fall	rise
large	small
low	high
luxury	economy
male	female
poor	well-off
professional	manual
rigid	flexible
sharply	gradually
short	tall
single	married
slightly	significantly
slow	rapid
traditional	modern
unskilled	skilled

3 Students can choose a suitable product for which they can try to identify the target markets and/or segmentation. This can be anything they wish: examples of products from Unit 5 (cars, holidays, etc.); electronic goods (music players, games, etc.); food or drink.

Inspiration for products can be had by looking at the Internet, particularly online shopping sites. Students can present their findings to the whole class or in groups.

6 PRODUCTS AND STRATEGIES

Unit 6 continues the theme of marketing. It focuses on the product, which is central to the marketing mix. Lesson 1 looks at a typical product life cycle in terms of costs, sales and cash flow. The reading text in Lesson 2 discusses how a company can assess the potential of its products, how it can analyse its product portfolio, and how it can extend the life of ageing products by rebranding and repackaging. The unit finishes with a case study of a marketing strategy in a mature market: the mobile phone company Vodafone.

Skills focus

Reading

- locating key information in complex sentences

Writing

- reporting findings from other sources: paraphrasing
- writing complex sentences

Vocabulary focus

- synonyms, replacement subjects, etc. for sentence-level paraphrasing

Key vocabulary

brand (n)	level (n)	profitable
cash cow	level off	profit margin
cash flow	life cycle	rebrand
cost (n and v)	life-span	relaunch
decline (n and v)	market share	repackage
design (n and v)	mature (adj and v)	sales figures
established (adj)	maturity	saturate
evaluate	merchandise	saturation
extend	model (n, v and adj)	sponsor (adj)
extension	peak (n, v and adj)	stabilize
identify	phase	stable (adj)
integrated	portfolio	trial (n and v)
introduce	position (n and v)	unit cost
launch (n and adj)	profit (n)	

6.1 Vocabulary

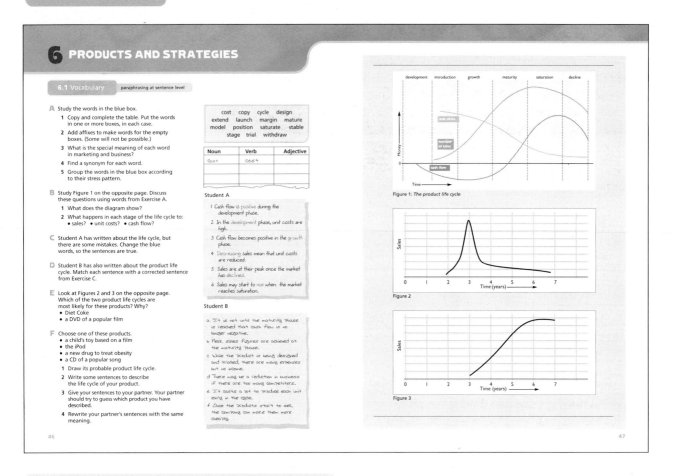

General note

Read the *Vocabulary bank* at the end of the Course Book unit. Decide when, if at all, to refer students to it. The best time is probably at the very end of the lesson or the beginning of the next lesson, as a summary/revision.

Lesson aims

● paraphrase at sentence level using passives, synonyms, negatives, replacement subjects

Further practice in:

● affixes
● words with different meanings in general English
● stress within words
● word sets – synonyms, antonyms

Introduction

1 Revise affixes, e.g., *re~*, *un~*, *in~*, *out~*, *~ize*, *~al*, *~ty*, *~ly*, *~ion*, *~ive*. Do this by dividing the class into small groups. Give each group one affix. Allow three or four minutes. The group which can list the most words is the winner.

2 Revise words describing graphs (from Unit 5). Draw a line graph on the board. The line should rise and fall, sharply and gradually, have a peak and a point where it levels off. Point to each part of the line and ask students to give you the appropriate verb and adverb. Alternatively, draw your own line graph and describe it. Students should try to draw an identical line graph from your description while you are talking.

Exercise A

1 Tell students to make a table with three columns and 15 rows in their notebooks. Go through the example in the Course Book. Set the exercise for individual work and pairwork checking. Tell students to use their dictionaries if they need to check meanings, grammatical category, etc. Feed back with the whole class, building the first three columns of the table in the Answers section on the board. Ask students to say what general meanings they can give for the words.

2 Refer to the example (*cost*) in the Course Book. Ask students to suggest a form of cost which is an adjective (*costly*). Set for pairwork. Students should try to fill as many empty boxes as possible with

words with appropriate affixes. They should continue to use their dictionaries to check meanings and spellings. Note that it is possible to use the past participle of a verb as an adjective if there is no other possibility. Feed back with the whole class, checking meanings of the words added to the table.

3 Add a fourth column on the board and give it the heading *Marketing/business meaning*. Underline or highlight the words as shown in the table below, and with the whole class, ask students to suggest (or find in their dictionaries) meanings specific to business/marketing for these words.

4 Work in a similar way with the fifth column, *Marketing/business synonym*. Limit the synonyms to those for the underlined words.

5 Set for pairwork. Feed back with the whole class, checking pronunciation.

Language note

Rules in language are made to be broken. The suffix ~*ly* normally makes an adjective into an adverb, but there are common cases where this is not what happens. Here, the noun *cost* is made into an adjective *costly* by the addition of ~*ly*. Other anomalies are:
hard – hardly
poor – poorly
kind – kindly

Note that *cost* is neutral, whereas *costly* is a stance adjective – it suggests that the writer or speaker thinks the price is too high. In this regard *expensive* is not a true synonym since it does not have the same connotation. *Pricey*, however, does.

Answers

Model answers:

Noun	Verb	Adjective	Marketing/business meaning	Marketing/business synonym
cost	cost	costly	(n) money needed to make a product	(n) expense, overhead
copy	copy	copied	(v) a competitor may make a similar product	(v) duplicate (can also be used as a noun or adjective)
cycle	cycle	cyclical	(n) the life of a product from its beginning to its end	(n) life-span
design	design	designed	(v) create a product	(v) develop
extension	extend	extended, extensive	(v) try to make sales of a product last longer	(v) prolong
launch	launch	launched	(v) put a product on the market	(v) introduce
margin	marginalize	marginal	(n) money received for a product after expenses	(n) profit
maturity	mature	mature	(adj) a mature market is where the product is well known and sales are good	(adj) established
model	model	modelled	(n) a type of product (n) an example of a new product which can be tested	(n) version (n) prototype
position	position	positioned	(v) decide what market segment a product is suitable for	locate
saturation	saturate	saturated	(n) a point in the cycle where there are too many competitors in the market	(n) oversupply
stable	stabilize	stable	(v) numbers become stable; a market can stabilize = sales remain much the same (adj) numbers remain the same	(v) level off (adj) level
stage	stage		(n) the different sales periods through which a product goes	(n) phase
trial	trial		(v) the product is tried out to see if it works properly	(v) test
withdrawal	withdraw	withdrawn	(v) take a product off the market	(v) remove (from the market)

5

one syllable	cost, launch, stage
Oo	copy, cycle, margin, model, stable, trial
oO	design, extend, mature, withdraw
oOo	position
Ooo	saturate

Language note

Some grammatical forms of the words may have particular meanings that are unlikely (though probably not impossible) in a business context, e.g., *model* (v), *stage* (v), *stable* (n). Point this out if necessary but don't spend much time on these words.

Exercise B

1 Set for pairwork discussion. Students should refer to the words they have looked at in Exercise A to help describe the stages shown in the diagram. Monitor but don't assist. Feed back with the whole class, checking that students can give the topic of the diagram, and the meanings of the vertical and horizontal axes. Elicit words which can be used from Exercise A (underlined below, including synonyms).

2 Set for pairwork discussion. Remind students about words they have already studied for describing trends in graphs. Feed back with the whole class, asking one or two students to describe the trends for each of the concepts. Make sure that students use the present simple tense to talk about the stages as this is a process.

Answers

Model answers:

1 The diagram shows the concept of the product life cycle. The vertical axis represents money and the horizontal axis represents time. As can be seen, a product goes through a series of stages over time and the unit cost, cash flow and sales vary with each stage.

   Development phase: ideas for a product are developed. A model may be designed and tested.

   Introduction phase: the new product is launched.

   Growth phase: people become aware of the product and start to buy it. So sales grow.

   Maturity phase: the product is selling well, so competitors may copy it and start to sell their own version. The product has now become established and market has stabilized.

   Saturation phase: as more and more companies enter the market, a saturation point may be reached where there are too many companies competing for

a share. Some companies leave the market because the margins are too small.

   Decline phase: in the final phase, fewer and fewer people buy the product until eventually it is withdrawn.

2 **Sales:** in the development phase there are no sales, obviously. After introduction, sales are few. Then they start to increase until the market is mature, when they level off. When the product is in the decline phase, sales fall.

   Unit costs: to begin with, the company may have a lot of expenses (for promotion, distribution, adapting or buying production machinery, etc.) so the unit costs are high. As sales increase, the unit costs start to fall.

   Cash flow: in the beginning cash flow is negative, which means that the company is spending more than it is earning. Although cash comes in from the introduction phase onwards, it takes some time before money from sales means that the company is earning more than it is spending and cash flow becomes positive. This happens during the maturity stage.

Note that companies often use marketing strategies to try to extend the life of a product, though this is not shown – it will be discussed in later lessons.

Exercise C

As well as requiring the use of antonyms, this exercise checks that students have understood the diagram in Exercise B. Set for individual work and pairwork checking. Feed back with the whole class. A good way to do this is to use an OHT with blanks for the blue words (see additional resources section, Resource 6B).

Answers

Model answers:

1 Cash flow is negative during the development phase.

2 In the introduction phase, unit costs are high.

3 Cash flow becomes positive in the maturity phase.

4 Increasing sales mean that unit costs are reduced.

5 Sales are at their peak once the market has stabilized/matured.

6 Sales may start to fall/drop/decline when the market reaches saturation.

Exercise D

Introduce the idea of paraphrasing – or restating. Elicit from the students the main ways to do this at sentence level, namely:

- using different grammar
- using different words
- reordering the information

Write these points on the board. Also make the point very strongly that a paraphrase is not a paraphrase unless 90% of the language is different. There are some words which must remain the same, but these are very few, and are likely to be words specific to the subject, such as *cash flow*. It is best to try to use all three of the above strategies, if possible.

Students should look carefully at the corrected sentences from Exercise C and then compare them with the paraphrases. The first step is to identify which sentences match. Set for individual work and pairwork checking. It may be helpful for the students if you reproduce the corrected sentences from Exercise C and the sentences in Exercise D on strips of paper so that they can move them around. Both sets of sentences are reproduced in the additional resources section (Resource 6C) to facilitate this.

Feed back with the whole class. A good way to do this is to reproduce the sentences on OHTs, with each sentence cut into a separate strip. Lay the sentences on the OHP one at a time, as you agree what is the correct match.

Once the sentences are correctly paired, ask students to locate the parts of each sentence which seem to match. They will need to look at the overall meaning of each phrase, using what they know about the subject, to make sure that the phrases are similar. Set for pairwork. Feed back with the whole group, using the OHT strips and highlighting the matching parts with coloured pens.

Answers

Model answers:

1 **Cash flow is negative** *during the development phase.*
c *While the product is being designed and trialled,* **there are many expenses but no income.**

2 **In the introduction phase,** *unit costs are high.*
e *It costs a lot to produce each unit* **early in the cycle.**

3 *Cash flow becomes positive* **in the maturity phase.**
a *It is not until* **the maturity phase is reached** *that cash flow is no longer negative.*

4 **Increasing sales mean that** *unit costs are reduced.*
f **Once the products start to sell,** *the company can make them more cheaply.*

5 *Sales are at their peak* **once the market has stabilized.**

b *Peak sales figures are achieved* **at the maturity phase.**

6 *Sales may start to fall* **when the market reaches saturation.**
d *There may be a reduction in business* **if there are too many competitors.**

A final step is to be specific about the details of the changes that have been made. Students should refer to the list of types of changes you have written on the board. Look at each paraphrase with the class and ask students what changes have been made. Be specific about the types of vocabulary or grammar changes. For example, in the first answer above, the paraphrase reorders the information, uses time clause/passive, uses replacement subject *there*, changes all vocabulary.

Exercise E

Put students in pairs to discuss the two figures, and which product is most likely to have which type of cycle. You could ask students to suggest a film to discuss. Feed back with the whole group. If you wish, you could write some descriptive sentences on the board.

Answer

Model answer:

These two graphs show extremes of product life cycle. Figure 2 shows a two-year development phase, a rapid increase in sales following introduction and an extremely rapid decline, but a low level of sales for a longish period – the likely product is a DVD of a popular film. Figure 3 shows a development phase of around three years, a rapid introduction and growth phase. The product is still selling well in a mature market. The likely product is Diet Coke.

Note: The Diet Coke project was started in 1979, and the product was launched in 1982. Diet Coke was an instant success, capturing 17% of the soft drinks market by a year later.

Exercise F

1/2 Set for individual work.

3 Set for pairwork. Go round and check what students have written, giving advice if necessary.

4 Set for individual work or for homework. Tell students to try to follow the advice for paraphrasing in Exercise D, i.e., to reorder the information and to change vocabulary and grammar as far as possible. You may wish to refer students to the *Vocabulary bank* at this point to provide a reminder for grammar structures to use.

Closure

Discussion:

1 Can students think of other products with life cycles similar to those shown in Figures 2 and 3?

2 What can a company do to prolong the life of a product with a life cycle similar to the one in Figure 2?

6.2 Reading

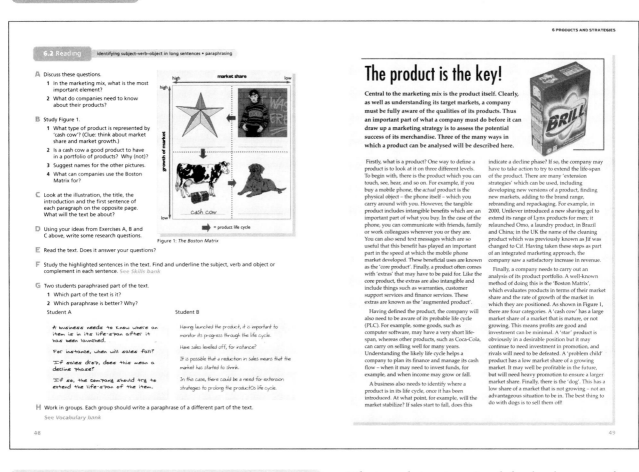

General note

Read the *Skills bank* at the end of the Course Book unit. Decide when, if at all, to refer students to it. The best time is probably after Exercise F, or at the very end of the lesson or the beginning of the next lesson, as a summary/revision.

Lesson aims

- identify the kernel SVC/O of a long sentence

Further practice in:

- research questions
- topic sentences
- paraphrasing

Introduction

Remind the class about techniques when using written texts for research. Ask:

What is it a good idea to do:

- *before reading?* (think of research questions)
- *while you are reading?* (look for topic sentences)
- *after reading?* (check answers to the research questions)

What words in a text signal the development of a topic in a new direction? (markers showing contrast such as *but, however, at the same time, on the other hand*, etc.) If you wish, refer students to Unit 4 *Skills bank*.

Exercise A

Set for general discussion. Allow students to debate differences of opinion. Encourage them to give examples if they can. Do not correct or give information at this point, as these topics will be dealt with in the text.

Exercise B

1/2 Set for pairwork discussion. Feed back with the whole class. Accept any reasonable answers. If students don't know, don't tell them, but say they may find out in the text.

3 Set for pairwork. Feed back with the whole class, giving the correct names. Ask students how these types of products are different from the cash cow.

4 Discuss with the whole class. Accept any sensible suggestions. Don't elaborate further at this point, as more information will be found in the text.

Answers

Model answers:

1 A cash cow is a product which has a large market share in a stable market (i.e., one that is no longer growing).

2 See text.

3 Star, problem child, dog.

4 See text.

> ### Subject note
>
> The arrows on the matrix show the common life cycle of a product, i.e.,
> It begins as a problem child.
> It becomes a star.
> It becomes a cash cow.
> It becomes a dog.
>
> On some versions of the Boston Matrix, the problem child phase is shown as a question mark.

Exercise C

Set for individual work. Elicit ideas, but do not confirm or correct.

Exercise D

Set for individual work and pairwork checking.

Exercise E

Set for individual work. Feed back with the whole class.

Exercise F

Draw a table with the headings from the Answers section on the board. If you wish, students can also draw a similar table in their notebooks. Explain that in academic writing, sentences can seem very complex. This is often not so much because the sentence structure is highly complex in itself, but that the subjects and objects/complements may consist of clauses or complex noun phrases. Often the verb is quite simple. But in order to fully understand a text, the grammar of a sentence must be understood. Subject+verb+object or complement is the basic sentence structure of English. Students need to be able to locate the subjects, main verbs and their objects or complements.

Elicit from the students the subject, main verb and object for the first sentence. Ask students for the *head word* of each subject, main verb and object (underlined in the table in the Answers section). Write them in the table on the board. Using high-speed questioning, get students to build the whole phrase that constitutes the subject/main verb/object/complement.

Example 1:

Underlined words shown:

<u>Understanding</u> the likely life cycle <u>helps</u> a <u>company</u> to plan its finance and manage its cash flow …

What is this sentence about? = understanding

What does understanding do? = it helps

What does it help? = a company

Which company? = a = any company

Write these head words in the table on the board.

Then elicit the remaining words and add to the table:

Understanding what exactly? = the likely cycle

Give me more information about how this will help a company = (it will help it) to plan its finance and manage its cash flow

Example 2:

This example shows how to deal with *is* + complement.

<u>The best thing</u> to do with dogs <u>is to sell</u> them off!

What is this sentence about in general? = dogs

More particularly? = the best thing to do with them

What's the main verb in this sentence? = is

*So what **is** the best thing to do?* = to sell off

Sell off what? = them = dogs

The idea is that students should be able to extract something which contains the kernel even if it does not make complete sense without the full phrase.

Ask students to identify the leading prepositional/adverbial phrase in the fourth sentence (*Having defined the product …*). Point out that this part contains information which is extra to the main part of the sentence. The sentence can be understood quite easily without it.

Set the remainder of the exercise for individual work followed by pairwork checking. Finally, feed back with the whole class.

You may wish to refer students to the *Skills bank – Finding the main information*.

Answers

See table on next page.

Model answers:

Subject	Verb	Object/complement
an important <u>part</u> of what a company must do before it can draw up a marketing strategy	<u>is</u>	to assess the potential <u>success</u> of its merchandise.
One way to <u>define</u> a product	<u>is</u>	to look at it on three different <u>levels</u>.
the tangible <u>product</u>	<u>includes</u>	intangible <u>benefits</u> which are an important part of what you buy.
the <u>company</u>	will also <u>need</u>	to be <u>aware</u> of its probable <u>life cycle</u> (PLC).
<u>Understanding</u> the likely life cycle	<u>helps</u>	a <u>company</u> to plan its finance and manage its cash flow …
The best thing to <u>do</u> with dogs	<u>is</u>	to <u>sell</u> them off!

Exercise G

Set for individual work and pairwork checking. Make sure that students identify the original phrases in the text first (the first four sentences of paragraph 4) before looking at the paraphrases.

Feed back with the whole class. A good way to demonstrate how Student A's text contains too many words from the original is to use an OHT and highlight the common words in colour. (A table giving the sentences plus commentary is included in the additional resources section – Resources 6D and 6E.) Check that students are able to say which parts of the paraphrase match with the original, and which structures have been used.

Answers

1 The first part of paragraph 4.
2 Student B's paraphrase is better, because it uses fewer of the words from the original text.

Language note

It is important that students understand that when paraphrasing, it is not sufficient to change a word here and there and leave most of the words and the basic sentence structure unchanged. This approach is known as 'patch-writing' and is considered to be plagiarism. It is also important when paraphrasing not to change the meaning of the original – also quite hard to do.

Exercise H

Refer students to the *Vocabulary bank* at this stage. Review paraphrasing skills with the whole class before starting this exercise.

Divide the text into parts. For example, each paragraph can be divided into two so that there are eight different sections (though of course you should not use the first part of paragraph 4). Give each section to different students to work on. Alternatively, you could choose one part of the text for all students to work on, for example the second part of paragraph 4. This can be done in class or if you prefer as individual work/homework.

If students are doing the work in class in groups or pairs, a good way to provide feedback is to get students to write their paraphrase on an OHT. Show each paraphrase (or a selection) to the class and ask for comments. Say what is good about the work. Point out where there are errors and ask for suggestions on how to improve it. Make any corrections on the OHT with a different coloured pen.

Closure

1 Divide the class into two teams. Write the five topic sentences from the reading text on strips, or photocopy them from the additional resources section (Resource 6F). One team chooses a topic sentence and reads it aloud. The other team must give the information triggered by that topic sentence. Accept only the actual paragraph content.

2 Dictate the following to the class:
   Think of a product which …
   … has a large share of a mature market.
   … is a 'dog'.
   … is a 'star'.
   … has recently been renamed.
   … has had new packaging in the last year.
   … has just been launched.
   … includes travel as part of its core product.
   … includes delivery as part of its augmented product.

   Students work in pairs to think of products which fit the descriptions. The first pair to find a product for each category are the winners. Feed back to the whole class.

6.3 Extending skills

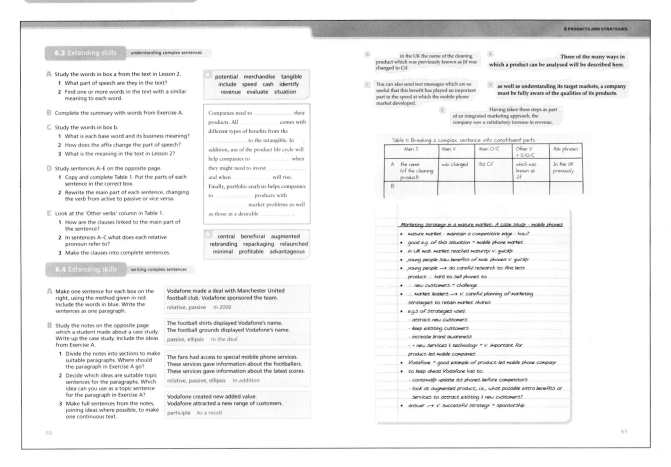

Lesson aims

- study sentence structure in more detail
- identify the main information in:
  an active sentence
  a passive sentence
  a complex sentence with participles
  a complex sentence with embedded clauses

Further practice in:

- vocabulary from Lesson 2

Introduction

Ask students to see how many phrases or compound nouns they can make with the words *market* or *marketing*. Feed back with the whole class.

Possible answers: *market characteristics, market share, market leader, market segment, target market, market size, market trends, growth market, gap in the market, marketing mix, marketing strategy*, etc.

Exercise A

Ask students to study the words in the box and to find the words in the text. Set for individual work and

pairwork checking. Tell students not to use their dictionaries to begin with but to use what they know to guess meanings and parts of speech. If necessary, they should use dictionaries when checking in pairs. Deal with any common problems with the whole class.

Answers

Model answers (paragraph numbers in brackets):

Word	Part of speech	Similar meaning
potential (1)	adj	likely, probable (3)
merchandise (1)	n (U)	products, goods, (2,3)
tangible (2)	adj	physical (2)
include (2)	v (T)	come with (2)
speed (2)	n	rate (5)
cash (3)	usually n (U); here part of compounds *cash flow* and *cash cow*, so in adjectival position	funds (3)
identify (4)	v (T)	be aware of (3)
revenue (4)	n (U)	income (3)
evaluate (5)	v (T)	assess, analyse (1)
situation (5)	n (C)	position (5)

Exercise B

Set for individual work and pairwork checking. Students should make use of all the words they have discussed in Exercise A (i.e., the synonyms as well as the words in the box). Feed back with the whole class.

Answers

Model answers:

Companies need to evaluate/assess/analyse their products. All merchandise comes (or: goods/products come) with different types of benefits from the tangible/physical to the intangible. In addition, use of the product life cycle will help companies to identify/be aware of when they might need to invest funds/cash and when income/revenue will rise. Finally, portfolio analysis helps companies to be aware of/identify products with potential/likely/probable market problems as well as those in a desirable position/situation.

Language note

The use of words as synonyms often depends on the context. For example, although the base meanings of *identify* and *be aware of* are not exactly synonymous, they could both be used in the third and final sentences of the summary text with very little difference in meaning.

Exercise C

Set for pairwork. Feed back with the whole class. Note that not all the base words have specifically business meanings. Tell students to explain the meaning in business terms as far as possible.

Answers

Model anwers:
See table below.

Word	Base and meaning	Effect of affix	Meaning in text
central	centre (n, C) – the middle	~al = adjective ending	most important
beneficial	benefit 1. (n, C) – something good or useful that a product has 2. (v, T) – have a good effect on; be useful	~(ci)al = adjective ending	helpful, useful, good
augmented	augment (v, T) – make something bigger	~ed = past participle ending, makes an adjective	something extra added to a core product
rebranding	brand (n, C) – the name which a business uses to identify a product as theirs. The brand also represents all the values and qualities which the business wants to associate with its product	re~ = do something again ~ing = gerund form indicating the process of creating a brand	making a new brand
repackaging	package 1. (n, C) – parcel 2. (v, T) – make into a package for selling	re~ = do something again ~ing 1. = noun ending: the materials used to make the package 2. = gerund ending: the process of making a package	putting the products in new packaging so that they seem to be a new version of the product
relaunched	launch (v, T) – put a new product on the market; begin selling a product	re~ = do something again ~ed = past simple ending	started to sell Omo again as if it was a new product
minimal	minimum (adj) – the smallest possible; can only be used in front of the noun, i.e., *The minimum amount* not *The amount is minimum*; sometimes a noun with *of*: *a minimum of ...*	~al = adjective ending; difference from *minimum*: only an adjective, and can be used after *be*: *The amount is minimal.*	very little
profitable	profit (n, C/U) – money from business activity	~able = adjective ending	produce profits
advantageous	advantage (n, C) – something that helps to bring a good result, especially compared to other people/companies	~ous = adjective ending	desirable, beneficial

Exercise D

1 Copy the table headings from the Answers section onto the board and complete the example with the students. Tell them that when they look at the 'Other verbs' column they may well find several, and should number each verb and subject/object/complement section separately. Point out that the order of each part of the sentence is not reflected in the table: the table is just a way to analyse the sentences.

Set the rest of the sentences for individual work and pairwork checking. Feed back with the whole class. Draw their attention to the 'main' parts of the sentence: it is very important in reading that they should be able to identify these. Notice also that the main parts can stand on their own and make complete sentences.

2 Set for individual work. If the clause is active it should be changed to passive, and vice versa.

Answers

Model answers:

1 See table below.

2 A   Unilever/The company changed the name of the cleaning product to Cif.

B   I/the author will describe three (of the many) ways (to analyse products).

C   Text messages can also be sent.

D   The qualities of (its) products must be fully understood (by a company/companies).

E   A satisfactory increase in revenue was seen (by the company).

Exercise E

This exercise involves looking carefully at the dependent clauses in sentences A–E.

1 Say that these clauses have special ways to link them to the main part of the sentence. Do this exercise with the whole class, using an OHT of the table in Exercise D, and a highlighter pen to mark the relevant words. (A version of the table without underlining is included in the additional resources section – Resource 6G.) Go through the clauses asking students what words or other ways are used to link the clauses to the main part of the sentence.

2 Set for individual work and pairwork checking. Students should look at each sentence and identify the antecedents of the relative pronouns. You could ask them to use a highlighter pen or to draw circles and arrows linking the words.

3 Students must be able to get the basic or kernel meaning of the clause. Take sentence A as an example and write it on the board. Point out that the relative pronouns and other ways of linking these clauses to the main clause will need to be changed or got rid of. Students should aim to write something that makes good sense as a complete sentence. They can break a sentence into shorter sentences if necessary. Set the remaining clauses for individual work. Feed back with the whole class. Accept anything that makes good sense.

	Main subject	Main verb	Main object/complement	Other verbs + their subjects + objects/complements	Adverbial phrases
A	the name (of the cleaning product)	was changed	(to) Cif	which* was known as Jif	In the UK previously
B	Three of the many ways	will be described		in which a product can be analysed	here
C	You	can also send	text messages	1. … which are so useful 2. … that this benefit has played an important part in the speed 3. … at which the mobile phone market developed.	
D	a company	must be	fully aware (of the qualities of its products)	As well as understanding its target markets, …	
E	the company	saw	a satisfactory increase in revenue.	Having taken these steps as part of an integrated marketing approach, …	

*underlined text = means by which dependent clause is joined to main clause

Answers

1 See table on previous page. Sentences A–C use relative clauses. D and E use participle clauses.

2 A *which* = the cleaning product

   B *which* = ways

   C (1) *which* = text messages
      (2) *which* = speed

3 Possible answers:

   A The cleaning product was previously known as Jif.

   B A product can be analysed in many ways.

   C (1) Text messages are (so) useful.
      (2) The text message benefit played an important part in the speed of development of the mobile phone market.
      (3) The speed of development of the mobile phone market was due to text messages.

   D A company must (also) understand its target markets.

   E The company took these steps as part of an integrated marketing approach.

Language note

A dependent clause contains a verb and a subject and is a secondary part of a sentence. It is dependent because it 'depends' on the main clause. A main clause can stand by itself as a complete sentence in its own right (usually). A dependent clause always goes with a main clause and cannot stand by itself as a sentence in its own right.

Dependent clauses are typically joined to main clauses with certain types of words: for example, relative pronouns (e.g., *who, which,* etc.), linking adverbials (e.g., *if, when, before, although, whereas,* etc.); words associated with reporting speech (e.g., *that,* a *Wh~* word such as *what* or *why*) and so on.

Some dependent clauses are non-finite, that is, they don't have a 'full verb' but a participle form (e.g., *having* finish*ed, open*ing*) and the subject may not be stated.

For more on this, see a good grammar reference book.

Closure

Write the following underlined beginnings and endings of words on the board or dictate them. Ask students to give the (or a) complete word.

<u>ob</u>(ject)

<u>bene</u>(fit)

<u>supp</u>(ort)

<u>fin</u>(ance)

<u>vers</u>(ion)

(serv)<u>ice</u>

(strat)<u>egy</u>

(succ)<u>ess</u>

(portfo)<u>lio</u>

(analy)<u>sis</u>

(custo)<u>mer</u>

6.4 Extending skills

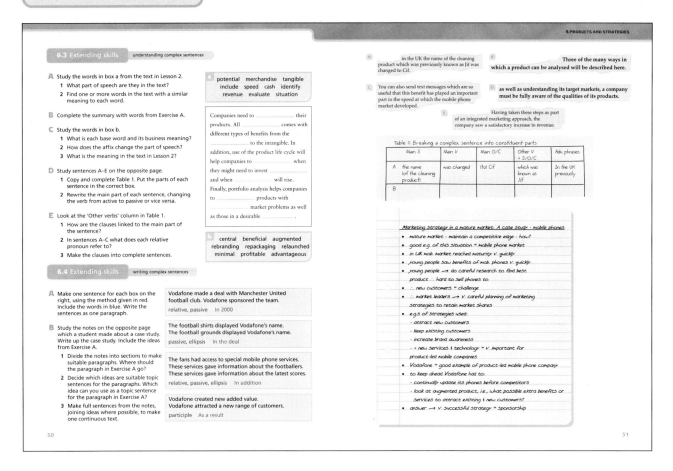

Lesson aims

- write complex sentences:
  with passives
  joining with participles
  embedding clauses
  adding prepositional phrases

Further practice in:

- writing topic sentences
- expanding a topic sentence into a paragraph

Introduction

Ask students to think about and discuss the following questions:

1 Give some examples of mobile phone companies.

2 Are these companies' approaches to marketing more likely to be product-led or market-led? (In other words, are these companies more likely to develop products in response to perceived market needs (= market-led) or are they more likely to develop new products and then try to promote them (= product-led)?).

3 Why?

4 What are some of the marketing strategies a mobile phone company might use?

Note: Some mobile phone companies (such as Vodafone) are very strongly focused on their products since they are in a field in which technological developments take place very rapidly.

Exercise A

Set for individual work and pairwork checking. If necessary, do the first box with the whole class. Make sure students understand that they should write the four sentences as a continuous paragraph.

Feed back with the whole class. Accept any answers that make good sense. Point out where the phrases in blue act as linkers between the sentences to make a continuous paragraph.

Answer

Possible answer:

In 2000, a deal was made by Vodafone with Manchester United football club in which the team was sponsored/the company sponsored the team. In the deal, Vodafone's name was displayed on the football shirts and at the football grounds. In addition, the fans had access to special mobile phone services through which they were given information about the footballers and the latest scores. As a result, having

109

created new added value, Vodafone attracted a new range of customers.

Note: Vodafone's sponsorship deal with Manchester United, which began in 2000, lasted until 2006.

Exercise B

In this exercise, students are required to use all they have practised about sentence structure as well as revise what they know about topic sentences and paragraphing. Set for pairwork. Do not feed back after each question but allow students to work through the questions, proceeding to write up the whole text. They will need to decide where is the best place for the paragraph in Exercise A, and should also add this to their text.

If possible, pairs should write their text on an OHT. Select two or three OHTs for display and comment by the whole class. Make any corrections on the text yourself with a coloured pen. Alternatively, circulate the transparencies to other pairs to correct and comment on. These pairs then display the corrected work and explain why they have made the corrections.

Answers

Possible answers:

1/2

Paragraph divisions are given below, with the possible topic sentences underlined. Note that other answers may be possible.

---

mature market – maintain a competitive edge – how?

- good e.g. of this situation = mobile phone market
- in UK mob. market: reached maturity v. quickly
- young people saw benefits of mob. phones v. quickly
- young people → do careful research to find best product
  - ∴ hard to sell phones to
- ∴ new customers = challenge

- ∴ market leaders → v. careful planning of marketing strategies to retain market shares
  e.g.s of strategies used:
  – attract new customers
  – keep existing customers
  – increase brand awareness
  – + new services & technology = v. important for product-led mobile companies

---

- Vodafone = good example of product-led mobile phone company
- to keep ahead Vodafone had to:
  – continually update its phones before competitors
  – look at augmented product, i.e., what possible extra benefits or services to attract existing & new customers?

- answer → v. successful strategy = sponsorship
  (= controlling idea for the paragraph from Exercise A)

---

3 How can a company maintain a competitive edge once the market has matured? One example of this situation is the mobile phone market. In the UK, the mobile phone market reached maturity very quickly. Young people especially were very quick to see the benefits offered by mobile phones. But young people are hard to sell mobiles phones to because they carry out careful research to find the best product. So finding new customers soon became quite challenging.

As a result, mobile phone companies which wanted to retain their positions as market leaders needed to plan their marketing strategies very carefully. There were many strategies considered by such companies, including trying to attract new customers, making sure that existing customers were not lost, and increasing brand awareness. In addition, for product-led mobile companies, developing new services and new technology were especially important.

Vodafone is a good example of such a mobile phone company. In order to keep ahead of its competitors Vodafone had to continually update its phones before they did, and was also obliged to look carefully at the augmented product. In other words, what extra intangible benefits or services, which would attract customers both existing and new, could it provide?

In answer to this question, Vodafone adopted a marketing strategy which was particularly successful, namely sponsorship. In 2000, a deal was made by Vodafone with Manchester United football club in which the company sponsored the team. In the deal, Vodafone's name was displayed on the football shirts and at the football grounds. In addition, the fans had access to special mobile phone services through which they were given information about the footballers and the latest scores. As a result, having created new added value, Vodafone attracted a new range of customers.

Closure

Give students some very simple three- or four-word SVO/C sentences from the unit (or make some yourself) and ask them to add as many phrases and clauses as they can to make a long complex sentence. Who can make the longest sentence?

For example:
Cash flow becomes positive.
→ It is not until the maturity phase, when sales are at their peak and demand for the product is established, that cash flow becomes positive and the company may have extra funds to start investing in a new product which they will develop over the next few years …
(48 words)

Extra activities

1 Work through the *Vocabuary bank* and *Skills bank* if you have not already done so, or as a revision of previous study.

2 Use the *Activity bank* (Teacher's Book additional resources section, Resource 6A).

   A Set the wordsearch for individual work (including homework) or pairwork.

   Answers

Verb	Noun
achieve	achievement
assess	assessment
create	creation
defeat	defeat
design	design
display	display
evaluate	evaluation
extend	extension
include	inclusion
indicate	indication
integrate	integration
launch	launch
predict	prediction
repackage	repackaging
retain	retention
saturate	saturation
sponsor	sponsorship
trial	trial
update	update
withdraw	withdrawal

B Students work in pairs or small groups and try to think of word pairs. They should be able to explain the meaning.

Alternatively, photocopy (enlarged) the words from the additional resources section (Resource 6H) and cut up into cards. Put the A and B words into separate envelopes. Put students into groups of four. Make one set of A and one set of B words for each group. Give one pair in each group the A words and the other pair the B words. Each pair takes it in turns to pick a word from their envelope. The other pair must try to find a word from their own envelope which can go with it.

Accept all reasonable word pairs.

Possible pairs are:

A	B
added	value
brand	awareness
brand	range
cash	cow
cash	flow
competitive	edge
customer	services
decline	phase
extra	benefits
integrated	approach
life	cycle
life	span
market	leader
marketing	strategy
mature	market
portfolio	analysis
problem	child
product	led
product	portfolio
text	message
unit	cost

7 OPERATIONS: PRODUCING THE GOODS

Operations management is covered in this unit and Unit 8. In this unit, the focus is on production methods and processes and associated issues. The first listening extract, from a lecture, looks at the input–transformation–output process and discusses how value is added at each stage of the process. It also describes the three main types of production: job, batch and flow. Finally, the importance of scheduling in planning the production process is emphasized. The second listening extract is from a seminar in which criteria for choosing a business location are discussed.

Skills focus

🎧 Listening

- understanding speaker emphasis

Speaking

- asking for clarification
- responding to queries and requests for clarification

Vocabulary focus

- compound nouns
- fixed phrases from business studies
- fixed phrases from academic English
- common lecture language

Key vocabulary

See also the list of fixed phrases from academic English in the *Vocabulary bank* (Course Book page 60).

assembly line	lean production	quality
batch production	linear	raw materials
capital (n)	locate	resource (n)
cash flow	location	revenue
component	manufacturing	scheduling
continuous	mass production	sequence (n and v)
delay (n)	method (n)	simultaneously
design (n and v)	operation	supply (n and v)
fixed cost	planning	supply chain
flow production	process (n)	value added
ingredient	productivity	variable costs
investment	project management	
job production	prototype	

7.1 Vocabulary

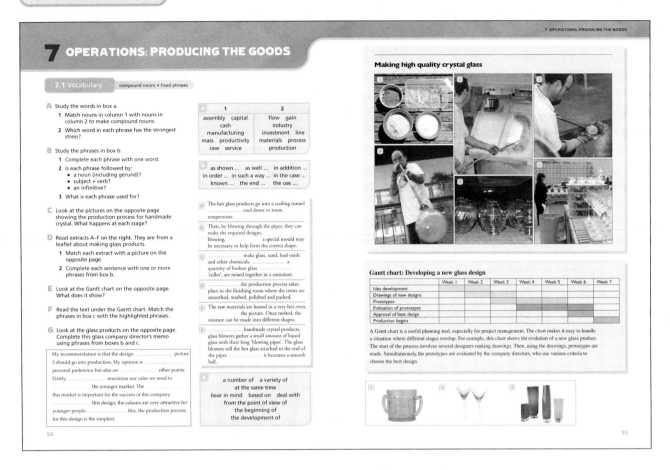

General note

Read the *Vocabulary bank* at the end of the Course Book unit. Decide when, if at all, to refer your students to it. The best time is probably at the very end of the lesson or the beginning of the next lesson, as a summary/revision.

Lesson aims

- understand and use some general academic fixed phrases
- understand and use fixed phrases and compound nouns from the discipline

Introduction

1 Revise some noun phrases (noun + noun, adjective + noun) from previous units. Give students two or three minutes to make word stars with a base word, trying to find as many possible combinations as they can (preferably without having to look at dictionaries).

For example:

```
            quantitative
              |
secondary           market
        \ research /
        /         \
   qualitative      primary
```

Other base words which could be used are *job*, *company*, *goods*, *management*. If they are stuck for ideas, tell them to look back at previous units.

2 Introduce the topic of the lesson by looking at the pictures of glass objects. Discuss what students know about the glass production process. How are things like vases and drinking glasses made?

Exercise A

Set for individual work and pairwork checking. Feed back with the whole class, making sure that the stress pattern is correct. Ask students to suggest other fixed phrases which could be made using the words in column 2.

Answers

Model answers:

a'ssembly line

capital in'vestment

'cash flow

manu'facturing process

project 'management

produc'tivity gain

i'dea development

'service industry

Exercise B

1/2 Set for individual work and pairwork checking. Feed back with the whole class, building the first three columns of the table in the Answers section on the board.

3 Add the fourth column with the heading 'Use to …'. Give an example of the kind of thing you are looking for, i.e., a phrase which can describe why you would choose to use this fixed phrase. Elicit suggestions from the students to complete the table, supplying the information yourself if students don't know the answer. If students are not sure about the meaning of some of the phrases, give them some example sentences and tell them that you will look further at how they are used shortly. Leave the table on the board as you will return to it.

Answers

Model answers:

Phrase		Followed by …	Use to …
as shown	in	noun	indicate a diagram or table
as well	as	noun/gerund	add information
in addition	to	noun/gerund	add information
in order	to	infinitive	give the purpose for doing something
in such a way	that*	subject + verb	give the result of doing something
in the case	of	noun/gerund	mention something
known	as	noun	give the special name for something
the end	of	noun	refer to the end of something
the use	of	noun	refer to the use of something

*as to is also possible after *in such a way*, although in this exercise, one word is required

Exercise C

Set for pairwork. Students should try to identify what each picture represents. One pair can describe each picture to the whole class. On the board, build up as many key words to describe the process as students can come up with. If students don't know some important words, tell them they will meet them shortly.

Answers

Answers depend on the students.

Exercise D

Explain that the information from the leaflet goes with the pictures they have just discussed. Each extract (A–F) goes with one picture. Students should first read the extracts, checking words they can't guess in the dictionary. They should not pay attention to the spaces at this point.

1 Set for pairwork. Feed back with the whole class. Add any key words which might have been useful in Exercise C to the board.

2 Set for individual work. Refer back to the table in Exercise B, which will help students to choose the correct phrase. Feed back with the whole class.

Answers

Model answers:

1	C	<u>In order to</u> make glass, sand, lead oxide and other chemicals, <u>as well as</u> a quantity of broken glass <u>known as</u> 'cullet', are mixed together in a container.
2	E	The raw materials are heated in a very hot oven, <u>as shown in</u> the picture. Once melted, the mixture can be made into different shapes.
3	F	<u>In the case of</u> handmade crystal products, glass blowers gather a small amount of liquid glass with their long 'blowing pipes'. The glass blowers roll the hot glass attached to the end of the pipes <u>in such a way that</u> it becomes a smooth ball.
4	B	Then, by blowing through the pipes, they can make the required designs. <u>In addition to</u> blowing, <u>the use of</u> a special mould may be necessary to help form the correct shape.
5	A	The hot glass products go into a cooling tunnel <u>in order to</u> cool down to room temperature.
6	D	<u>The end of</u> the production process takes place in the finishing room where the items are smoothed, washed, polished and packed.

If you wish, ask students to return to the table in Exercise B and write one sentence for each of the fixed phrases to show their meaning. If you can put this into the context of a production process which students are very familiar with, such as a recipe, so much the better.

Exercise E

Introduce the Gantt chart – if students have not seen one before – by saying that it is a highly important tool in project management. It shows how different stages in a process might overlap.

Set for pairwork discussion. Feed back with the whole class, making sure that students understand the concept behind the chart. Do not correct or confirm students' views of the content at this point.

Subject note

The Gantt chart was the invention of Henry Laurence Gantt (1861–1919), who was a mechanical engineer. Gantt developed his charts in the early 20th century. His invention was hugely important in management then as well as now. It can be used for large-scale construction projects as well as for small pieces of work that an individual person may have to do.

Exercise F

Set for individual work and pairwork checking. Students should use their dictionaries if they are not sure of the meaning of the phrases. Note that some phrases can be used for the same thing – it is a good idea to use a different word to avoid repetition. Ask students to say which sentence goes with which part of the chart. Which part of the diagram is not mentioned?

Answers

Model answers:

A Gantt chart is a useful planning tool, especially (*for*) from the point of view of project management. The chart makes it easy to (*handle*) deal with a situation where (*different*) a number of stages overlap. For example, this chart shows (*the evolution of*) the development of a new glass product. (*The start of*) The beginning of the process involves (*several*) a number of designers making drawings. Then, (*using*) based on the drawings, prototypes are made. (*Simultaneously*) At the same time, the prototypes are evaluated by the company directors, who (*use*) bear in mind (*various*) a number of/a variety of criteria to choose the best design.

Language note

The fixed phrases here are used in a situation which describes a series of chronological stages. However, the same words can be used when writing or talking in more general abstract academic terms, for example when introducing an essay or lecture or piece of research. This use of these words will be covered later in the unit.

Exercise G

Set for pairwork. Feed back with the whole class.

Answers

Model answers:

My recommendation is that the design (as) shown in picture 3 should go into production. My opinion is based on personal preference but also on a number of other points. Firstly, in order to maximize our sales we need to bear in mind the younger market. The development of this market is important for the success of this company. In the case of this design, the colours are very attractive for younger people. In addition to/ as well as this, the production process for this design is the simplest.

Closure

Tell students to cover the text and then describe:

- the typical main stages of a design process, e.g., glass-making
- what a typical Gantt chart looks like and what it includes

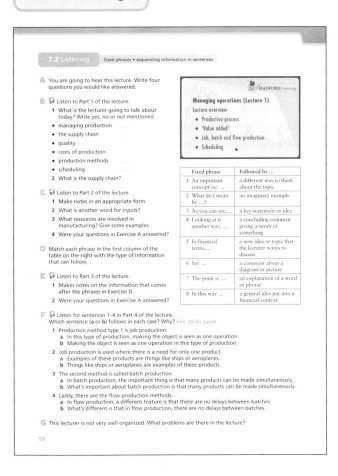

Lesson aims

- improve comprehension through recognition of fixed phrases and what follows them in terms of words/type of information
- understand how information can be sequenced in different ways within a sentence, e.g., for emphasis (see *Skills bank*)

Further practice in:

- understanding fractured text

General note

Read the *Skills bank – 'Given' and 'new' information in sentences* at the end of the Course Book unit. Decide when, if at all, to refer students to it. The best time, as before, is probably at the very end of the lesson or the beginning of the next lesson, as a summary/revision. Alternatively, use the *Skills bank* in conjunction with Exercise F.

Introduction

Review key vocabulary by writing a selection of words from Lesson 1 on the board and asking students to put them into phrases of two or more words.

Exercise A

Remind students about preparing for a lecture. If you wish, review Unit 1 *Skills bank – Making the most of lectures*. Remind students that, when they begin their talks, lecturers usually provide their listeners with an outline in order to aid comprehension. Elicit from the students the kinds of signpost words lecturers might use (e.g., *To start with, … , Firstly, … , I'll begin/start by …ing, discuss, examine,* etc.). If necessary, refer students to Unit 5.

Refer students to the lecture slide. Tell them to look at the title and bullet points and to list ideas/make questions for each bullet point. At this stage do not explain any words from the slide, or allow students to check in their dictionaries, as the meanings will be dealt with in the lecture. Set the exercise for pairwork.

Feed back with the whole class: ask several students to read out their questions. Write some of the questions on the board.

🎧 Exercise B

Tell students they are going to hear the introduction to the lecture – not the whole thing. Give students time to read questions 1 and 2. Remind them they will only hear the recording once. Play Part 1. Allow students to compare their answers.

Feed back. Confirm the correct answers. Note that 'scheduling' is mentioned on the slide, but not in the introduction, so we have no idea if this will be covered or not.

Answers

Model answers:

1

managing production	yes
the supply chain	no
quality	no
costs of production	no
production methods	yes
scheduling	not mentioned

2 The supply chain is the flow of resources through the stages of getting the raw materials, making the products, to getting the products to the consumer.

Transcript 🎧 1.29
Part 1

Good morning, everyone. What I'm going to talk about today is the core activity of business: that is, how the business does what it does. In other words, how does a company manage its production processes? Bearing in mind that this process also depends on many other operations, beginning with getting raw materials. Plus, of course, transporting the finished products to a place where they can be sold. This whole operational sequence is also known as the 'supply chain'. What I mean is … it's everything from getting the raw materials, making the products, to getting the products to the consumer. It's the flow of resources through these stages. Anyway, we'll look at the supply chain later on, I mean, another time.

So, er … in later lectures, we'll also go on to consider how companies balance the quality of their goods or services with the need to control costs of production. Today, however, we will deal with production processes and methods.

🎧 Exercise C

Refer students to the first point on the lecture slide ('production process'). Ask students to suggest an appropriate type of notes. The key word here is process, which should instantly trigger the idea of a flowchart (see Unit 1).

Give students time to read the questions. Ask if they remember the model of business given in Unit 1. Can they suggest the other key words which accompanied *input?* (i.e., *transformation* and *output*). Write these on the board. Play Part 2.

Put students in pairs to compare their diagrams and discuss the questions. With the whole class, ask students how many answers to their questions in Exercise A they heard.

Build the flowchart from the Answers section on the board, at the same time checking the answers to questions 2 and 3, and eliciting synonyms for the words *transformation* (manufacturing and/or production processes) and *output* (finished products).

Answers
Model answers:

1 **input**

| raw materials
other components |

↓

transformation

| manufacturing
production processes | ← | transforming
resources
e.g., buildings
machinery
people
computers |

↓

output

| finished product |

2 Resources.
3 Buildings, machinery, computers, people.
4 Answers depend on students' questions.

Transcript 🎧 1.30
Part 2

As we have seen in an earlier session, the production process can be thought of as input, transformation and output. As we know, the inputs include all the raw materials and other components that are needed for the transforming, or manufacturing, process. Now, another term for these inputs is *resources*. Of course, as well as the raw material resources, the production processes themselves will also involve resources. In other words, the buildings, machinery, computers and people that are necessary to carry out the production – or transforming – processes. In this case, we call these resources the 'transforming resources'. And then, finally, as we saw previously, at the end of the manufacturing process, we have the output – or finished product.

Exercise D

Explain that these are common phrases in an academic context such as a lecture. Knowing the meaning of the phrases will help a lot with comprehension. Make sure students understand that the items in the second column are not in the correct order.

Set for individual work and pairwork checking. Tell students to check the meaning of any words they don't know in a dictionary. They should be able to guess the meanings of the phrases, even if they don't actually know the phrases.

Feed back with the whole class, completing the first two columns of the chart in the Answers section for Exercise E on the board. (Alternatively, make an OHT from Resource 7D in the additional resources section.) Once the 'Followed by …' column is completed, this will act as a predictive support for Part 3 of the lecture.

Methodology note

Two-column activities are good for pair checking and practice. Once students have got the correct answers they can test each other in pairs. Student A covers the first column and tries to remember the phrases, then B covers the second column and tries to remember the purpose of each phrase.

You can then check memory by getting students to close their books and giving a phrase; students (as a group or individually) must give its purpose. Then change roles.

Exercise E

1 Tell students that in the next part of the lecture they will hear the phrases in Exercise D. They know now what *type* of information is likely to follow. Now they must try to hear what *actual* information is given. If you wish, photocopy the table in the additional resources section (Resource 7D) for students to write their answers on.

Do the first one as an example. Play the first sentence and stop after '*value added*'. Ask students: *What is the important concept?* (Answer: '*value added*'.)

Play the rest of the recording, pausing briefly at the points indicated by a // to allow students to make notes. Put students in pairs to check their answers.

Feed back with the whole class, asking questions based on the words in the 'Followed by …' column. For example:

After phrase number 2, what is the word or phrase that is explained?

After phrase number 3, what is the diagram that is commented on?

2 Refer back to students' questions in Exercise A. Discuss with the whole class whether they heard any answers to their questions.

Answers

1 Model answers: see table below.

2 Answers depend on students' questions.

Transcript 🎧 1.31

Part 3

Now, an important concept in business is the notion of 'value added'. What do I mean by value added? Well, to help you understand this idea clearly, can you look for a moment at the leaflet I have given you from the Monckton Crystal Company? // As you can see, the ingredients for making glass – i.e., sand, lead oxide and other chemicals – go though several stages of production in order to be made into beautiful glass objects that customers will want to pay money for. // However, looking at it another way, when a business makes raw materials into something else, it is actually 'adding value' to the raw materials. In fact, at each *stage* of production, value is added to the raw materials. // In financial terms, we can calculate added value by comparing the cost of the raw materials and the price which the goods are actually sold for. //

Let's look at an example of this. Say the company buys in some raw materials for £3,000. From these materials, the company makes 2,000 glass products which it sells for £4 each. The income from sales will be £8,000. Subtract the cost of the raw materials from the income from sales. The difference between these two figures is £5,000, and that's the 'value added'. //

Why is value added so important? Well, the point is that if companies know exactly which stages of production add the most or least value, then they can develop and improve their products and their production methods. // In this way they can maximize the benefits of the production operation to the business.

	Fixed phrase	Followed by …	Actual information (suggested answers)
1	An important concept (is) …	a new idea or topic that the lecturer wants to discuss	value added
2	What do I mean by …?	an explanation of a word or phrase	explanation of value added
3	As you can see, …	a comment about a diagram or picture	the glass-making process
4	Looking at it another way, …	a different way to think about the topic	value is added to the raw materials in the production process
5	In financial terms, …	a general idea put into a financial context	added value can be calculated financially
6	Say …	an imaginary example	some examples of figures for costs of raw materials, number of products and income from sales
7	The point is …	a key statement or idea	value added helps companies to improve products and production methods
8	In this way …	a concluding comment giving a result of something	the benefits of production can be maximized

🎧 Exercise F

The purpose of this exercise is to look at how information tends to be structured in sentences. It also requires very close attention to the listening text.

Before listening, allow students time to read through the sentences. In pairs, set them to discuss which sentence (**a** or **b**) they think will follow the numbered sentences.

Play Part 4 all the way through. Students should choose sentence **a** or **b**. Put them in pairs to check and discuss why **a** or **b** was the sentence they heard.

Feed back with the whole class. Deal with sentences 1 and 2 first. Tell students that all the sentences are correct, but sentence **a** 'sounds better' when it comes after the first sentence. This is because of the way that sentences go together and the way in which information is organized in a sentence. Draw the table below on the board. Show how the underlined words in the second sentence have been mentioned in the first sentence. In the second sentence the underlined words are 'old' or 'given' information. When sentences follow each other in a conversation (or a piece of writing), usually the 'given' information comes in the first part of a sentence.

Now look at sentences 3 and 4. These are different. The normal choice would be the **a** sentences. However, here the speaker wanted to emphasize the idea of 'important' and 'different'. So a *Wh~* cleft sentence structure was used, which changes the usual order of information. Show this on the table as below. This 'fronting' of information has the effect of special focus for emphasis.

Language note

In English, important information can be placed at the beginning or at the end of a sentence. There are two types of important information. The first part of the sentence contains the topic and the second part contains some kind of information or comment about the topic. Usually the comment is the more syntactically complicated part of the sentence.

Once a piece of text or a piece of conversation (i.e., a piece of discourse) has gone beyond the first sentence, a 'given'/'new' principle operates. Information which is 'given', in other words that has already been mentioned, goes at the beginning of the sentence. Normally speaking, information which is new goes at the end of the sentence. So in the second sentence of a piece of discourse, an aspect of the comment from the previous sentence may become the topic. Thus the topic of the second sentence, if it has already been mentioned in the previous sentence, is also 'given'. Of course, the given information may not be referred to with exactly the same words in the second sentence. Other ways to refer to the given information include reference words (*it, he, she, this, that, these, those,* etc.) or vocabulary items with similar meanings.

Information structure is covered in the *Skills bank* in the Course Book.

First sentence		Second sentence	
		Given information	**New information**
1 Production method type 1 is <u>job production.</u>		**a** In <u>this type of production,</u> ... one operation.	... making the object is seen as
2 Job production is used when there is a need for only <u>one product.</u>		**a** Examples of <u>these products,</u> ...	... are things like ships or aeroplanes.
3 The second method is called <u>batch production.</u>	normal order	**a** In <u>batch production,</u> ...	... the important thing is that many products can be made simultaneously.
	special focus	**b** What's <u>important</u> about batch production is ...	... that many products can be made simultaneously.
4 Lastly, there are the <u>flow production methods.</u>	normal order	**a** In <u>flow production,</u> ...	... a different feature is that there are no delays between batches.
	special focus	**b** What's <u>different</u> is ...	... that in flow production, there are no delays between batches.

Further examples of different ways to 'front' information and more practice will be given in Lesson 3.

Transcript 🎧 1.32
Part 4

Now ... er ... let's see ... oh dear, I see we're running short of time ... but perhaps I *should* just say something about production methods.

There are three main types of production method. To start with, production method type 1 is *job production*. In this type of production, making the object is seen as one operation. So, because it's one operation, it has to be finished before the next one can start. Job production is used where there is a need for only one product. Examples of these products are things like ships or aeroplanes. In other words, very big things. In the early days, cars were made like this, too, before Henry Ford came along with his mass production ideas. Projects with one customer in mind can also be seen as a type of job production: for example, building an extension to a house, or repairing a car.

On the other hand, making one thing at a time is clearly not very economical. So the second method is called *batch production*. What's important about batch production is that many products can be made simultaneously. It's what happens, for example, in a bakery, where a baking company will make, say, 50 cakes all at the same time, and then start the process again with another 50, and so on. Batch production is suitable for products such as food or clothes. The glasses that we have looked at are also made in batches. At the same time, disadvantages of this system are that sometimes people have to wait around for a batch to finish before they can start a new batch, so the process is not continuous.

Lastly, there are the *flow production* methods. What's different is that in flow production, there are no delays between batches while workers wait for each batch to be finished. Instead, the products move along an assembly line and are made in a continuous, linear sequence as each worker does his or her part. This method of production is of course associated with car manufacturing, mechanical parts for machines, and products such as toys.

Now ... oh dear, I was going to mention the advantages and disadvantages of these methods of production, but ... ah ... I see that time is moving on. So instead, I'm going to ...

Exercise G

Set for pairwork discussion. Feed back with the whole class. Note that the lecture has not yet finished. The last part will be heard in Lesson 3.

Answers

Model answers:

Scheduling was not mentioned in the introduction, but is on the lecture slide.

The lecturer is running out of time.

The lecturer has not had time to talk about advantages and disadvantages of the different production methods.

Closure

Ask students to group these products according to whether they think they are most likely to be made with job, batch or flow production methods.

bicycles	houses
biscuits	music CDs
bridges	public buildings
buses	restaurant meals
cakes	roads
cameras	shirts
cheese	TVs
computers	washing machines
frozen pizzas	watches

7.3 Extending skills

Answers

calculate	7
component	10
continuous	1
delay	8
financial	11
ingredient	2
linear	9
manufacturing	5
maximize	12
resource	4
sequence	6
simultaneously	3

Transcript 🎧 1.33

1   con'tinuous

2   in'gredient

3   simul'taneously

4   re'source

5   manu'facturing

6   'sequence

7   'calculate

8   de'lay

9   'linear

10 com'ponent

11 fi'nancial

12 'maximize

Lesson aims

- extend knowledge of fixed phrases commonly used in lectures
- give sentences a special focus (see *Skills bank*)

Further practice in:

- stress within words

Introduction

As in Units 3 and 5, tell students to ask you questions about the information in the lecture in Lesson 2 as if you were the lecturer. Remind them about asking for information politely. If they need to revise how to do this, tell them to look back at the *Skills bank* for Unit 3.

🎧 Exercise A

Remind students of the importance of stressed syllables in words (see the teaching notes for Unit 3, Lesson 3, Exercise A). Play the recording, pausing after the first few to check that students understand the task.

Feed back, perhaps playing the recording again for each word before checking. Ideally, mark up an OHT of the words. Finally, check students' pronunciation of the words.

🎧 Exercise B

Write these words on the board and ask students to say what symbols you can use for them when taking notes. Put the symbols on the board.

∵	because
e.g.	for example
=	is, means
→	invented, leads to*
∴	therefore, so
& +	and
numbers or bullet points	a list
/	or

*the arrow has a wide range of possible meanings, including *made*, *produced*, *did*, *causes*, *results in*, etc.

121

Tell students they will hear the final part of the lecture. Ask them to read the notes through. Remind them also to listen for their research task. Play Part 5.

Put students in pairs to compare their symbols. Feed back with the whole class, if possible using an OHT of the notes. Discuss acceptable alternatives, e.g., *start & finish* instead of *start / finish*.

Answers

Model answers:

1 Production planning $=$ complex $\because$

   1) some factors $=$ outside control of company

      e.g. weather $\rightarrow$ clothes demand

   2) design $\rightarrow$ production method

  Scheduling $=$ what processes? When start $/$ finish?

  Henry Gantt $\rightarrow$ Gantt charts (early 1900s)

  In batch $\&$ flow production $=$ waste of time if workers have to wait $\therefore$ Gantt charts used for scheduling

2 They must research the criteria for business location.

Transcript 🎧 1.34

Part 5

I'm going to finish with some comments on the planning of production – in other words, scheduling.

Now, the fact of the matter is, it's a highly complex task to plan production. The reason for this is that planning decisions are based on a wide variety of different factors – not to mention the fact that some of these factors are totally outside the control of the company. Let's take clothes: a change in the weather can affect the demand for clothes, which of course companies can't control. Plus

there's the fact that the design of the product affects the type of production method, as we've just seen.

OK. Where was I ? Oh, yes ... So scheduling means working out what the different processes are, when they start, when they finish, etcetera, in relation to other processes. You've probably heard about Gantt charts? It was Henry Gantt who came up with a very simple idea to help with scheduling – the Gantt chart. Many organizations use Gantt charts to help with organizing and planning these types of production methods. The advantage of Gantt charts is that they show what processes are happening at any one time. In batch and flow production, it is very expensive and a waste of time if workers have to wait for one job to finish before another one can start. So, although it was in the early 1900s that Gantt invented his charts, they are still very much used today.

To sum up, then, production must be carefully planned. Let me put it another way ... Planning must take into account the necessary processes and variables if the company is to succeed.

Oh, I almost forgot to mention your research topics. OK, well, what's very important for the whole operation is the location of the business. So I'd like you to find out what are the main criteria that need to be borne in mind in deciding where to locate a business.

Exercise C

Set for pairwork. Feed back with the whole class. If necessary, play the relevant sections again. Ask for other phrases which have similar meanings, particularly from Lesson 3, and also from Unit 5. Build the table in the Answers section on the board. Accept any suitable words or phrases for the third column.

Answers

Model answers:
See table below.

Use	Fixed phrase	Other phrases
to introduce a new topic	You've probably heard of ...	Now, an important concept is ...
to make a major point	The fact of the matter is, ...	Actually, ... In fact, ... The point is that ...
to add points	Not to mention the fact that ... Plus there's the fact that ...	also, and, too
to finish a list	et cetera	and so on
to give an example	Let's take ...	For example, ... e.g., ... Let's look at an example of this. For instance, ...
to restate	Let me put it another way. In other words, ...	What I mean is ... That is to say, ... By that I mean ... To put it another way, ...

Exercise D

Students need to decide which word(s) should receive the particular focus and then try to rewrite the sentences. Depending on the class, they can work in pairs or individually first.

Feed back with the whole class. Take each sentence in turn. Ask for suggestions as to which aspect could receive special emphasis (actual words are underlined below). Accept any reasonable answers. Replay Part 5 at this stage if you wish students to check their answers. Note that:

- sentences 1, 2 and the first part of 4 use an *It* construction to give the special focus
- sentence 3 uses a *Wh~* cleft sentence already seen in Lesson 2
- sentences 4 and 5 introduce new, general words (often found in academic contexts) followed by *is* plus a *that* clause

Answers

Model answers:

1 <u>Henry Gantt</u> came up with an idea to help with scheduling. (*It*)

It was Henry Gantt who came up with an idea to help with scheduling.

2 Gantt invented his charts <u>in the early 1900s</u>. (*It*)

It was in the early 1900s that Gantt invented his charts.

3 The location of the business is very <u>important</u> for the whole business operation. (*What*)

What's very important for the whole operation is the location of the business.

4 Production planning is <u>complex because</u> planning decisions are based on a wide variety of different factors. (*Two sentences. First = 'It'; Second = 'The reason'*)

It's a complex task to plan production. The reason for this is that planning decisions are based on a wide variety of different factors.

5 Gantt charts show what processes are happening at any one time. (*The advantage*)

The advantage of Gantt charts is that they show what processes are happening at any one time.

After completing Exercises C and D, students can be referred to the *Vocabulary bank* and the *Skills bank* for consolidation and preparation for Exercise E.

Exercise E

Set the initial preparation for individual work. Students can refer to their notes in Lesson 2 (Exercises C and E) or the notes for completion in Lesson 3 (Exercise B). They should think about how they can use the phrases they have looked at, and ways of giving special focus/emphasis. (Note: They should not write out exactly what they are going to say in complete sentences and then read!)

Put students in pairs to give their oral summaries to each other, preferably pairing students who have chosen different sections to summarize.

Go around the class noting any problems or especially good examples of language use. You may wish to choose one or two individuals to give their summary to the whole class.

With the whole class, feed back any language or other difficulties which you noticed.

Exercise F

1 Set for pairwork. Suggest simple activities like making a cup of tea or a sandwich or writing an essay. Students should first list all the different processes and then decide how to order them and which processes overlap. They should make a Gantt chart and put the activities in it. They should decide what time units to use.

2 Put the pairs in groups of four to present their charts to each other.

Closure

Dictate some words for which students have learnt note-taking symbols or abbreviations such as *and, minus, approximately, less than, results in, therefore, because, etc., as, since, for example, approximately*. Students should write the symbol or abbreviation.

Remind them of the list of symbols and abbreviations at the back of the Course Book.

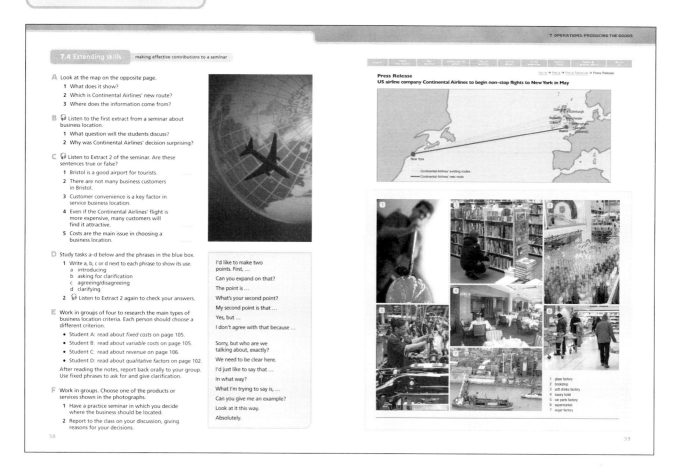

7.4 Extending skills

Lesson aims

- make effective contributions to a seminar:

  using pre-organizers – *I'd like to make two points; I don't agree with that because ...*

  responding to queries by clarifying – *What I'm trying to say is .../What I meant was ...*

Introduction

Revise phrases from the previous lessons. Give a word or phrase and ask students to give one with a similar meaning. Ask for phrases from the previous lesson which can be used to:

- introduce a new topic
- emphasize a major point
- add a point
- finish a list
- give an example

Exercise A

Set for pairwork discussion. Feed back.

Answers

Possible answers:

1 It shows several routes which Continental Airlines operates from New York to the UK.

2 The new route from Bristol to New York.

3 The headline comes from a press release.

🎧 Exercise B

Allow students time to read the two questions. Play Extract 1 once only. Check answers in pairs. Feed back with the whole class.

Answers

Model answers:

1 Why did Continental Airlines establish a new non-stop route from Bristol to New York in 2005?

2 They already had routes to several other places in the UK. At least two of these places are not far from Bristol (Birmingham and London). There are already many flights provided by other airlines to the USA from London airports.

124

Transcript 🎧 **1.35**

Extract 1

Now, as we know, the location of their operations is one of the most important decisions that companies have to make. I asked you to look at the case of Continental Airlines, which in 2005 established a new non-stop route from Bristol Airport in the south-west of the UK to New York. Why did they do this? They already had routes to several other places in the UK, including London (Gatwick) and Birmingham, which are not far away. Also, there are many other airlines flying from the London airports to the USA. So, let's have some views.

🎧 **Exercise C**

Allow students time to read the questions. Play Extract 2 straight through once while they mark the answers true or false. Check in pairs and/or with the whole class. Check any unknown vocabulary, such as *expand on*, *untapped potential*.

Answers

1	true	
2	false	Bristol is an important regional business centre.
3	true	
4	true	
5	false	There are many factors; other factors also mentioned are revenue and investment potential.

Transcript 🎧 **1.36**

Extract 2

Note: The underlining relates to Exercise D.

JACK: Well. <u>I'd like to make two points. First,</u> Bristol gives easy access to several popular tourist destinations.

LEILA: <u>Can you expand on that</u>, Jack?

JACK: Sure, Leila. Bristol is near Wales, and the south-west peninsula of the UK.

LEILA: So?

JACK: So <u>the point is</u> that both areas are famous for their beaches and natural beauty.

LECTURER: OK. So, <u>what's your second point</u>, Jack?

JACK: I was coming to that! <u>My second point is that</u> Bristol is an important regional business centre.

LEILA: <u>Yes, but</u> that's true for London, too. Even more so, I'd say. So there's no need to expand outside London.

MAJED: Well, <u>I don't agree with that</u>, Leila, <u>because</u> from what I've read, there's huge untapped potential for business customers based in or near Bristol.

EVIE: <u>Sorry, but who are we talking about, exactly?</u> People flying into the UK from the USA? Or people going to the USA?

LEILA: Yes, <u>we need to be clear here</u>. It must be both. Anyway, <u>I'd just like to say that</u> according to what I've read, in the case of a service industry like travel, convenience for customers is a major factor in location.

EVIE: <u>In what way?</u>

LEILA: Well, if you can bring your service nearer to the customer, you can charge a bit more. Also, you may be able at the same time to offer a more attractive service than the competitors.

EVIE: I don't get that. How can it be more attractive if it's more expensive?

LEILA: <u>What I'm trying to say is</u>, the company can charge more for their product but actually the customer might get the product more cheaply overall.

EVIE: I still don't understand. <u>Can you give me an example</u>, Leila?

LEILA: OK. <u>Look at it this way</u>. People who live near Bristol would have to travel to London or Birmingham to fly to the USA. That will cost them money – say, £100. If they go from Bristol they don't have to spend that money. If Continental Airlines charge £50 more for the flight than a flight from London, the customers still get the flight for £50 less.

MAJED: So everybody wins! It's all about money, in fact.

LECTURER: <u>Absolutely</u>. In making a decision on location, companies have to think about their fixed and variable costs, as well as the revenue they're likely to get from a particular site.

MAJED: Yes, and I'd just like to say something else. As I mentioned before, there are potentially a lot of business customers who might use the Bristol flight. So it's a good investment, as business usage is likely to increase in the future.

🎧 Exercise D

Check the meaning of 'introducing' phrases. This means a phrase to use before your main statement to announce that you are going to say something. It may also signal how much you are going to say, or how important you think what you are going to say is.

1 Set for individual work and pairwork checking. Feed back.

2 Play Extract 2 from Exercise C. Ask students to tell you to stop when they hear each phrase (underlined in the transcript above). Check what kind of phrase they think it is. Get students to repeat the phrase to copy the intonation.

Answers

Model answers:

I'd like to make two points. First, …	a
Can you expand on that?	b
The point is …	d
What's your second point?	b
My second point is that …	a
Yes, but …	c
I don't agree with that because …	c
Sorry, but who are we talking about, exactly?	b
We need to be clear here.	d
I'd just like to say that …	a
In what way?	b
What I'm trying to say is, …	d
Can you give me an example?	b
Look at it this way.	d
Absolutely.	c

Exercise E

With the whole class, revise asking for information. Tell students to look at the *Skills banks* in Unit 3 and Unit 5. Remind students also about reporting information to people (see Unit 3 *Skills bank*).

Set students to work in groups of four. Each student should choose one aspect of location and turn to the relevant page to make notes on the information. When everyone is ready they should feed back to their group, giving an oral report on the information. It's important that they do not simply read aloud the information, but use it to inform their speaking.

Alternatively, the research activity can be done as a 'wall dictation' as follows. Use Resource 7E in the additional resources section. Make large A3 (or A4) size copies of the location information (one type of research per page) and pin the sheets on the classroom walls. Each student should leave his/her seat and go to the wall to find the information he/she needs. Students should not write anything down: instead they should read and try to remember the information. Then they

return to their group and tell them the information. If they forget something they can go back to the wall to have another look.

Circulate, encouraging students to ask for clarification and to use the appropriate phrases when giving clarification. Note where students are having difficulty with language and where things are going well. When everyone has finished, feed back to the class on points you have noticed while listening in to the discussions.

Exercise F

Move on from Exercise E to this simulation. Encourage students to make this as realistic as possible by choosing a product or service that they know or can identify with. The location could be in your area. If students decide on an international location, remind them that there will be other factors to consider such as language barriers, political stability, exchange rate fluctuations, and so on. If you wish, the whole class could work on the same product or service, but with the location decision discussed in groups.

Alternatively, you could have a 'pyramid discussion'. Choose one product or service for the whole class to debate and put students in pairs to discuss a suitable location. After a short while, the pair should join together with another pair. This group of four should then come to an agreement on a suitable location. The group of four should then join another group of four. One or two people from each group of eight should then present the decision and the reasons for the decision to the class. It will help their presentation if they use visual aids such as maps or diagrams. Finally, the whole class should try to reach agreement on the site decision, taking a vote if necessary.

Remind students about agreeing and agreeing, and about good and bad ways to contribute to seminar discussions (refer to Unit 5 if necessary).

While the representatives are presenting their group decisions, you should occasionally interrupt with a wrong interpretation so that students are forced to clarify their statements. Or you could ask for clarification.

Closure

Choose three cities in your country. Ask students to first discuss and then *describe* and *evaluate* the characteristics of each city according to the following:

- location
- logistics and transport systems
- people
- industries
- economy
- environment
- quality of life
- image
- cost of living

Extra activities

1 Work through the *Vocabulary bank* and *Skills bank* if you have not already done so, or as a revision of previous study.

2 Use the *Activity bank* (Teacher's Book additional resources section, Resources 7A–C).

A Set the crossword for individual work (including homework) or pairwork.

Answers

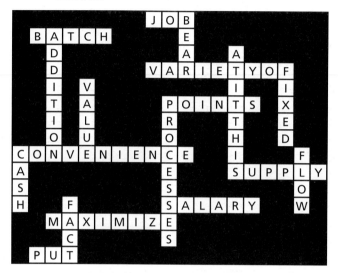

B Put students in pairs to play 'word battleships'. The idea behind this game is that each word represents a battleship, which is 'sunk' when all the letters of the word have been located; the aim of the game is to be the first to sink all the ships.

Give Resource 7B to Student A; give Resource 7C to Student B. Make sure they can't see each other's information. Students take turns to ask about individual squares, e.g., *Is there a letter in (1C)?* The other student answers either *No* or *Yes, it's (F)*. They mark their empty grid accordingly – either putting a letter or a cross in each square. If a student finds a letter, he/she can continue asking until he/she gets a negative answer (i.e., an 'empty' square). Students continue asking one question each until one of them thinks they have found a word, when they can say *Is the word ... ?* The first student to find all their words is the winner.

The words for each category are:

Student A:

- four words for production types: *batch, flow, job, mass*
- two verbs ending in ~ate: *calculate, evaluate*
- four words which can be nouns or verbs: *delay, design, handle, supply*

Student B:

- two ways to show an idea for a new product: *drawing, prototype*
- four types of cost from a location: *fixed, variable, loan, rent*
- two ways to refer to raw materials: *ingredients, resources*
- two words for the place of business: *location, site*

3 Make some statements about what you're going to do after the class and ask students to transform them into *Wh~* cleft sentences. For example:

I'm going to have a coffee after the class.

→ *What you're going to do after the class is have a coffee.*

I might go to a film tonight.

→ *What you might do tonight is go to a film.*

Put students in pairs to practise.

8 OPERATIONS: EFFICIENCY, COSTS AND QUALITY

This is the second of two units on aspects of operations management. This unit looks at how improvements in efficiency can make companies more profitable and more successful. Concepts such as economies of scale and capacity utilization are examined. The reading text discusses Japanese management practices such as just-in-time and other 'lean production' techniques, as well as quality control techniques such as Total Quality Management.

Skills focus

Reading
- understanding dependent clauses with passives

Writing
- paraphrasing
- expanding notes into complex sentences
- recognizing different essay types/structures:
  descriptive
  analytical
  comparison/evaluation
  argument
- writing essay plans
- writing essays

Vocabulary focus

- synonyms
- nouns from verbs
- definitions
- common 'direction' verbs in essay titles (*discuss, analyse, evaluate*, etc.)

Key vocabulary

assemble	initiative	profitability
bulk	inventory	quality
capacity utilization	large-scale (adj)	quality control
consistency	machinery	retailer
cost savings	manpower	savings
defect (n)	manufacturer	stock (n)
economical	materials	technique
economies of scale	maximize	waste (n and v)
efficiency	monitor (v)	wholesaler
elimination (of waste)	plant (n)	workforce
inefficiency	premises	

8.1 Vocabulary

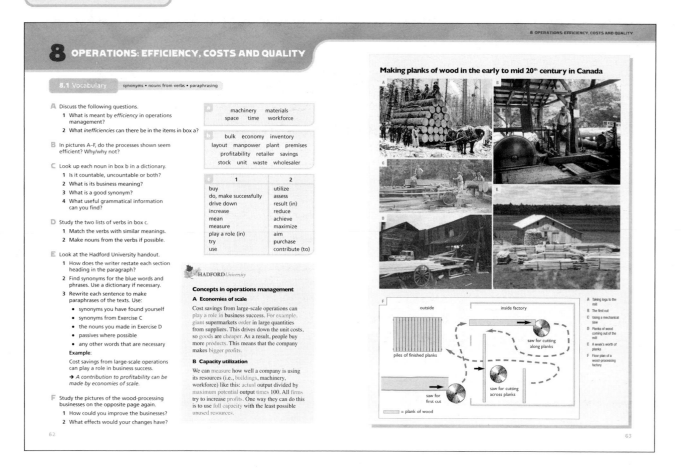

Lesson aims

- extend knowledge of synonyms and word sets (enables paraphrasing at word level)
- make nouns and noun phrases from verbs (enables paraphrasing at sentence level)

Further practice in paraphrasing at sentence level with:

- passives
- synonymous phrases
- negatives
- replacement subjects

Introduction

Revise ways of paraphrasing sentences. Write the following sentences from Unit 6 on the board and ask students to say what changes have been made to the paraphrased sentences.

Original sentence: *Increasing sales mean that unit costs are reduced.*

Paraphrase: *The company can make products more cheaply once they start to sell well.*

(answer: change in word order, passive to active, use of synonyms)

Original sentence: *In the introduction phase, unit costs are high.*

Paraphrase: *It costs a lot to produce each unit early in the cycle.*

(answer: change in word order, use of synonyms, replacement subject)

Exercise A

Answers

Possible answers:

1 Having an efficient operation means keeping the costs of production as low as possible so that the biggest possible profits are achieved – without a negative effect on the desired quality.

2 **machinery:** machinery may be old and liable to break down; new machinery could possibly increase production speed or reduce the workforce.

materials: at any one time, a company may have too much raw material for its needs, so money is tied up in stock unnecessarily.

space: there may be too much (increasing overhead costs), or the design of the operation in the factory or company buildings may be poor so that goods take a long time to move through the production process.

time: production of a good may be taking more time than it needs to, therefore involving people in unnecessary work.

workforce: a company may have too many people doing a particular job, or the wrong people; or people with the wrong or outdated skills.

Exercise B

Set for pairwork discussion. Check that students understand the technical vocabulary shown in the pictures (*log, saw, plank, cart, sawmill*). Tell students to bear in mind the points they have just discussed. Feed back with the whole class.

Answers

Possible answers:

A Several men are transporting logs through some woods using horses. This looks inefficient because there are only two horses but quite a lot of logs and men. Tying the logs onto the cart takes time. There is no proper road – the ground looks rough. The whole process looks very slow.

B A man is are using a machine to cut the logs. He is beginning the process of turning logs into planks. The process is again probably rather inefficient compared to nowadays because the logs must be moved around and the process is not automatic. The process looks dangerous and slow – only one log can be cut at a time. The machine is outside – presumably once cut, the wood must be carried somewhere else.

C Here we can see several people involved in the process. Some are only watching and doing nothing.

Also we can see that the machine looks rather old: it's likely that it works rather slowly and inefficiently.

D The planks of wood are coming out of the mill and going onto a cart. They look very disorganized. Some planks are on the ground. It looks rather wasteful.

E The planks are waiting to be transported somewhere. Why haven't they already gone to a place where they can be sold? The company is not going to get its money quickly.

F The floor plan shows that the factory is rather disorganized and does not make the best use of space. The planks do not follow a simple route.

Exercise C

Set for pairwork. You may wish to divide the work up between different pairs. For question 4 (useful grammatical information), tell students to look out for words that can have the same form when used as a noun or verb, nouns that can be only singular or only plural, nouns that change their meaning when used as U or C, etc.

Feed back, building up the table in the Answers section on the board.

Answers

Model answers:
See table on next page.

Exercise D

Set for individual work and pairwork checking. Make sure students understand that they should find a verb in column 2 with a similar meaning to one of the verbs in column 1.

Feed back with the whole class, discussing the extent to which the verbs are exact synonyms, and if not, identifying any differences in meaning.

Answers

Model answers:

Verb	Noun	Verb	Noun
buy	–	purchase	purchase
do, make successfully		achieve	achievement
drive down	–	reduce	reduction
increase	increase	maximize	maximization
mean	no noun in this meaning	result (in)	result
measure	measurement	assess	assessment
play a role (in)	–	contribute (to)	contribution
try	try	aim	aim
use	use, usage	utilize	utilization

Word	C/U	Meaning in business	Synonym	Useful grammatical information
bulk	C/U	large quantity	large quantity, large volume	usual use is in phrase: *in bulk*. Can be found as countable in fixed expressions
economy	C/U	1. careful use of money 2. all the business of a country= the economy of the UK	1. saving	U or C depends on use: *to practise economy; to make some economies* C = money system of a country adj = economical v = economize
inventory	C	(a list of) stock held by a company	list	
layout	C	how a shop or factory space is arranged	plan, design	
manpower	U	workers for a job	workforce	
plant	C/U	machinery, factory	machinery	U = machinery C = a factory (also a tree or flower)
premises	C	the building(s) used for	building(s) the business	plural noun only
profitability	U	the difference between income and expenditure; therefore, a company's ability to be successful financially	business success	
retailer	C	an organization or person selling to the public	seller (e.g., food retailer = supermarket)	
savings	C	money that has been saved	economies	always plural
stock	C/U	1. supply of goods, both at the input and at the output stages 2. another word for *shares*	1. finished products	v = stock
unit	C	a single product	a product, good, item	*unit* is the word which usually goes with *cost* = the cost of one item
waste	C/U	resources that were not needed or used, causing unnecessary expense	unused or unwanted materials or resources	C = always singular adj = wasteful
wholesaler	C	the organization or person supplying a retailer	supplier	

Exercise E

This is an exercise in paraphrasing based on word and sentence level techniques. As well as finding their own synonyms from memory and using the synonyms already discussed in Exercises C and D, students will use noun phrases in place of verb phrases as a technique in paraphrasing. Students should also make passive sentences wherever they can.

1 Set for individual work. Feed back with the whole class.

2 Set for individual work and pairwork checking.

3 Set for pairwork; pairs then check with other pairs. Alternatively, tell some students to write their answers on an OHT for discussion by the whole class.

Answers

Model answers:

1 A Economies of scale = cost savings from large-scale operations

B Capacity utilization = how well a company is using its resources

2 Possible synonyms (including synonyms from Exercises C and D):

A **Economies of scale**
Cost savings from large-scale operations can *(play a role in)* contribute to business success. *(For example)* For instance, *(giant)* big/large/huge supermarkets *(order)* buy in large quantities from suppliers. This drives down the unit costs, so *(goods)* products are *(cheaper)* less expensive. As a result, people buy more *(products)* items. This means that the company makes *(bigger profits)* more revenue.

B **Capacity utilization**
We can *(measure)* assess how well a company is using its resources (i.e., *(buildings)* premises, machinery, workforce) like this: *(actual)* real output divided by *(maximum potential)* highest possible output *(times)* multiplied by 100. All *(firms)* companies try to increase *(profits)* revenue. One way they can do this is to use *(full capacity)* all their resources with the least possible *(unused resources)* waste.

3 Possible paraphrases:

A **Economies of scale**
A contribution to profitability can be made by economies of scale.

For instance, big food retailers buy in bulk from wholesalers.

The (resulting) reduction in the unit costs means that products are less expensive.

So more items are purchased.

The result is that increased revenue is achieved (by the company).

B **Capacity utilization**
Capacity utilization (i.e., use of premises, plant, manpower) can be assessed by dividing real output by highest possible output multiplied by 100.

The aim of all companies is the maximization of revenue.

This can be achieved by the utilization of all their resources with the smallest possible waste.

Exercise F

Set for pair or small group discussion. Feed back with the whole class. Accept any reasonable suggestions.

Answers

Possible answers:

Invest in some modern plant and transport:

- (pictures A and D)
  large trucks for transport and machines to load the trucks – this would make the transport of the logs to and planks from the mill faster and more efficient

- (pictures B and C)
  bigger and more modern saws which can hold and turn the logs without the need for two men – just one to oversee the process

- (picture E)
  use the trucks to make sure that the planks are delivered for sale as quickly as possible so that the stock does not accumulate – the company needs to get money for its products as fast as possible

Reduce the size of the workforce or retrain some of the workers – there are too many employees (picture A).

Improve the premises and buildings:

- (picture F)
  redesign the way in which the planks move from one place to another so that the shortest route is used. For example, move the first cut saw nearer to the door. Make a new entrance on the right side of the factory so that the finished planks can go straight out

- (picture D)
  redesign the end of the process so that the finished planks are loaded accurately onto trucks for transport so there is no waste

- (picture E)
  build new premises to store the finished planks so that they do not get wet

Closure

Ask students to work in pairs or small groups to draw a new design for the layout of the sawmill and then to present their solutions.

8.2 Reading

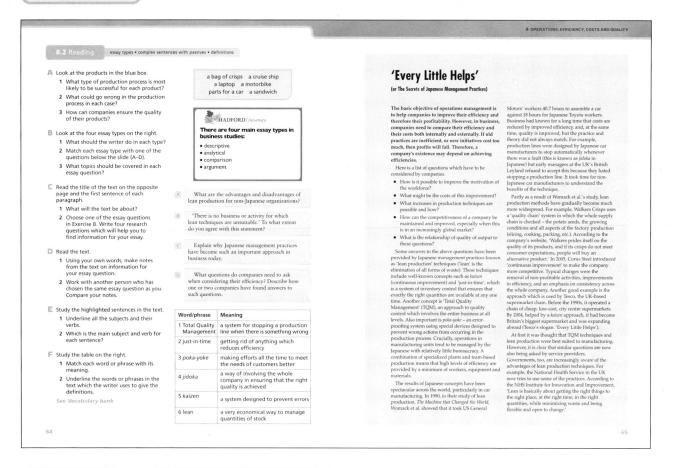

General note

Read the *Vocabulary bank* and *Skills bank* at the end of the Course Book unit. Decide when, if at all, to refer students to them. The *Vocabulary bank* section *Understanding new words: using definitions* is relevant to Lesson 2; the *Skills bank* will be more relevant to Lessons 3 and 4.

Lesson aims

- understand essay types
- interpret essay titles
- find the main information in a passive clause
- understand internal definitions (see *Vocabulary bank*)

Further practice in:

- reading research
- finding the kernel of a long sentence

Introduction

With the whole class, discuss how to use written texts as sources of information when writing an answer for an essay question. Ask students:

1 *How can you choose useful sources?* (to get an idea of whether a text might be useful, survey the text, i.e., look at the title, look at the beginning and the end and the first line of each paragraph; in other words, skim-read to get an approximate idea of the text contents)

2 *If you decide that a text is going to be useful, what is it a good idea to do …*

- … before reading? (think of questions related to the essay question to which you would like to find some answers)

- … while reading? (identify useful parts of the text; make notes in your own words)

- … after reading? (check answers to the questions)

Exercise A

Revise production methods from Unit 7. Elicit the words *job*, *batch*, *flow* and ask for examples of products these are used with. Remind students that 'batch' is where a large number of the same items are made simultaneously. When one batch is finished, another can be started. Production may stop between the end of one batch and the start of another. 'Flow' is where items proceed individually along a production line and components are added. There are no pauses in production activity.

Revise concepts from Lesson 1 of this unit: ask for suggestions of areas in which companies can become more efficient (elicit *materials*, *workforce*, *machinery*, *space*, *time*; also *money/investment* (though this was not covered in Lesson 1).

Set the three questions for pairwork discussion with whole class feedback.

Answers

Possible answers:

1

Product	Probable production method
a bag of crisps	batch
a cruise ship	job
a laptop	flow
a motorbike	flow
parts for a car	batch
a sandwich	batch

2 Accept any reasonable answers, e.g., crisps are not crisp, have too much salt, not enough in the bag; cruise ship is late/is over budget; laptop has faulty battery which will catch fire (= real example!); motorbike doesn't work/has the wrong parts in it; sandwich is not hygienically produced so could poison people (many real examples!); etc.

3 One way companies can ensure the quality of their products is through checking samples of products. Another way is 'Total Quality Management' in which *everyone* in the company has an awareness of the need to 'continually increase (in) customer satisfaction at continually lower real costs' (http://en.wikipedia.org/wiki/Total_Quality_Management).Introduce the idea of Japanese management practices, which TQM is associated with. Tell students that they will find out more about this subject in this lesson.

Exercise B

1 Refer students to the lecture slide. Discuss this question with the whole class. Build up the table in the Answers section on the board.

2 Set for pairwork. Feed back with the whole class. Ask the class to say which are the key words in each title that tell you what type of writing it is.

3 Set for pairwork. Feed back using the second table in the Answers section, discussing with the whole class what topics which will need to be included in each essay. Add the notes in the third column.

Answers

Possible answers:

1

	What the writer should do
Descriptive writing	describe or summarize key ideas/key events /key points. Give the plain facts. Could involve writing about: a narrative description (a history of something); a process (how something happens); key ideas in a theory; main points of an article (answers the question *What is/are …?*)
Analytical writing	try to analyse (= go behind the plain facts) or explain something or give reasons for a situation; may also question accepted ideas and assumptions (answers the question *Why/how …?*)
Comparison	compare two or more aspects/ideas/things/people, etc.; usually also evaluate, i.e., say which is better/bigger, etc.
Argument writing	give an opinion and support the opinion with evidence/reasons, etc.; may also give opposing writing opinions (= counter arguments) and show how they are wrong

2/3

Key words are underlined:

Type of writing	Question	Topics
Descriptive writing	D <u>What questions</u> do companies need to ask when considering their efficiency? <u>Describe</u> how one or two companies have found answers to such questions.	• efficiency: what is it? Why important? • how to evaluate efficiency: types of questions • examples of companies and what they did
Analytical writing	C <u>Explain why</u> Japanese management practices have become such an important approach in business today.	• Japanese management practices: what are they? • the extent and reasons for their importance • examples of current businesses which use them
Comparison	A <u>What are the advantages and disadvantages</u> of lean production for non-Japanese organizations?	• lean production: what is it? • advantages for Japanese organizations • examples of advantages for non-Japanese organizations • examples of disadvantages for non-Japanese organizations
Argument writing	B 'There is no business or activity for which lean techniques are unsuitable.' <u>To what extent do you agree</u> with this statement?	• lean techniques: what are they? • businesses originally associated with lean techniques • businesses which use it successfully/ unsuccessfully • other types of business which could/ could not use it

Exercise C

1 Set for individual work. Feed back with the whole class.

2 If necessary, remind students of the purpose of research questions and do one or two examples as a class. Set for individual work and pairwork checking. Feed back, getting good research questions for each essay topic on the board.

Answers

Possible answers:

1 The title of the text suggests that the text will look at Japanese management techniques. The word *secrets* suggests these techniques have benefits for business, i.e., they are positive features of management. The title implies that small details are important in these techniques – together these detailed aspects will help a company perform better. ('Every Little Helps' carries this meaning: it is also Tesco's slogan, a fact which is in the text.)

Paragraph 1 explains the basic concept of the text: operations management is necessary in order to help companies improve and be more efficient and productive.

Paragraph 2 is going to provide a list of important questions.

Paragraph 3 will provide answers to the questions in paragraph 2.

Paragraph 4 is about important results of the Japanese techniques, especially in the car industry.

Paragraph 5 will show that these techniques have become more common in business; it also gives some terms and definitions and a reference (Womack et al.).

Paragraph 6 will suggest that other sectors of business can also benefit from Japanese techniques.

2 Answers depend on the students.

Exercise D

Set for individual work then pairwork comparison/checking. If you wish, students can make notes under the headings in the 'Topics' column of the table in Exercise B above. Encourage students to make notes in their own words.

Answers

Possible notes:

A *What are the advantages and disadvantages of lean production for non-Japanese organizations?*

- lean production = production techniques which avoid unnecessary waste. Involves, e.g., Total Quality Management, 'just-in-time', *poka-yoke*, *jidoka*, *kaizen*

- advantages for Japanese organizations: Japanese management practices v. successful, e.g., car manufacturing: as shown in Womack et al. 1990, Toyota workers could make car in less than half time of US workers; not much bureaucracy needed; team-based production; v. efficient with low resources (workforce, plant, etc.)

- examples of advantages for non-Japanese organizations: improved efficiency, e.g., Walkers Crisps (control and quality in whole supply chain); Corus Steel (stopped anything not profitable, increased efficiency in processes, consistency in company); Tesco supermarket chain (*kaizen*); the UK National Health Service

- disadvantages of lean for non-Japanese organizations: not much here – just negative reactions by workforce (need to research this more)

B *'There is no business or activity for which lean techniques are unsuitable.' To what extent do you agree with this statement?*

- lean = production techniques which avoid unnecessary waste. Involves, e.g., Total Quality Management = quality control method which concerns whole organization; 'just-in-time' = way to control production/stock; *poka yoke* = error-proofing system; *jidoka* = production line stops if there is a problem; *kaizen* = everyone works toward continuous improvement

- businesses associated with 'lean' – Japanese car manufacturers first used it and became v. successful

- businesses which use it successfully/unsuccessfully: other companies used the methods to improve efficiency, e.g., Walkers Crisps (control and quality in whole

supply chain); Corus Steel (stopped anything not profitable, increased efficiency in processes, consistency in company); Tesco supermarket chain (*kaizen*); UK National Health Service

- other types of business which could/could not use it: could be used by service industries. Also used in some government services

C *Explain why Japanese management practices have become such an important approach in business today.*

- Japanese management practices: what are they? Lean production: Total Quality Management = quality control method, an approach to quality control which concerns whole organization; 'just-in-time' = way to control production/stock; *poka-yoke* = error-proofing system; *jidoka* = production line stops if there is a problem; *kaizen* = everyone works toward continuous improvement

- extent and reasons for their importance: now used very widely because of success, esp. in car industry; famous study (Womack et al.) made results of Japanese methods known to world. Clear that the methods provided answers to question re. how to increase efficiency in operations

- examples of current businesses which use them: Walkers Crisps (control and quality in whole supply chain); Corus Steel (stopped anything not profitable, increased efficiency in processes, consistency in company); Tesco supermarket chain (*kaizen*); the UK National Health Service (accuracy in stock control; openness to change)

D *What questions do companies need to ask when considering their efficiency? Describe how one or two companies have found answers to such questions.*

- importance of efficiency – helps companies to maximize their profits; operations management plays a part in this; without efficiency company may fail

- how to evaluate efficiency? Look at internal and external costs; old practices, new plans; motivation of employees; production techniques; global competition; role of quality

- examples of companies and what they did – Walkers Crisps (control and quality in whole supply chain); Corus Steel (stopped anything not profitable, increased efficiency in processes, consistency in company); Tesco supermarket chain (*kaizen*); the UK National Health Service (accuracy in stock control; openness to change)

Exercise E

Set for individual work and pairwork checking. Students could copy out the sentences in their notebooks and then underline all the verbs and subjects.

Feed back with the whole class, building up the table in the Answers section on the board. Point out that each sentence has two verbs, which means that each sentence has two *clauses*. This means that the sentences are complex. (A simple sentence has only one main verb and subject.) To enable students to identify which is the 'main' part of the sentence (in bold in the table), ask how the two clauses are 'joined' and add the joining words (here: a time word, a *that* which follows a verb of saying/thinking, and a relative pronoun). The main part of the sentence is linked to the *dependent* part with these words.

Check understanding of the passives in each case by asking how each clause and sentence could be rephrased with an active verb, e.g.,

1 How can we maintain and improve the competitiveness of a company, especially when this is an increasingly global market?

2 A combination of specialized plants and team-based production means that a minimum of workers, equipment and materials can provide high levels of efficiency.

3 Tesco, the UK-based supermarket chain, uses an approach which is another good example.

Language note

The choice of whether to use an active or a passive construction often depends on how the writer wants to structure the information. Refer to Unit 7 *Skills bank* for a note on information structure.

Answers

Possible answers:

	Joining word	Subject	Verb	Object/complement
1		**competitiveness**	**can ... be maintained**	
		(can ... be) improved		
	when	this	is	in an increasingly global <u>market</u>?*
2		**A combination of specialized <u>plants</u> and team-based <u>production</u>**	**means**	
	that	high levels of <u>efficiency</u>	are provided	by a minimum of <u>workers</u>, <u>equipment and materials</u>.
3		**Another good <u>example</u>**	**is**	**the <u>approach</u>**
	which		is used	by <u>Tesco</u>, the UK-based supermarket chain.

*the underlined noun is the head word of the noun phrase

Exercise F

Set for individual work and pairwork checking. In question 2, tell students to look for the actual words used and the punctuation, grammatical and vocabulary devices which are used to indicate meanings.

Feed back with the whole class, pointing out the structures given in the third column of the table for question 2 in the Answers section. If you wish, refer students to the *Vocabulary bank – Understanding new words: using definitions*.

Answers

1

	Word/phrase	Meaning
1	Total Quality Management	a way of involving the whole company in ensuring that the right quality is achieved
2	just-in-time	a very economical way to manage quantities of stock
3	*poka-yoke*	a system designed to prevent errors
4	*jidoka*	a system for stopping a production line when there is something wrong
5	*kaizen*	making efforts all the time to meet the needs of customers better
6	lean	getting rid of anything which reduces efficiency

Closure

Tell students to make a list of products and/or services in the local environment – this could be something they have brought with them today, something in the room, or something that can be found in the college/school. For example:

- students: mobile phones/MP3s/stationery/ books/clothes/shoes/bags/laptops
- classroom and beyond: furniture and fittings/carpets/tables/chairs/computers/AV equipment/drinks machines/tables and chairs
- services: canteen/library/bookshop/institution administration/students' services/computing services

Students should work in small groups and choose one or two items. Then they should discuss the following:

1 Does the item meet their needs? Why/how?

2 How was the item produced?

3 How has quality been incorporated into the design and production?

4 How could the item/service be improved?

2 Model answers:

Word/phrase	Actual words giving the meaning	Punctuation/vocab/structure
Total Quality Management	… , an approach to quality control which involves the entire business at all levels.	word/phrase followed by comma + noun + *which*
just-in-time	… , which is a system of inventory control	word/phrase followed by comma + *which is a*
poka-yoke	… – an error-proofing system using special devices designed to prevent wrong actions from occurring in the production process.	word/phrase followed by a dash + noun phrase + elided relative and past participle (*which are designed*)
jidoka	… stop automatically whenever there was a fault (this is known as …)	word/phrase followed by name in brackets (*this is known as …*)
kaizen	… (continuous improvement)	word/phrase followed by definition in brackets
lean	('lean' is the elimination of all forms of waste)	definition in brackets; noun phrase + *is* + noun phrase

8.3 Extending skills

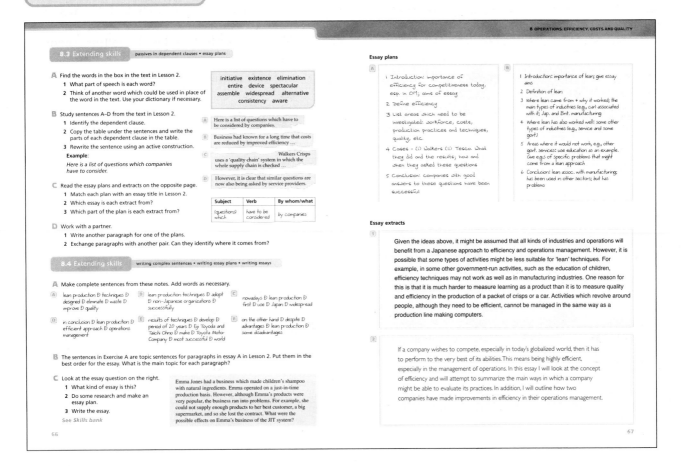

Lesson aims

- find the main information in a passive dependent clause
- recognize appropriate writing plans for essay types

Further practice in:

- vocabulary from Lesson 2

Introduction

Choose about 10–15 words from the previous unit which you think that students should revise. Write them in a random arrangement and at different angles (i.e., not in a vertical list) on an OHT or on the board. Allow students two minutes to look at and remember the words, and then take them away. Students should write down all the words they can remember.

Exercise A

Set for individual work and pairwork checking. Feed back with the whole class.

Answers

Model answers:

Word	Part of speech	Another word
initiative	n (C)	plan, proposal, scheme
existence	n (U)	survival
elimination	n (U)	removal, eradication
entire	adj	whole
device	n (C)	machine, mechanism
spectacular	adj	amazing, dramatic, fantastic
assemble	v	manufacture, make
widespread	adj	common, prevalent
alternative	adj	another, different
consistency	n (U)	uniformity, evenness (of quality)
aware	adj	conscious (of), familiar (with)

Exercise B

Set for individual work and pairwork checking. Make sure that students can correctly identify the main clause, the dependent clause and the linking word. Do the first transformation with the class to check that they know what to do. Note that they do not need to rewrite the main clauses. Also, if no agent is given they will need to supply one themselves.

Answers

Model answers:

1/2

	Main clause	Linking word	Dependent clause		
			Subject	Verb	By whom/what
A	Here is a list of questions	which	(questions) which*	have to be considered	by companies
B	Business had known for a long time	that	costs	are reduced	by improved efficiency ...
C	Walkers Crisps uses a 'quality chain' system	in which	the whole supply chain	is checked ...	
D	However, it is clear	that	similar questions	are now also being asked	by service providers.

*note that in A the relative pronoun is the subject of the dependent clause. In C it is not the subject – instead, the subject is *the whole supply chain*

3   A Here is a list of questions which companies have to consider.

B Business had known for a long time that improved efficiency reduces costs.

C Walkers Crisps uses a 'quality chain' system in which they check the whole supply system.

D However, it is clear that service providers are now asking similar questions.

Exercise C

Tell students to look back at the essay questions in Lesson 2. You may also need to remind them of the topics which you decided are suitable for the essay.

Set all three questions for individual work and pairwork checking. Feed back with the whole class. Ask students to say what aspects of the plans and the extracts enabled them to be identified. Check that students can match the parts of the extracts with the corresponding parts of the essay plan.

Answers

Model answers:

1 Plan A = essay title D: *What questions do companies need to ask when considering their efficiency? Describe how one or two companies have found answers to such questions.*

   Plan B = essay title B: *'There is no business or activity for which lean techniques are unsuitable.' To what extent do you agree with this statement?*

2 Extract 1 = plan B
   Extract 2 = plan A

3 Extract 1 = Plan B, point 5: **Areas where it would not work**, *e.g., other govt. services: use education as an example. Give e.g.s of specific problems that might come from a lean approach*
   Extract 2 = Plan A, point 1: *Introduction:* **importance of efficiency for competitiveness today, esp. in** OM; *aims of essay*

Language note

Sometimes topic sentences are not the first sentence of a paragraph. As can be seen in point 5 of essay B, the first sentence of the paragraph links with the previous paragraph. The topic is given in the second sentence.

Exercise D

Remind students about writing topic sentences. Set for pairwork. Students who chose these two questions in Lesson 2 can refer to their notes. Students who did not make notes on these two questions in Lesson 2 can refer back to the reading text for information. In all cases, students should write using their own words, i.e., paraphrase the ideas in the text.

If you wish, you could ask some students – perhaps those who finish early – to write their paragraphs on an OHT for all the class to look at. Comment on the extent to which students have managed to paraphrase, whether they have successfully covered the point in the plan, and whether their topic sentence is supported well by the sentences that follow.

Closure

Ask students to finish the following sentences as quickly as possible.

The basic objective of operations management is …

'Lean production' is …

'Kaizen' means …

'Just-in-time' is a … which …

TQM is …

'Jidoka' means …

A good example of kaizen implementation is …

8.4 Extending skills

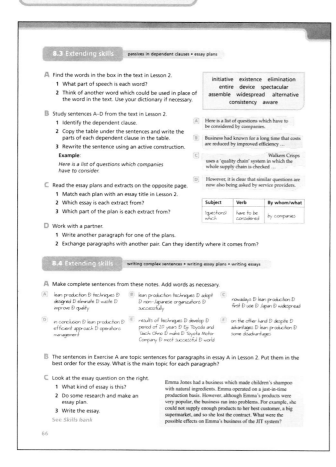

Lesson aims

- expand notes into complex sentences
- make an essay plan
- write an essay

Further practice in:

- writing topic sentences
- expanding a topic sentence into a paragraph
- writing complex sentences with passives
- identifying required essay type

Introduction

Remind students about complex and compound sentences – that is, sentences with more than one clause. Remind students that academic texts typically consist of sentences with several clauses. Give the following simple sentences (or make your own) and ask students to add some more clauses to them:

Efficiency means reducing waste.

Undercapacity means lower profits.

Companies must look at their fixed costs.

Efficiency requires excellent management.

High-quality goods are more expensive to produce.

Low-quality goods can be mass-produced.

Exercise A

Set for individual work and pairwork checking. Remind students that they should try to make sentences in a good 'academic' style. Also remind them to use passives where necessary/possible, and to look out for ways of making dependent clauses, such as relative pronouns, linking words, etc. They will also need to pay attention to making correct verb tenses.

Feed back with the whole class.

Answers

Possible answers:

A Lean production is a collection of techniques which are designed to eliminate waste and improve quality.

B Lean production techniques have been successfully adopted by many non-Japanese organizations.

C Nowadays, the concept of lean production, which was first used in Japan, has become widespread.

D In conclusion, as we can see, lean production is a highly efficient approach to operations management.

E The results of these techniques, which were developed over 20 years by Eiji Toyoda and Taiichi Ohno, made the Toyota Motor Company one of the most successful in the world.

F On the other hand, despite the many advantages of Japanese-style lean production, there are some disadvantages in the concept.

Exercise B

Set for individual work. Feed back with the whole class. Point out how this comparison essay is organized by discussing all the advantages first and then all the disadvantages. (See *Skills bank* for an alternative approach to comparison.)

If you wish, you could take this exercise further, asking students to build on the topic sentences by suggesting what ideas could follow the topic sentence in each paragraph. For this they will need to refer to ideas in the text. Note that disadvantages of lean production techniques are not fully discussed in the text, so ideas for this paragraph would need to be researched further. A Web search is a good place to start for this. For example (at the time of writing): www.referenceforbusiness.com/management/Int-Loc/Japanese-Management.html

Answers

Model answers:

Topic sentences	Paragraph topic
C Nowadays, the concept of lean production, which was first used in Japan, has become widespread.	introduction
A Lean production is a collection of techniques which are designed to eliminate waste and improve quality.	definition
E The results of these techniques, which were developed over 20 years by Eiji Toyoda and Taiichi Ohno, made the Toyota Motor Company one of the most successful in the world.	advantages for Japanese companies
B Lean production techniques have been successfully adopted by many non-Japanese organizations.	advantages for non-Japanese companies
F On the other hand, despite the many advantages of Japanese-style lean production, there are some disadvantages in the concept.	disadvantages of lean production
D In conclusion, as we can see, lean production is a highly efficient approach to operations management.	conclusion

Exercise C

Discuss question 1 with the whole class. Set the research and planning (question 2) for group work and the writing for individual work (this could be done at home). Students can do Web searches to find more information on just-in-time (JIT) and its possible problems.

Answers

1 Model answer:
  This essay is largely analytical since it requires (possible) reasons why something happened. It also asks students to think critically about possible problems with a system that is thought to be very good.

2 Possible essay plan:
  - Introduction: popularity of JIT; aims of essay.
  - Definition and description of JIT (i.e., everything from raw materials to parts to finished products are supplied 'just in time' so that money is not tied up unnecessarily in stock held in the company; plus description/examples of how the system works).

- Aspects of JIT which can cause problems, e.g.,
  - needs very good organization and administration
  - needs reliable suppliers
  - may be more expensive to administer ordering system (more ordering is needed)
  - fewer bulk-buying cost advantages
  - if machinery breaks down, there can be problems in supplying finished products
  - difficult to cope with sudden increase in demand
  - customers may go elsewhere if deliveries of stock are late or stock is not available
- Conclusion: suitability of JIT for Emma's business; general comments about JIT.

Closure

Ask students if they can remember a word from the unit …

	Example(s)
beginning with *c*	capacity
beginning with *i*	initiative
ending with *y*	economy
ending with *s*	assess
with two syllables	common, layout, device
with three syllables	contribute, existence
with four syllables	economy, manufacture
which is a verb	assemble, maximize
which is an uncountable noun	machinery, profitability
which is an adverb	automatically
which goes together with another word	quality control
which is difficult to pronounce	competitiveness (students' answers will vary)

Extra activities

1 Work through the *Vocabulary bank* and *Skills bank* if you have not already done so, or as a revision of previous study.

2 Use the *Activity bank* (Teacher's Book additional resources section, Resource 8A).

A Set the wordsearch for individual work (including homework) or pairwork. Establish that the words are uncountable in the context in which they are used in the unit, although some can be countable in other contexts.

Answers

```
D  E  L  I  M  I  N  A  T  I  O  N  T  P  B
W  M  A  N  A  G  E  M  E  N  T  G  Y  R  Y
U  T  I  L  I  Z  A  T  I  O  N  R  Q  T  L
F  V  O  L  U  M  E  M  G  N  E  Y  I  V  L
E  C  A  P  A  C  I  T  Y  N  C  L  Y  A  K
K  F  T  E  K  W  K  P  I  N  I  Q  V  K  R
M  P  F  L  X  D  J  H  E  B  W  I  N  P  Y
N  Y  U  I  Q  I  C  T  A  T  V  A  F  R  T
K  B  P  T  C  A  S  T  Q  R  B  R  S  J  P
V  Y  K  J  M  I  I  T  U  U  C  D  D  T  R
H  F  Q  T  S  F  E  S  E  R  A  V  M  R  E
P  C  V  N  O  Y  T  N  T  N  L  L  H  K  N
K  N  O  R  V  B  Z  B  C  D  C  Y  I  H  F
G  C  P  X  N  Y  Y  R  C  Y  T  E  W  T  B
P  R  O  D  U  C  T  I  O  N  F  V  L  K  Y
```

B Set the spelling exercise for individual work and pairwork checking. If students are having difficulty, give them the first letter of the word.

Answers

Jumbled word	Correct spelling
bamslase	assemble
cuaarclstep	spectacular
ecpas	space
eeialtrr	retailer
feetcd	defect
frwookecr	workforce
mireseep	premises
quetchnie	technique
tineer	entire
tskco	stock

3 Check word stress by writing the following words on the board *without* stress markings. Students have to mark the stress and pronounce the words correctly.

> *spec'tacular*
>
> *ma'chinery*
>
> *'maximize*
>
> *sur'vival*
>
> *a'ssemble*
>
> *'concept*
>
> *e'conomy*
>
> *de'vice*

4 Remind students of how to give definitions (see Lesson 2). Then select five or six familiar items (e.g., iPod, laptop, sunglasses, pen, mobile phone) and ask students to think of definitions (e.g., it's something that you use to listen to music; you need these when it is sunny; etc.).

This can also be done the other way round by giving the definitions and asking students to guess the word; once they get the idea students can come up with items, questions and definitions themselves. Other forms for definitions can include:

> *This is a place where …*
>
> *This is a company which …*
>
> *If you want to buy a(n) X, you need to go to …*

Other categories which can be used to practise both the language of definition and general business and cultural knowledge include:

- brand or company names, e.g., Marks & Spencer (well known in the UK for food and for quality); also use global multinationals
- familiar places in the town or college where the students are studying
- famous people
- movies and TV programmes

An alternative is the Weakest Link TV quiz show format, e.g., *What 'A' is a well-known brand of computer?* (Apple.)

9 MANAGING FINANCIAL ACCOUNTS

This is the first of two units on financial management. This unit focuses on two aspects: financial accounting and management accounting. The key differences between these two types of accounting are analyzed. Useful financial terms such as *balance sheet, profit and loss account, cash flow, profit margin, turnover*, etc. are defined.

Skills focus

🎧 Listening
- using the Cornell note-taking system
- recognizing digressions in lectures

Speaking
- making effective contributions to a seminar
- referring to other people's ideas in a seminar

Vocabulary focus
- fixed phrases from finance
- fixed phrases from academic English

Key vocabulary

See also the list of fixed phrases from academic English in the Vocabulary bank (Course Book page 76).

accounting	document	net profit
accounts	documentation	operating costs
annual budget	equity	ownership
annual sales	expenditure	profit and loss account
asset	expense	profit margin
balance sheet	finance (n)	profitability
break even	financial tool	profitable
budget (n and v)	fixed asset	revenue
capital investment	income	sales volume
cash flow	interest (n)	share price
cost price	invest	shareholders' equity
cost savings	investment appraisal	statement
cost-benefit analysis	investor	stock (n)
credit (n)	liabilities	tax inspector
creditor	liquid (adj)	turnover
debt	liquidity	variable costs
debtor	loan (n)	
dividend	loss	

9.1 Vocabulary

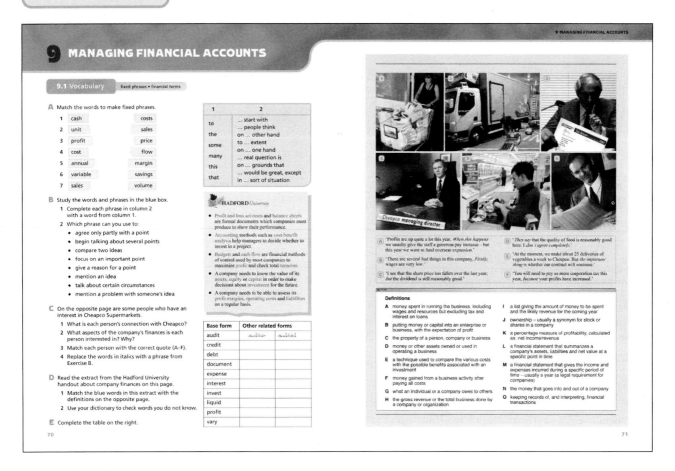

General note

Read the *Vocabulary bank* at the end of the Course Book unit. Decide when, if at all, to refer your students to it. The best time is probably at the very end of the lesson or the beginning of the next lesson, as a summary/revision.

Lesson aims

- understand and use some fixed phrases/compound nouns from business studies
- understand and use some fixed phrases from academic English

Introduction

Introduce the topic for the next two units. Ask students to say what accounting is and arrive at a definition on the board, such as:

Accounting is the 'recording, classifying, summarizing and interpreting' of financial transactions and events (Adapted from www.investor dictionary.com/definition/accounting.aspx)

Exercise A

This gives revision of some compound noun phrases (noun + noun, adjective + noun) connected with finance from previous units.

Set for individual work or pairwork. Check that students remember the meanings and that they can pronounce the compounds with the main stress on the correct word. Accept any reasonable alternatives which apply to the topic of finance.

Answers

Model answers:

1	'cash	flow
2	'unit	price; costs
3	'profit	margin
4	'cost	savings, price
5	annual	'sales, 'costs
6	'variable	costs*
7	'sales	volume

* when contrasted with *fixed*, the adjective not the noun takes the primary stress

Exercise B

Set for individual work and pairwork checking. Point out that some of the words on the left must be used more than once and that there is more than one phrase for some of the functions. Feed back with the whole class.

Answers

Model answers:

to start with	to begin talking about several points
many/some people think	to mention an idea
on the other hand	to compare two ideas
to some extent	to agree only partly with a point
on the one hand	to compare two ideas .
the real question is	to focus on an important point
on the grounds that	to give a reason for a point
that would be great, except	to mention a problem with someone's idea
in this/that sort of situation	to talk about certain circumstances

Exercise C

1/2 Set for pairwork discussion.

3 Set for individual work and pairwork checking.

4 Set for individual work. Check with the whole class, asking students to read out the quotation with the alternative phrase inserted in place of the original words in italics.

Answers

Model answers:

1/2

1 is a customer – likely to be interested in prices and quality.

2 is a vegetable supplier – likely to be interested in how much Cheapco will pay for goods and whether the contract to supply will carry on.

3 is a tax officer – likely to be interested in how much tax Cheapco must pay.

4 is the boss of Cheapco Supermarkets – likely to be interested in profits and losses.

5 is an employee of Cheapco (a cashier) – likely to be interested in wages/salary.

6 is an investor in Cheapco – likely to be interested in share price and dividend.

3 A (boss): 'Profits are up quite a lot this year. *When this happens* we usually give the staff a generous pay increase – but this year we want to fund overseas expansion.'

B (employee): 'There are several bad things in this company. *Firstly*, wages are very low.'

C (shareholder): 'I see that the share price has fallen over the last year; *but* the dividend is still reasonably good.'

D (customer): '*They say* that the quality of food is reasonably good here. I *don't agree completely*.'

E (supplier): 'At the moment, we make about 25 deliveries of vegetables a week to Cheapco. But *the important thing* is whether our contract will continue.'

F (tax officer): 'You will need to pay us more corporation tax this year, *because* your profits have increased.'

4

A	*When this happens*	*In this sort of situation* we usually give the staff a generous pay increase.
B	*Firstly,*	*To start with*, wages are very low.
C	*but*	… *on the other hand* the dividend is still reasonably good.
D	*They say*	*Many/Some people think* that the quality of food is reasonably good here.
D	*don't agree completely*	I *agree to some extent.*
E	*the important thing is*	But *the real question is* whether our contract will continue.
F	*because*	You will need to pay us more corporation tax this year *on the grounds that* your profits have increased.

Exercise D

This exercise gives some key business financial terms – and so is rather technical.

Set students to read the handout extract first and ask them to discuss in pairs which of the blue words they know and which are new to them. Feed back with the whole class, to establish how much is known. Where students give correct explanations tell them they are right, and where they are wrong also tell them, but do not give the right answer at this point.

Set the exercise for individual work and pairwork checking. Feed back with the whole class, checking the meaning of other possibly unknown words. In particular, make sure students know *gross* and *net*.

The words will be used throughout the next two units, so don't worry too much about practice at this point. However, for extra practice at this point if you wish, set students to work in pairs. One student should shut the book. The other student should say one of the words for the first student to explain. Then change over.

Answers

Model answers:

profit and loss accounts	M	a financial statement that gives the income, costs and expenses incurred during a specific period of time – usually a year (a legal requirement for companies).
balance sheets	L	a financial statement that summarizes a company's assets, liabilities and net value at a specific point in time
accounting	O	keeping records of, and interpreting, financial transactions
cost-benefit analysis	E	a technique used to compare the various costs with the possible benefits associated with an investment
budgets	I	a list giving the amount of money to be spent and the likely revenue for the coming year
cash flow	N	the money that goes into and out of a company
profit	F	money gained from a business activity after paying all costs
turnover	H	the gross revenue or the total business done by a company or organization
assets	C	the property of a person, company or business
equity	J	ownership – usually a synonym for stock or shares in a company
capital	D	money or other assets owned or used in operating a business
investment	B	putting money or capital into an enterprise or business, with the expectation of profit
profit margins	K	a percentage measure of profitability, calculated as: net income/revenue
operating costs	A	money spent in running the business, including wages and resources but excluding tax and interest on loans
liabilities	G	what an individual or a company owes to others

Language note

There are many differences between financial terms used in the US and in Europe, which is sometimes confusing. For example, *revenue* is used in the US and *turnover* in Europe for the money that a company receives for its products or services. *Net income* is used in the US while *net profit* is used in Europe for the actual income that a company receives after deducting the costs of doing business (i.e., costs of resources and raw materials, salaries, tax and interest payments).

Exercise E

Set for individual work. Tell students to use their dictionaries to check the meanings and grammatical categories of the words if they are not sure. Explain that many of the base words only have one other related form.

Feed back with the whole class, pointing out that most of the words have a particular use in the area of finance (those that can have more general use are shaded in the table in the Answers section). Check students can pronounce all the words correctly, particularly those words where the word stress shifts.

Answers

Model answers:

Base form	Other related form(s)
'audit n (C), v	'auditor n (C) 'audited*
'credit n (C/U), v	'creditor n (C)
debt n (C/U)	'debtor n (C)
'document n (C), v	documen'tation n (U)
ex'pense n (C/U)	ex'penditure n (U) ex'pensive
'interest n (C/U), v	'interesting
in'vest v	in'vestment(s) n (C/U) in'vestor n (C)
'liquid n (C/U), adj	li'quidity n (U)
'profit n (C/U), v	profita'bility n (U) 'profitable
'vary v	va'riety n (C/U) 'variable

*often used in the phrase *audited accounts*

Language note

With a good class, you can spend plenty of time on the issue of whether each noun is used as countable or uncountable or both, i.e., can the word be made plural, and if so, does that change the meaning?

Closure

It is important that students are familiar with the finance terminology from this lesson. On the board, write some terms from the lesson and ask students to give a definition; choose items from Exercises A and D. Or read out a definition and ask students to tell you the appropriate word or phrase. Check the pronunciation. This exercise can also be done as a dictation exercise.

Alternatively, write the words and definitions on different cards and give a card to each student. The student then reads out the word or the definition and the rest of the class must produce the correct answer.

9.2 Listening

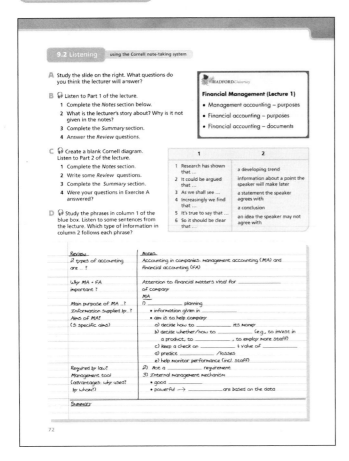

Introduction

1 Review key vocabulary from this unit by writing a selection of words from Lesson 1 on the board and asking students to put the words in groups, giving reasons for their decisions.

2 Revise note-taking symbols and abbreviations by using extra activity 4 at the end of this unit.

3 Introduce the elements of the Cornell note-taking system. Try to elicit some of the R words. Ask students to try to think of five words beginning with *re-* with six or seven letters that are good strategies to use when studying and taking notes. Write the words as follows on the board:

$$RE \_ \_ \_ \_ \quad = record$$
$$RE \_ \_ \_ \_ \quad = reduce$$
$$RE \_ \_ \_ \_ \quad = recite$$
$$RE \_ \_ \_ \_ \_ \quad = reflect$$
$$RE \_ \_ \_ \_ \quad = review$$

Discuss with the class what each word might mean when taking notes. Try to elicit the following, helping where needed.

record	Take notes during the lecture.
reduce	After the lecture, turn the notes into one- or two-word questions or 'cues' which help you remember the key information.
recite	Say the questions and answers aloud.
reflect	Decide on the best way to summarize the key information in the lecture.
review	Look again at the key words and the summary (and do this regularly).

Tell students that in this lesson they will be introduced to this system of note-taking – which can be used both for lectures, and also for reading and for revision for exams later. Do not say much more at this point; they will see how the system works as the lesson progresses.

General note

Read the *Skills bank – Using the Cornell note-taking system* at the end of the Course Book unit. Decide when, if at all, to refer students to it. The best time is probably at the very end of the lesson or the beginning of the next lesson, as a summary/revision.

Lesson aims

- use the Cornell note-taking system

Further practice in:

- listening for an established purpose
- understanding fractured text
- recognition of fixed phrases and what type of information comes next
- using abbreviations and symbols in note-taking

Subject note

The Cornell system was developed by Walter Pauk at Cornell University, USA. (Pauk, W. and Owens, R. (2004). *How to Study in College* (8th ed.). Boston: Houghton Mifflin). Pauk advised students to use a large, loose-leaf notebook, with holes punched for filing. This is better than a bound notebook, because you can organize the notes in a file binder. You can also take out notes and rewrite them. Pauk's method, which is now called the Cornell system, is based on a specific page layout.

Pauk told students to divide up the page into three areas. The first area is a column 5 cm wide on the left side of the page. This is the cue area. The main part of the page is the note-taking area. At the bottom of the page is a row 8 cm high, which is the summary area. This basic grid, with information on what each section should contain, is reproduced in the additional resources section (Resource 9B).

The note-taking and learning process involves the *Five Rs* in the order listed in the introduction to this lesson (and in the *Skills bank*). There are many useful references on the Internet for this system. Two useful ones at the time of writing are:

www.yorku.ca/cdc/lsp/notesonline/note4.htm

www.clt.cornell.edu/campus/learn/LSC%20 Resources/cornellsystem.pdf

Exercise A

Set for pairwork discussion. Refer students to the lecture slide. Tell them to look at the title and bullet points, and for each bullet point to make questions which they expect the lecturer to answer. Do not explain any words from the slide or allow students to check in their dictionaries at this point, as the meanings of the words will be dealt with within the lecture.

Feed back with the whole class, asking several students to read out their questions. Write some of the questions on the board if you wish.

🎧 Exercise B

1/2/3 Refer students to the notes at the bottom of the page. Tell them that this student has used the Cornell system to take notes, but has not managed to complete everything and so has left some gaps. (Note that this is quite a normal occurrence in note-taking – details may need to be filled in later, for example by checking with other people.)

Allow students time to read the gapped notes. Also make sure they read question 2 and are ready to listen out for a story.

Play Part 1, pausing after each major point if you wish.

Tell students to work in pairs to compare their answers to questions 1 and 2, and to complete the summary in 3. Feed back with the whole class, using an OHT or other visual display of the answers if you wish. (The completed notes are reproduced in the additional resources section – Resource 9C – to facilitate this.)

4 Now focus on the *recite* element of the Cornell system. Point out that here the student has completed the *Review* section. Cover up the *Notes* section of the answer and ask students if they can say anything about the first and second questions in the *Review* section. Then put students in pairs to test each other on the remaining notes.

Answers

Model answers:

1/3/4 See table below and Resource 9C.

2 The lecturer talks about her own experience of bad financial management. It is not in the notes because it is a digression – that is, as a personal experience it is not essential information for the subject.

Review	Notes
2 types of accounting are ...?	Accounting in companies: management accounting (MA) and financial accounting (FA)
Why MA + FA important?	Attention to financial matters vital for *success* of company
	MA
Main purpose of MA ...?	1) *Forward* planning
Information supplied by ...?	• information given in *annual budgets*
Aims of MA? (5 specific aims)	• aim is to help company
	a) decide how to *spend* its money
	b) decide whether/how to *borrow funds* (e.g., to invest in a product, to *buy new equipment*, to employ more staff)
	c) keep a check on *cash flows* & value of *investments*
	d) predict *profits*/losses
	e) help monitor performance (incl staff)
Required by law?	2) Not a *legal* requirement
Management tool (advantages: why used? by whom?)	3) Internal management mechanism
	• good *practice*
	• powerful → *decisions* are based on the data

Summary

There are two types of accounting: management and financial. Management accounting is a useful management tool. It's not a legal requirement. It's used internally.

Transcript 🎧 2.1

Part 1

Good morning, everyone. I'm going to talk to you this morning about accounting, and in particular, two important types of accounting. These two types of accounting are known as management accounting and financial accounting and, as you can probably guess from the names, they are both methods for dealing with a company's finance in one form or another. I'm going to talk first about the topic of management accounting and I will outline some of the major points connected with this type of accounting. After I've described management accounting then I will go on and do the same for financial accounting. I'll also give you a summary of the major differences between them at the end.

But before we begin I have a little story to tell you … I once worked for a small publishing company with a very dynamic boss who had lots of good ideas and was very good with people. However, he wasn't very good at the financial side of the company. He didn't like working with numbers and details and he was very forgetful. Sadly, the person he relied on for his finance management was also not good at numbers. I lost my job after a year because the company went bust.

Of course the point of that story is that it is really very dangerous for managers – from both your own and your employees' point of view – if you don't pay enough attention to financial matters! So … to get back to the main part of my lecture.

Now, as we have already noticed, finance and financial matters are vital for companies if they're going to be successful. So to help them manage their finances effectively, it's important to stress that they need to make use of both management accounting and financial accounting methods. There are major differences between these two approaches to managing finance and it's the first of these approaches than I'm going to focus on now.

OK, so to start with let's take a few moments to consider the role of management accounting. What is it exactly that management accounting is supposed to do? Well, research has shown that there are three important aspects of management accounting. It could be argued that these three aspects also exist for financial accounting. But, as we shall see here, these tend to have a different emphasis – I'll come back in a little while and tell you some of the similarities and differences.

The first important point to note here is that management accounting often deals with the forward planning aspect of business, that is to say, with how a company is going to perform, rather than concentrating on how well or how badly it has performed in the past. From the point of view of management, for example, it is fair to say that it is management accounting which provides detailed financial information which helps managers to plan for the future. One form of financial information is the annual budget, and the main aim here, of course, is to help a company to decide how to spend the money it has available, or – and this is also very likely – whether and how to borrow further funds if it needs them. So as a result of this we find that management accounting deals with questions such as what kind of financing a company will need in the future. This might be needed, for example, to invest in a product or to buy new equipment, or to employ more staff and so on. Management accounting also helps to keep a check on cash flows and the value of investments, and to calculate profits – or indeed losses – for the future. Increasingly we find that businesses and other organizations use this predicting or future-oriented role of management accounting as an internal management tool. The kind of things it is used for is to help monitor the performance of divisions or separate units of the company (this is especially important, for example, if the company is a very big one like ICI or BP).

So as we can see, management accounting is used extensively to both control and predict financial aspects. Just to recap for a moment, as we have seen, these aspects cover a lot of different areas but two good examples here would be a company's borrowing, how much it needs to borrow, and its profitability – that is, how likely it is to be able to make a profit in the future (and of course predictions about how much that profit might be). It's true to say that a lot of aspects of a company can be measured using management accounting, and that's the reason why companies use it. Even staff performance, for instance, can be measured by some management accounting techniques.

The second major point in relation to management accounting is that management accounting, unlike financial accounting, is not actually essential. What I mean, in other words, is that it's not required by company law. It may be considered good practice (in fact it usually is) but companies do not *have* to use management accounting. When we look at financial accounting we'll find that there are some legal requirements which a company must adhere to. However, as far as management accounting is concerned, there are no requirements or legal matters that a company must pay attention to. They can decide whether they want to use management accounting techniques, employ people such as management accountants and so on, or not.

Thirdly, management accounting is an internal company management mechanism. Crucially, because management accounting is able to look at various different parts or units of the company as required, and because it can provide financial data inside a company for managers to use, it is a powerful management tool. The power of management accounting within this context – the internal one – lies in the fact that decisions can be made inside a company, based on the data and conclusions which come from management accounting techniques. So it should be clear that management accounting is very useful for a company. Let's turn now to financial accounting …

Exercise C

1 Tell students to divide up a page of their notebooks into the three sections of the Cornell system. They should try to make notes in the *Notes* section as they listen. Warn them that they may not be able to complete their notes while writing so they should leave spaces which they can fill in later.

Play Part 2 straight through. Then put the students in pairs to complete any gaps in their notes. Feed back with the whole class. Build up a set of notes on the board.

2/3 Tell students to work in pairs to complete the review questions and the summary. Feed back with the whole class.

4 Discuss with the class the extent to which their pre-questions in Exercise A have been answered.

Subject note

The Enron case, which first came to light in 2002 in the USA, was a major financial scandal and illustrated how companies can disguise their true financial positions. The following links provide more information at the time of writing:

http://en.wikipedia.org/wiki/Enron

http://news.bbc.co.uk/1/hi/business/5017298.stm

www.digitalspy.co.uk/ustv/a32821/enron-director-plans-corruption-series.html

Answers

Possible answers:

See table below.

Review	Notes
FA:	Financial accounting:
Concerned with …?	● looks at past
What documents …?	● documents = company balance sheet & profit and loss account
What do they show …?	● shows cash flow & assets and liabilities (= financial strengths/weaknesses for period)
Legal?	
What is the process?	FA = legal requirement
	● accounts → checked ('audited') by independent accountants
	● results → shareholders & Companies House
	● if illegal practices → serious charges (e.g., Enron scandal)
Who sees accounts?	
	people outside company can see accounts/performance, e.g., investors, customers, analysts, tax inspector

Summary
FA looks at the past and uses certain documents. It's a legal requirement. People outside the company can see the accounts.

Transcript 🎧 2.2

Part 2

Let's turn now to financial accounting: as opposed to management accounting, we find that financial accounting is exclusively concerned with the past and with what has already taken place financially. And in the sense that financial accounting records what has happened in the past, there are specific prescribed documents required, usually in the form of a company balance sheet and a profit and loss account (and often a cash flow statement). Thus financial accounting shows how the business has performed over a specific period of time. The balance sheet describes the assets and liabilities of a company and – quite important this – it will give a 'snap-shot' viewpoint of the company's finances at a particular point in time. OK. Now, we also need to remember the fact that unlike management accounting, companies do not have a choice about financial accounting. All registered companies must provide a financial report in a particular form. In the UK and the USA, for example, this is a legal requirement and is monitored against professional standards such as GAAP (Generally Accepted Accounting Principles). Accounts have to be checked ('audited' as this is known) and this checking must be done by independent accountants, provided in a standard format (for example, the balance sheet) and the results must be sent to shareholders and to Companies House. There are agreed standards and principles that financial accounting must use to provide this information, and if any illegal practices are discovered then this can result in serious charges against company directors. If you want a good example of how this can happen and the problems it can cause then you may well remember or have heard about the Enron scandal (Enron was the biggest power company in the USA at the time) in which senior company officials were found to have been hiding the debts of the parent company in other companies; the whole question of accounting practices was opened up and the directors and the accountancy firm of Arthur Andersen were prosecuted. So the real question is: Is a company doing what it needs to do within the law?

Now, where was I? Oh, yes, right, I was talking about the importance of the regulation of financial accounting – which is, of course, not the same as for management accounting, which as we have already seen, does not have any legal requirements.

Yes … and a further important point about financial accounting is that it deals with the whole company, rather than just some bits or sections of it, and is available to external observers. This means that lots of different people, for example, investors, potential shareholders, customers and financial analysts as well as bankers and the tax inspector, can all see how well or badly a company has done over the past year or more.

So what exactly have we looked at this morning? Well, to sum up, we need to understand that the major differences between management accounting and financial accounting can be seen to happen in three distinct ways (although it is fair to say that these three different ways are also connected!). Firstly, whereas financial accounting looks at the past, management accounting is much more concerned with the present and future; secondly, financial accounting is part of the legal regulations that companies must observe, while management accounting is in a sense optional (a company can choose whether to use it or not, although many now do); and a third major difference is that management accounting produces information for an internal audience while the results of financial accounting are available to outsiders. These three main differences between management accounting and financial accounting are also reflected in the kind of documentation which is provided for accounting purposes …

🎧 Exercise D

Allow students time to read the phrases and the types of information, making sure that they understand any difficult words. Note that they are being asked not for the words that the speaker uses but what *type* of information the words represent. Note also that the information types may be needed more than once.

Play the sentences one at a time, allowing time for students to identify the type of information which follows. Check answers after each sentence, making sure that students understand the actual information is that follows.

Answers

Model answers:

See table on next page.

	Fixed phrase	Type of information which follows	Actual words/information
1	Research has shown that …	a statement the speaker agrees with	there are three important aspects of management accounting
2	It could be argued that …	an idea the speaker may not agree with	these three aspects also exist for financial accounting
3	As we shall see, …	information about a point the speaker will make later	these [three aspects] tend to have a different emphasis
4	Increasingly we find that …	a developing trend	businesses and other organizations use this … as an internal management tool
5	It's true to say that …	a statement the speaker agrees with	a lot of aspects of a company can be measured using management accounting approaches
6	So it should be clear that …	a conclusion	management accounting is very useful for a company

Transcript 🎧 2.3

1 Well, research has shown that there are three important aspects of management accounting.

2 It could be argued that these three aspects also exist for financial accounting.

3 But, as we shall see here, these tend to have a different emphasis – I'll come back in a little while and tell you some of the similarities and differences.

4 Increasingly we find that business and other organizations use this predicting or future-oriented role of management accounting as an internal management tool.

5 It's true to say that a lot of aspects of a company can be measured using management accounting.

6 So it should be clear that management accounting is very useful for a company.

Closure

Predicting information: play short sections from Part 2 of the lecture again. Stop the recording just before a word or phrase you want the students to produce and ask them what comes next in the lecture. For example:

Let's turn now to financial accounting: as opposed to management accounting, which looks forward, we find that financial accounting is much more concerned with [STOP] … *the past (and with what has already taken place financially)*.

And we also need to remember the fact that unlike management accounting, companies do not [STOP] … *have a choice (over FA)*.

All registered companies must provide [STOP] … *a financial report (in a particular form)*.

Alternatively, do this exercise by reading out parts of the transcript.

9.3 Extending skills

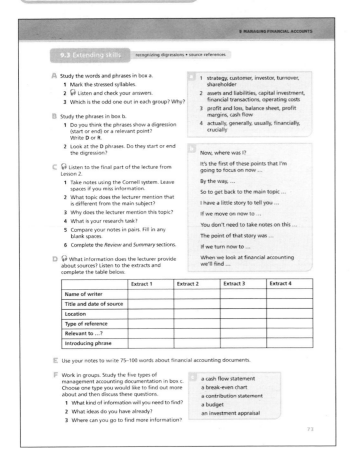

Feed back with the whole class, checking students' pronunciation, especially of the compound words, and eliciting the odd ones out.

Answers

Model answers:

1/3 (odd one out in italics)

1 'strategy, 'customer, *in'vestor* (stress is on second syllable), 'turnover, 'shareholder

2 ‚assets and lia'bilities, ‚capital in'vestment, fi‚nancial trans'actions, *'operating costs* (stress on first word)

3 *'profit and 'loss* (two equally stressed words), 'balance sheet, 'profit margins, 'cash flow

4 'actually, 'generally, 'usually, *fi'nancially* (stress is on second syllable), 'crucially

Transcript 🎧 2.4

'strategy, 'customer, in'vestor, 'turnover, 'shareholder

‚assets and lia'bilities, ‚capital in'vestment, financial tran'sactions, 'operating costs

'profit and 'loss, 'balance sheet, 'profit margins, 'cash flow

'actually, 'generally, 'usually, fi'nancially, 'crucially

Exercise B

Set for individual work and pairwork checking. Feed back with the whole class. Note that most of these phrases occurred in the lecture in Lesson 2. Some have occurred in previous units and one or two are new. Note also that the end of a digression is actually a transition back to the main point.

Answers

Model answers:

1/2 Now, where was I …? D (end)

It's the first of these points that I'm going to focus on now … R

By the way, … D (start)

So to get back to the main topic … D (end)

I have a little story to tell you … D (start)

If we move on now to … R

You don't need to take notes on this … D (start)

The point of that story was … D (end)

If we turn now to … R

When we look at financial accounting we'll find … R

Lesson aims

- recognize digressions: start and end
- understand reference to other people's ideas: source, quotes, relevance

Further practice in:

- stress within words and phrases
- leaving space in notes for missing information

Introduction

Revise the lecture in Lesson 2 by asking students to use their Cornell notes. They should cover up the *Notes* section and use the *Review* and *Summary* sections to help recall the contents of the lecture. They could work in pairs to do this.

🎧 Exercise A

1 Set for individual work and pairwork checking. Students can underline the stressed syllables.

2 Play the recording for students to check their answers.

3 Set for individual work and pairwork checking. Tell students they need to identify the odd one out in terms of stress (not the meaning of the words).

🎧 Exercise C

Refer the students to the lecture slide in Lesson 2. Ask them what they know already about financial accounting documents. What would they like to know?

Tell them to prepare a page to take notes using the Cornell system. Remind them that they may not get all the information. If they miss something, they should leave a space. They can fill it in after the lecture.

Let them read the questions through and tell them to listen out for the answers to questions 2, 3 and 4.

1 Play Part 3 straight through. Students should complete the Notes section.

2–4 Set for pairwork. Feed back with the whole class. Ask for suggestions for phrases to use to find out about the importance of digressions, e.g., *Why did he/she start talking about …? I didn't understand the bit about … Is it important?* and so on (see *Skills bank*).

5/6 Set for pairwork. Students compare their notes, complete any blank spaces and then write the *Review* and *Summary* sections.

Feed back with the whole class, building a set of notes on the board.

Answers

Possible answers:

1 See notes below.

2 The Cornell note-taking system.

3 It's important to know how to take good notes.

4 To find out about management accounting documents.

5/6 See notes. Note: The summary here is concerned with the section on financial accounting only – not the lecturer's overall summary of the differences between management accounting and financial accounting.

Transcript 🎧 2.5

Part 3

OK, so moving on to look at some financial documentation. Now, it's important to remember here that the three major differences that we saw between management accounting and financial accounting are also reflected in the kind of documentation which is provided for accounting purposes. Today I'm going to focus on the three types of documents which you will typically find in the area of financial accounting: balance sheets, profit and loss accounts and cash flow statements. Let's begin then with the basic document: the balance sheet. Now, we already know from what I have said earlier that this particular document is a

Review	Notes
	Financial accounting documentation
Balance sheet gives …? (3 things)	1 Balance sheet (NB legal requirement) • assets = fixed (e.g., factories, vehicles) or current (money in bank/stock) • liabilities = what co. owes, e.g., bank loan • capital and reserves, incl. shareholders' equity (also share capital) = money raised through shares NB amount of assets = amount of liabilities (incl. share capital)
Profit & loss acct shows …? (give example)	2 Profit and loss account (shows gross and net profit or loss) e.g., sales income • less cost of sales = gross profit • less other expenditure (e.g., salaries, rent) = net profit
US term for profit & loss acct …?	• US: profit and loss acct = 'income statement'
Who must have cash flow statements? CFS gives information on …?	3 Cash flow statement (NB req. only for plc) = info. on finance for activities, i.e., where the money came from (e.g., inside or outside the company)

Summary
FA documents are: balance sheet, profit & loss account, cash flow statement.
These documents give a good picture of company's finances.

requirement for companies – that is, it is necessary for legal reasons. In other words a company has to produce one, it doesn't have a choice.

So let's look in a bit more detail at the different sections you will find in a typical balance sheet. It's fairly obvious if you look at a balance sheet that it is usually divided into three main sections, and the three main pieces of information are as follows.

Number one is a company's assets. That is, what a company owns and how much this is worth. There are two types of assets: fixed and current assets. Typical fixed assets could include factories or vehicles, for instance. The things which can be used many times. Current assets are things like money – for instance, money that is held in an account at the bank. Current assets can also be stocks of materials used in production and amounts owed by debtors.

Number two is a summary of the liabilities of a company, which if you like is the kind of opposite of the assets. Liabilities as we have already seen are what a company – or an individual, we can use the same word – owes to others. This could be a bank loan which needs to have interest paid on it or some other debt.

Thirdly, and this is the final main section on the balance sheet, we have capital and reserves. Part of this is made up of what is usually called the shareholders' equity; this is also sometimes called share capital and is defined as the amount of money which a company has raised through shares. In other words, this is the money which is helping to finance the company. You can see, of course, that share capital is also money owed by the company to its shareholders. The key point about the balance sheet, as Baker points out in *Principles of Business Finance* (which is one of your core texts – the 2nd edition was published in 2002) – the key point is that it must balance. In other words, the value of what the company holds or owns, its assets, which it is using for its activities, should be the same as its liabilities, and share capital and reserves – but you don't need to worry about this at this stage.

OK, so now we can see that these three sections or parts of the balance sheet – the assets, the liabilities and the capital and reserves section – together can provide shareholders and others with a good accurate picture of a company. To quote Baker again, 'At a specific point in time, these three parts of a balance sheet can give investors an idea about what the company has (that is, what it owns) as well as describing its debts (what it owes).'

By the way, I see that some of you are using the Cornell note-taking system. That's very good. Do you all know about this? No? Right, well, if you want to know more about it, I suggest you look at *How to Study in College* by Walter Pauk, P-A-U-K, the 8th edition, published in 2004. It's very good, and it should be in the university library. I'm sure that you all know the importance of taking good notes – and this system is particularly useful.

So to get back to the main topic … There is some other documentation that is required for financial accounting. The second element is a profit and loss account, which can show whether a company is financially healthy (and perhaps also whether it is being managed successfully or not). One definition of the profit and loss account given by thefreedictionary.com on the Web is: 'An account compiled at the end of an accounting period to show gross and net profit or loss.' Typically, this account shows, for example, the cost of sales, which if taken away from the sales income, gives the gross profit. You then deduct other items of expenditure, such as salaries or rent, and you are left with a net profit (or perhaps a loss!). In the US a profit and loss account is known as an income statement.

Now the third element of financial accounting, that's the cash flow statement, is slightly different because it is not always necessary. To be more precise, this third element is only required when a company is a plc (that's a public limited company whose shares can be bought on the stock exchange). So to summarize briefly: this particular part of the accounting process, the cash flow statement, answers questions about how a company was able to find the cash to finance its recent activities and where the money came from (for example, whether this money came from inside or from outside the company).

Now I think that's all I'm going to say for the moment on the basic parts of financial accounting documentation. Are there any questions so far? No, good. Now when I see you in tutorials we'll look in more detail at management accounting. In the meantime, I'm going to set you a research task. Right, now listen carefully … your task is to find out about the different documents that are used in management accounting. I'd like you to work in groups of four. Each group should find out about the various management accounting documents that are used and report back on your findings.

🎧 Exercise D

Tell students that lecturers will often give references while they talk and it is important to note down any references. The kinds of information may differ – they may just be names of books or articles, they may be an exact quotation (a 'direct quote') or they may be a paraphrase (sometimes called an 'indirect quotation'). Refer students to the table and check that they know what each row represents.

Play each extract and allow students time to complete the sections of the table. Check with the whole class.

Answers

Model answers:
See table below.

Language note

A 'core text' is the main text used for the course. Students are usually told they should buy a copy of the core text for their course.

Transcript 🎧 2.6

Extract 1

Thirdly, and this is the final main section on the balance sheet, we have capital and reserves … The key point about the balance sheet, as Baker points out in *Principles of Business Finance* (which is one of your core texts – the 2nd edition was published in 2002) – the key point is that it must balance. In other words, the value of what the company holds or owns, its assets, which it is using for its activities, should be the same as its liabilities, and share capital and reserves – but you don't need to worry about this at this stage.

Extract 2

OK, so now we can see that these three sections or parts of the balance sheet – the assets, the liabilities and the capital and reserves section – together can provide shareholders and others with a good, accurate picture of a company. To quote Baker again, 'At a specific point in time, these three parts of a balance sheet can give investors an idea about what the company has (that is, what it owns) as well as describing its debts (what it owes).'

Extract 3

By the way, I see that some of you are using the Cornell note-taking system. That's very good. Do you all know about this? No? Right, well, if you want to know more about it, I suggest you look at *How to Study in College* by Walter Pauk, P-A-U-K, the 8th edition, published in 2004. It's very good, and it should be in the university library.

Extract 4

The second element is a profit and loss account, which can show whether a company is financially healthy (and perhaps also whether it is being managed successfully or not). One definition of the profit and loss account given by thefreedictionary.com on the Web is: 'An account compiled at the end of an accounting period to show gross and net profit or loss.'

Exercise E

Set for individual work – possibly homework – or else a pair/small group writing task. If the latter, tell students to put their writing on an OHT or other visual medium so that the whole class can see and comment on what has been written. You can correct language errors on the OHT.

	Extract 1	Extract 2	Extract 3	Extract 4
Name of writer	Baker	Baker	Walter Pauk	
Title and date of source	*Principles of Business Finance* 2nd edition 2002	as in 1	*How to Study in College* 8th edition 2004	thefreedictionary.com
Location	core text	as in 1	university library	Web
Type of reference	indirect quotation/ paraphrase	direct quotation	name of book	direct quotation
Relevant to …?	balance sheet	the (three sections of the) balance sheet	Cornell note-taking	profit and loss account
Introducing phrase	As Baker points out in …	To quote Baker …	I suggest you look at …	One definition of … given by …

Exercise F

Tell students to work in groups of three or four. Either give each group a topic (i.e., a type of documentation) or allow them to choose. Make sure that each topic is covered by at least one, or preferably two groups.

Feed back on questions 1–3 with the whole class. Tell students that each student should now carry out research into the group's topic. They should each look at a different source and so will need to decide who is going to look at each one. You will also need to arrange the date for the feedback and discussion of the information – this is the focus of Exercise D in Lesson 4. Tell students that in Lesson 4 they will take part in a seminar on this topic.

Answers

Possible answers:

1 Information to find: What are these documents? What are the purposes and uses of each type of document: Who? When? What for? Are there different categories within each type of document?

3 Use subject course books, the library and the Internet to find out the necessary information. Some example websites are:

www.investopedia.com/

www.freedictionary.com

Alternatively (or in addition) – depending on your teaching situation and access to the sources of information – you can refer the students to the information for their group on page 107 of the Course Book. Some additional websites are given in Resource 9D in the additional resources secton.

Closure

Resource 9E is a (simplified) balance sheet for a large US company. Ask students to go to *Google define* and find out the meanings of the words below if they don't know them. Then tell them to use the words to fill the spaces on the balance sheet.

cash
inventories
fixed assets
net receivables

accounts payable
long-term debt
shares outstanding

Answers

Model answers:

cash – assets held as money in bank accounts

inventories – also called stock. Refers to raw materials, unfinished and finished products

fixed assets – something tangible that is owned by the business such as equipment, buildings, etc.

net receivables – money that is owed to the business

accounts payable – money that is owed by the business to others (e.g., suppliers)

long-term debt – money owed to paid back over a long period

shares outstanding – all the shares a company has that are held by investors

	Jan 06	Jan 05	Jan 04
Assets			
Cash	6,414	5,488	5,199
Net receivables	2,662	1,715	1,254
Inventories	32,191	29,447	26,612
Fixed assets	79,290	68,567	58,530
Other current assets	2,557	1,841	1,356
Total assets	123,114	107,058	92,951
Liabilities			
Accounts payable	40,178	35,107	31,051
Short-term debt	8,648	7,781	6,367
Long-term debt	30,171	23,669	20,099
Other liabilities	6,019	4,270	3,772
Total liabilities	85,016	70,827	61,289
Shareholders' equity			
Shares outstanding	4,165	4,234	4,296

9.4 Extending skills

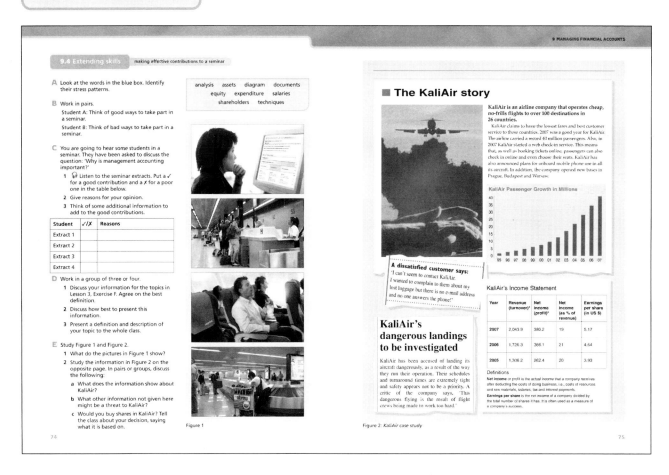

Lesson aims

- make effective contributions to a seminar

Further practice in:

- stress within words

Introduction

Use a few of the review cues from the Cornell system notes in Lesson 3 for students to try to recall the ideas on financial accounting in the lecture. If students appear to be having difficulty remembering, ask them to look again at their own notes from Exercise C in Lesson 3. Check that students are clear about the difference between management and financial accounting. Ask them to give the three main differences:

- financial accounting looks at the past and management accounting at the present and future as well

- financial accounting is a legal requirement whereas management accounting is just good management practice

- management accounting is only available to managers inside the company while the results of financial accounting are available to outsiders

Exercise A

Set for individual work and pairwork checking.

Answers

Model answers:

Oo	assets
oO	techniques
Ooo	diagram, documents, equity, salaries, shareholders
oOoo	analysis, expenditure

Exercise B

This is revision from Unit 5. Set for individual work and pairwork checking. Feed back with the whole class. Give a time limit and see which pair can think of the most Do's and Don'ts in the time. Refer to Unit 5 Lesson 4 for suggestions if you need to.

Answers

Possible answers:
See table at top of next page.

Do's	Don'ts
ask politely for information	demand information from other students
try to use correct language	
speak clearly	mumble, whisper or shout
say when you agree with someone	get angry if someone disagrees with you
contribute to the discussion	sit quietly and say nothing
link correctly with previous speakers	
answer the question	make points that aren't relevant
be constructive	be negative
explain your point clearly	
listen carefully to what others say	start a side conversation
bring in other speakers	dominate the discussion
give specific examples to help explain a point	
paraphrase to check understanding	
use clear visuals	
prepare the topic beforehand	

🎧 Exercise C

Check that students understand the topic for the seminar discussion. Ask them what they might expect to hear. Work through these extracts one at a time. Complete questions 1–3 for each extract before moving on to the next.

1 Set for individual work.

2 First check that students have understood the extract as well as possible. Then ask for opinions from the whole class on the contribution.

3 Once everyone has a clear notion of whether the contribution is a good one, ask for suggestions for additional points. Alternatively, set this part for pairwork after you have completed questions 1 and 2.

Answers

Model answers:

See table below.

	✓/✗	Reasons	Possible additional information
Extract 1	✓	speaks clearly explains the point clearly answers the question uses good fixed phrases	any of these: company can 1. decide how to spend its money 2. decide whether/how to borrow funds, e.g., to invest in a product, to buy new equipment, to employ more staff 3. keep a check on cash flows & value of investments 4. predict profits/losses
Extract 2	✗	does not speak clearly does not answer the question is talking about FA vs MA poor use of visuals	
Extract 3	✗	speaks clearly, but doesn't answer the question the points are not relevant to the question – is talking about accountants, not MA	
Extract 4	✓	speaks clearly explains the point clearly answers correctly uses good fixed phrases has prepared well has a good visual	any of the other management accounting documents that students have researched into: break-even chart; contribution statements; budgets; investment appraisal

Transcript 🎧 2.7

Extract 1

… It seems quite clear that management accounting is a very useful way of controlling what happens in a company. Let's look at three basic advantages: firstly, management accountants can show where the strengths and weaknesses are in a company; secondly, it's possible to look at a wide range of different types of performance in different sections or units of a company; and thirdly, pretty important this, …

Extract 2

… erm, I think one big difference is management accounting. This is very important. It is possible, we can see, how this is very important. So let's look at the chart and … oh sorry, that's the wrong chart, just a minute … right, so here is some difference between financial and management … er you can see I think, this difference … do you have any questions about this chart? …

Extract 3

… We could ask the question: how much does it cost to use an accountant? Usually, this is very expensive but it is necessary because if you use an accountant you can get a good balance sheet and then you can show the customers how well the company is performing. On the other hand, a good accountant is also very important for the public because in England you have to have a balance sheet for the public and this balance sheet is the basic sheet for the whole company. Here we must look also at the profit and loss account because that is …

Extract 4

… So this is the main difference – the fact that unlike financial accounting which is public, management accounting is an internal mechanism. This difference shows us one of the main functions of management accounting. In fact we could say that this summarizes the main importance of this type of accounting, and it also explains why more and more companies are using financial accounting methods to improve their efficiency. If we look at the chart I've prepared here we can see the main areas that management accounting will be looking at. For example, if we examine in a bit more detail the section called *cash flow forecasting* we can see that this can be a very effective method for a company to examine its profitability. Another area is …

Exercise D

Students should work in the same groups as their research groups from Lesson 3, Exercise F. They will need to have with them the research they have done individually on the group's chosen topic.

Decide how you want students to present their information, e.g.,

- short talk with/without PowerPoint, OHT or other visual medium
- to the whole class or to another group

Make sure that students understand the options for the presentation types.

1 Tell each group to discuss the information that they have found and agree on the best definition and description of the type of documentation they have researched.

2 In discussing this question, students will need to decide who is going to speak when and say what. Encourage them to practise their presentation to each other before talking to the whole class.

3 Allow each group a maximum of five minutes for the presentation. Then allow some time for questions. If more than one group have done the same topic, encourage disagreement and critical analysis. Remind the groups when discussing to use all the good techniques and phrases they have learnt.

Exercise E

This is a case study of a fictitious 'no-frills' airline which will give more practice in discussion.

1 To set the context, first refer students to the pictures of an air journey in Figure 1. With the whole class, elicit the words needed to discuss the different stages of air travel (for example, booking a ticket; checking in luggage; on the plane; collecting luggage from the baggage hall/carousel, etc.).

Discuss air travel with the class. Ask them about air journeys they have taken. Did they travel with an ordinary or a cheap airline? What aspects of the journey do they think a 'cheap' airline will need to focus on in order to cut costs and make journeys cheaper for their passengers?

2 Put the students in pairs (or threes). At stage c, each pair can join another pair and agree a decision.

a In their pairs, students can divide the information between them and then summarize the information for their partner. If there are words that they do not understand they will need to check meanings in dictionaries or online.

b Students will need to think here about social, political or environmental factors which might have a negative effect on KaliAir's business. For example, as air travel is considered to be a big polluter, countries may decide to impose more tax on air travel in the future.

c In coming to a conclusion on this, students should use the financial information as well as the factual information given in the short texts, or any other factors they feel are relevant.

Closure

Use the *Vocabulary bank* to check that the group can remember the meaning, spelling and pronunciation of the financial vocabulary. You may also want to refer students to the information on financial documentation on page 107 of the Course Book.

Extra activities

This unit contains a lot of technical and semi-technical vocabulary. Students will need plenty of practice with the vocabulary.

1 Work through the *Vocabulary bank* and *Skills bank* if you have not already done so, or as revision of previous study.

2 Use the *Activity bank* (Teacher's Book additional resources section, Resource 9A).

A Set the crossword for individual work (including homework) or pairwork.

Answers:

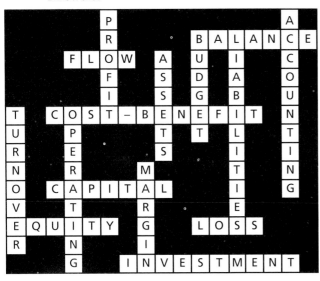

B Ask students to look at the nouns in the box: are plural forms of the nouns possible? Tell students to use an English–English dictionary or online definitions to help them find out the answers to the following questions.

1 Which forms are countable and which uncountable?

2 Do the countable and uncountable forms have different meanings?

Answers:

Noun	Countable or uncountable?	Notes
asset	C	
cash	U	
cost	C/U	
economy	C/U	*The economy usually refers to that part of a country's affairs*
liability	C/U	
loss	C/U	profit and loss account
margin	C	
profit	C/U	
sale	C/U	
share	C/U	
taxation	U	

3 Copy the extracts from company financial figures on Resource 9F. Ask students to make some comparisons between the companies and prepare a short presentation of the performance of Dell and Nike. Students can also look for the share history of these companies on the Internet for the period shown if they wish.

4 Revise note-taking symbols – see the list at the back of the Course Book. Check back to Unit 5 if necessary. Give the meanings and ask students to write down the symbol (or do it the other way round). Then ask students to think about and discuss which ones they actually use. Are there any other ones that they have come across that they think are useful?

Alternatively, write the meanings on a set of cards. Put students in groups of about six with two teams in each group. Give each group a pile of cards. A student from each team picks a card and, without showing the members of his/her team, draws the appropriate symbol. The members of his/her team must say what the symbol stands for. If the student writes the correct symbol and the team gets the meaning right, the team gets a point. If the student writes the wrong symbol and/or the team gets it wrong, the team loses a point. The teams take it in turns to pick a card.

5 Identify finance and company abbreviations which will be useful for your students. Give the abbreviation or acronym and ask students to give the meaning (or do it the other way round). For example, if they are studying in a UK or European-based context:

Business abbreviation	Meaning
FTSE100	Financial Times top 100 companies
AIM	alternative investment market
Nasdaq	National Association of Securities Dealers Automated Quotations (US electronic stock exchange)
HBOS	Halifax Bank of Scotland
RBS	Royal Bank of Scotland
AGM	annual general meeting
GAAP	generally accepted accounting practice
ROCE	return on capital employed
M&S	Marks and Spencer
AMEX	American Express
Co	company
plc	public limited company
NGO	non-governmental organization
CEO	chief executive officer
SME	small–medium enterprise
AOL	America online
FedEx	Federal Express
KFC	Kentucky Fried Chicken
VW	Volkswagen
GE	General Electric

Some useful glossaries are at:

www.spanish-translator-services.com/english-abbreviations/financial/index.htm

www.lse.co.uk/FinanceGlossary.asp

www2.hemscott.com/equities/GLOSS.HTM

or for USA:

www.nysfaaa.org/docs/student_family/terms_acronyms.html

10 FUNDING COMPANY ACTIVITIES

This is the second of two units on aspects of financial management. It looks at how different types of business raise capital to begin trading or to expand, and the different forms this funding may take: start-up loans, overdraft facilities, trade credit, shares issues, corporate bonds, etc.

Skills focus

Reading

- recognizing the writer's stance and level of confidence or tentativeness
- inferring implicit ideas

Writing

- writing situation–problem–solution–evaluation essays
- using direct quotations
- compiling a bibliography/reference list

Vocabulary focus

- 'neutral' and 'marked' words
- fixed phrases from finance
- fixed phrases from academic English

Key vocabulary

acquire	fixed asset	shares issue
acquisition	hire purchase (n)	slump (n and v)
adjustment	insolvency	soar (v)
asset sale	investor	start-up (n)
bankruptcy	lease (n and v)	stock exchange
bill (n and v)	loan (n and v)	stock market
collapse (n and v)	merger	stocks
corporate bond	overdraft (facility)	takeover (n)
depreciation	overhead (n)	term
entrepreneur	personal loan	trade credit
equity	raise (capital)	venture capital
finance (n and v)	repay	working capital

10.1 Vocabulary

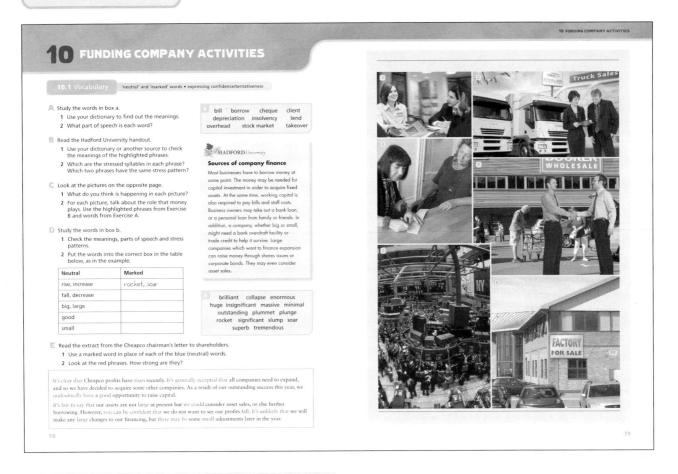

10 FUNDING COMPANY ACTIVITIES

10.1 Vocabulary · 'neutral' and 'marked' words • expressing confidence/tentativeness

A Study the words in box a.
1 Use your dictionary to find out the meanings.
2 What part of speech is each word?

B Read the Hadford University handout.
1 Use your dictionary or another source to check the meanings of the highlighted phrases.
2 Which are the stressed syllables in each phrase? Which two phrases have the same stress pattern?

C Look at the pictures on the opposite page.
1 What do you think is happening in each picture?
2 For each picture, talk about the role that money plays. Use the highlighted phrases from Exercise B and words from Exercise A.

D Study the words in box b.
1 Check the meanings, parts of speech and stress patterns.
2 Put the words into the correct box in the table below, as in the example.

Neutral	Marked
rise, increase	rocket, soar
fall, decrease	
big, large	
good	
small	

E Read the extract from the Cheapco chairman's letter to shareholders.
1 Use a marked word in place of each of the blue (neutral) words.
2 Look at the red phrases. How strong are they?

It's clear that Cheapco profits have risen recently. It's generally accepted that all companies need to expand, and so we have decided to acquire some other companies. As a result of our outstanding success this year, we undoubtedly have a good opportunity to raise capital.

It's fair to say that our assets are not large at present but we could consider asset sales, or else further borrowing. However, you can be confident that we do not want to see our profits fall. It's unlikely that we will make any large changes to our financing, but there may be some small adjustments later in the year.

Box a:
bill borrow cheque client depreciation insolvency lend overhead stock market takeover

HADFORD *University*

Sources of company finance

Most businesses have to borrow money at some point. The money may be needed for capital investment in order to acquire fixed assets. At the same time, working capital is also required to pay bills and staff costs. Business owners may take out a bank loan, or a personal loan from family or friends. In addition, a company, whether big or small, might need a bank overdraft facility or trade credit to help it survive. Large companies which want to finance expansion can raise money through shares issues or corporate bonds. They may even consider asset sales.

Box b:
brilliant collapse enormous huge insignificant massive minimal outstanding plummet plunge rocket significant slump soar superb tremendous

78

79

General note

Read the *Vocabulary bank* at the end of the Course Book unit. Decide when, if at all, to refer your students to it. The best time is probably at the very end of the lesson or the beginning of the next lesson, as a summary/revision.

Lesson aims

- understand when words are 'neutral' and when they are 'marked' (see *Vocabulary bank*)
- understand and use phrases expressing confidence/tentativeness (see *Vocabulary bank*)

Further practice in:

- fixed phrases/compound nouns from the discipline
- fixed phrases from academic English
- stress within words and phrases
- synonyms

Introduction

1 Revise finance words and phrases from the previous unit. Give definitions and ask students for the words/phrases. For example:

fixed assets – buildings, equipment, etc. necessary to operate the business

cash flow – the money that goes into and out of a company

operating costs – day-to-day expenses incurred in running a business

profit margin – net profit divided by net revenues

balance sheet – a financial statement that summarizes a company's position at a specific point in time

budget forecast – a prediction of revenue and money to be spent

liabilities – what an individual or a company owes to others

management accounting – an internal system for managing the finances of a company

turnover – the total business done by a company or organization

2 Revise the following phrases used in academic writing. Ask students what sort of information will follow these phrases.

> *On the other hand ...*
>
> *In conclusion ...*
>
> *To put it another way ...*
>
> *As Smith (2002) pointed out ...*
>
> *Research has shown that ...*
>
> *Part of the difficulty is ...*
>
> *To start with ...*
>
> *This can be defined as ...*
>
> *As a result ...*
>
> *Finally ...*
>
> *Given what has been shown above ...*

Exercise A

Set for individual work and pairwork checking. Feed back with the whole class.

Answers

Model answers:

Word	Part of speech	Meaning/synonym
bill	n (C), v (T)	invoice
borrow	v (T)	use or take on a temporary basis something belonging to someone else (lend = antonym)
cheque	n (C)	a piece of paper supplied by a bank to their customers (in a book) instructing the bank to pay money; similar in meaning is a *draft,* though these have different uses
client	n (C)	customer
depreciation	n (U)	reduction in value
insolvency	n (usually U)	bankruptcy
lend	v (T)	loan
overhead	n (C)	indirect cost (i.e., a cost such as electricity that cannot be directly linked to the production of a specific item)
stock market	n (C)	stock exchange
takeover	n (C)	acquisition

Language note

Stock exchange and *stock market* are not completely synonymous. A stock exchange is an *organization* (such as the New York Stock Exchange, or the London Stock Exchange) which provides the facilities for traders to buy and sell stocks. A stock market is a *market* in which stocks and shares are bought and sold.

Takeover/acquisition/merger: takeover is used for public companies and *acquisition* for private companies. A *merger* is like a takeover or acquisition except that it usually implies that there is agreement to the action by both sides. A takeover can be 'hostile' – that is, a company's shares are bought up against the wishes of the board.

Exercise B

1 Set for individual work and pairwork checking. Other sources besides dictionaries could be business textbooks, other reference books, or the Internet.

2 Show students how they can draw the stress pattern for the whole word as well as just locating the stressed syllable. If they use the system of big and small circles shown in the Answers section, they can see the pattern for the whole phrase quite easily.

Answers

Model answers:

1

capital investment	the money paid to buy a capital (fixed) asset
working capital	current assets minus current liabilities
bank loan	money lent by/borrowed from a bank
personal loan	money lent by/borrowed from a friend or family member
bank overdraft facility	not a loan, but money which a bank has agreed that a client can borrow from time to time
trade credit	when a firm supplies goods or services to a company and allows them to pay later
shares issues	the stock a company sells publicly in order to raise capital
corporate bonds	an alternative to shares, issued by companies to raise capital; a kind of IOU for borrowers
asset sales	property or other goods owned by a company or person which are sold to raise money

2

capital investment	Ooo oOo
working capital	Oo Ooo
bank loan	O O
personal loan	Ooo O
bank overdraft facility	O Ooo oOoo
trade credit	O Oo
shares issues	O Oo
corporate bonds	Ooo O
asset sales	Oo O

Shares issues and *trade credit* have the same stress pattern.

Exercise C

Set for pairwork or class discussion. Encourage students to speculate about what might be happening. Students should use the highlighted phrases and other words that are useful from the text in Exercise B; they can also use words from Exercise A.

Feed back with the whole class. Accept anything reasonable.

Answers

Possible answers:

1 Two business people are in a bank talking to the member of staff. Perhaps the clients want to borrow some money. In other words, they could be asking for either a **bank loan** or an **overdraft facility.**

2 A business person is looking at some new trucks/lorries. He will need some money to pay for the new lorries. In other words, he will need some money for **capital investment.**

3 A woman is writing a **cheque** – perhaps she is lending some money to a friend or family member – in other words, a **personal loan.** Or she could be paying a **bill.**

4 An owner of a small business is discussing/agreeing something with a supplier. Perhaps the supplier wants his/her money but the business person can't pay the bill at the moment. The business person will need to negotiate **trade credit.**

5 This shows the inside of a **stock exchange.** This is where **stocks, shares** and **bonds** are bought and sold. It's a **stock market.**

6 The company that owns this factory wants to sell it. In other words, this is an **asset sale.** Perhaps the company needs the money for something. Or possibly the factory is being sold as a result of **insolvency.**

(see *Language note* below and *Vocabulary bank*)

Language note

Stocks is used in the US, and *shares* in the UK, for shares held in a company. In the UK, *stocks* refers to *bonds* – which are loans taken out for a fixed period of time and repaid with interest.

Exercise D

Introduce the idea of 'neutral' and 'marked' vocabulary (see *Language note* below and *Vocabulary bank*). Set for individual work and pairwork checking.

Feed back, discussing any differences of opinion about whether the words are marked, and in what sense they are marked. (Some students may argue that *minimal, significant* and *insignificant* are not marked, for example. Others may argue that they are marked, because they suggest not just that something is big/small, but that it is important/unimportant. Compare *There is a small problem with the program* and *There is an insignificant problem with the program.*)

Answers

Model answers:

Neutral	Marked
rise, increase	'rocket, soar (v)
fall, decrease	co'llapse (v and n), 'plummet (v), plunge (v and n), slump (v and n)
big, large	e'normous, huge, 'massive, sig'nificant, tre'mendous* (adj)
good	'brilliant, out'standing, su'perb, tre'mendous* (adj)
small	insig'nificant, 'minimal (adj)

* *tremendous* can mean both very large and very good, so students may place this word in either category

Language note

One way of looking at vocabulary is to think about 'neutral' and 'marked' items. Many words in English are neutral, i.e., they are very common and they do not imply any particular view on the part of the writer or speaker. However, there are often apparent synonyms which are 'marked' for stance or opinion. Neutral words are usually thought of as basic vocabulary (the adjectives often have opposites, e.g., *big/small; light/dark*). Marked words tend to be less frequent and are therefore learnt later.

The marked words in Exercise D are not totally synonymous. Their appropriate use and interpretation will be dependent on the context and also on collocation constraints. For example, one can say that a building is 'massive' but not (in the same sense) 'significant'.

Exercise E

1 Set for individual work and pairwork checking. Make sure that students understand any words they are not sure of. Feed back with the whole class by asking individual students to read out a sentence. Make sure that the pronunciation and stress patterns of the marked words are correct.

2 Put the table from the Answers section on the board. Make sure that students understand *confident* and *tentative*. Elicit answers from the whole class and complete the table. Point out that these phrases are usually found in conversation or in informal writing such as this. Academic writing also requires writers to show degrees of confidence and tentativeness. The mechanisms for this will be covered in the next lesson.

Answers

Model answers:

1 It's clear that Cheapco profits have (*risen*) <u>soared</u>/<u>rocketed</u> recently. It's generally accepted that all companies need to expand, and so we have decided to acquire some other companies. As a result of our outstanding success this year, we undoubtedly have a (*good*) <u>tremendous</u>/<u>superb</u> opportunity to raise capital.

It's fair to say that our assets are not (*large*) <u>enormous</u>/<u>huge</u>/<u>massive</u> at present but we could consider asset sales, or else further borrowing. However, you can be confident that we do not want to see our profits (*fall*) <u>plummet</u>/<u>plunge</u>/<u>slump</u>/<u>collapse</u>. It's unlikely that we will make any (*large*) <u>massive</u>/<u>significant</u>/<u>huge</u> changes to our financing, but there may be some (*small*) <u>minimal</u>/<u>insignificant</u> adjustments later in the year.

2

	Very confident	Fairly confident	Tentative (= not confident)
It's clear that	✓		
It's generally accepted that		✓	
we undoubtedly have	✓		
It's fair to say that		✓	
we could			✓
you can be confident that	✓		
It's unlikely that		✓	
there may be			✓

Closure

1 For further practice of neutral and marked vocabulary, ask students to write down some basic words, e.g., four verbs, four nouns and four adjectives. Put a list of these on the board and ask students if they are neutral or marked. See if you can find any opposites. Ask students to find some synonyms for neutral words – they can use a dictionary. A synonyms dictionary or Microsoft Word thesaurus can be useful here as well.

2 Ask pairs or groups to define as accurately as they can three of the fixed business phrases from the *Vocabulary bank*. Give them a few minutes to think of their definitions, then feed back and discuss as a class.

10.2 Reading

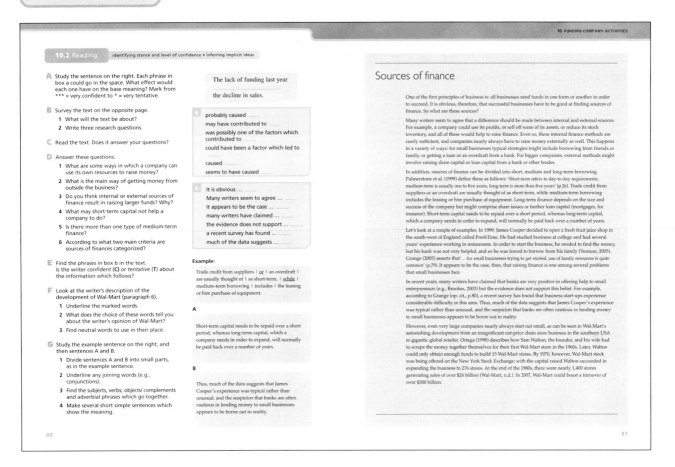

10.2 Reading — identifying stance and level of confidence • inferring implicit ideas

A Study the sentence on the right. Each phrase in box a could go in the space. What effect would each one have on the base meaning? Mark from *** = very confident to * = very tentative.

B Survey the text on the opposite page.
1 What will the text be about?
2 Write three research questions.

C Read the text. Does it answer your questions?

D Answer these questions.
1 What are some ways in which a company can use its own resources to raise money?
2 What is the main way of getting money from outside the business?
3 Do you think internal or external sources of finance result in raising larger funds? Why?
4 What may short-term capital not help a company to do?
5 Is there more than one type of medium-term finance?
6 According to what two main criteria are sources of finances categorized?

E Find the phrases in box b in the text. Is the writer *confident* (C) or *tentative* (T) about the information which follows?

F Look at the writer's description of the development of Wal-Mart (paragraph 6).
1 Underline the marked words.
2 What does the choice of these words tell you about the writer's opinion of Wal-Mart?
3 Find neutral words to use in their place.

G Study the example sentence on the right, and then sentences A and B.
1 Divide sentences A and B into small parts, as in the example sentence.
2 Underline any joining words (e.g., conjunctions).
3 Find the subjects, verbs, objects/ complements and adverbial phrases which go together.
4 Make several short simple sentences which show the meaning.

The lack of funding last year ____
the decline in sales.

a
probably caused ____
may have contributed to ____
was possibly one of the factors which contributed to ____
could have been a factor which led to ____
caused ____
seems to have caused ____

b
It is obvious ... ____
Many writers seem to agree ... ____
It appears to be the case ... ____
many writers have claimed ... ____
the evidence does not support ... ____
a recent survey has found ... ____
much of the data suggests ... ____

Example:

Trade credit from suppliers | or | an overdraft | are usually thought of | as short-term, | while | medium-term borrowing | includes | the leasing or hire purchase of equipment.

A

Short-term capital needs to be repaid over a short period, whereas long-term capital, which a company needs in order to expand, will normally be paid back over a number of years.

B

Thus, much of the data suggests that James Cooper's experience was typical rather than unusual, and the suspicion that banks are often cautious in lending money to small businesses appears to be borne out in reality.

Sources of finance

One of the first principles of business is: all businesses need funds in one form or another in order to succeed. It is obvious, therefore, that successful businesses have to be good at finding sources of finance. So what are these sources?

Many writers seem to agree that a difference should be made between internal and external sources. For example, a company could use its profits, or sell off some of its assets, or reduce its stock inventory, and all of these would help to raise finance. Even so, these internal finance methods are rarely sufficient, and companies nearly always have to raise money externally as well. This happens in a variety of ways: for small businesses typical strategies might include borrowing from friends or family, or getting a loan or an overdraft from a bank. For bigger companies, external methods might involve raising share capital or loan capital from a bank or other lender.

In addition, sources of finance can be divided into short, medium and long-term borrowing. Palmerston et al. (1999) define these as follows: 'Short-term refers to day-to-day requirements, medium-term is usually one to five years, long-term is more than five years' (p.26). Trade credit from suppliers or an overdraft are usually thought of as short-term, while medium-term borrowing includes the leasing or hire purchase of equipment. Long-term finance depends on the size and success of the company but might comprise share issues or further loan capital (mortgages, for instance). Short-term capital needs to be repaid over a short period, whereas long-term capital, which a company needs in order to expand, will normally be paid back over a number of years.

Let's look at a couple of examples. In 1999, James Cooper decided to open a fresh fruit juice shop in the south-west of England called FreshTime. He had studied business at college and had several years' experience working in restaurants. In order to start the business, he needed to find the money, but his bank was not very helpful, and so he was forced to borrow from his family (Venture, 2005). Grange (2005) asserts that'... for small businesses trying to get started, use of family resources is quite common' (p.79). It appears to be the case, then, that raising finance is one among several problems that small businesses face.

In recent years, many writers have claimed that banks are very positive in offering help to small entrepreneurs (e.g., Brookes, 2003) but the evidence does not support this belief. For example, according to Grange (op. cit., p.80), a recent survey has found that business start-ups experience considerable difficulty in this area. Thus, much of the data suggests that James Cooper's experience was typical rather than unusual, and the suspicion that banks are often cautious in lending money to small businesses appears to be borne out in reality.

However, even very large companies nearly always start out small, as can be seen in Wal-Mart's astonishing development from an insignificant cut-price chain store business in the southern USA to gigantic global retailer. Ortega (1998) describes how Sam Walton, the founder, and his wife had to scrape the money together themselves for their first Wal-Mart store in the 1960s. Later, Walton could only obtain enough funds to build 15 Wal-Mart stores. By 1970, however, Wal-Mart stock was being offered on the New York Stock Exchange; with the capital raised Walton succeeded in expanding the business to 276 stores. At the end of the 1980s, there were nearly 1,400 stores generating sales of over $26 billion (Wal-Mart, n.d.). In 2007, Wal-Mart could boast a turnover of over $300 billion.

General note

Read the *Skills bank – Identifying the parts of a long sentence* at the end of the Course Book unit. Decide when, if at all, to refer students to it. The best time is probably at the very end of the lesson or the beginning of the next lesson, as a summary/revision.

Lesson aims

- identify the writer's stance on information from the use of marked words
- identify the writer's level of confidence in the research or information
- infer implicit ideas

Further practice in:
- finding the main information in a sentence

Introduction

Introduce the idea of degree of confidence in information, which is usually shown in academic writing. More often that not, writers will avoid very categorical statements such as 'X was the cause of Y' and will demonstrate the extent to which they are sure about something through various different linguistic devices, such as modals and hedging words and phrases.

Put this table on the board to help explain the idea:

100% *** definitely true. The writer is very confident	X caused Y
75% ** probably true. The writer is a little tentative	X probably/is likely to havecaused Y
50% * possibly true. The writer is very tentative	X may/might/could have/ possibly caused Y

Exercise A

Set the exercise for pairwork. Students should refer to the table on the board to explain the rating system. Feed back with the whole class, pointing out the aspects of the language that contribute to the degree of confidence.

Answers

Model answers:

Word/phrase	Rating	Words which show less than 100% confidence
probably caused	**	probably
may have contributed to	*	may contributed (i.e., there were other reasons)
was possibly one of the factors which contributed to	*	possibly one of the factors (i.e., there were several factors) contributed
could have been a factor which led to	*	could a factor (i.e., there were other factors)
caused	***	–
seems to have caused	**	seems

Exercise B

Remind students that surveying the text means skim-reading to get an approximate idea of the text contents. They should:

- look at the title
- look at the first few lines and the final few lines of the text
- look at the first sentence of each paragraph

Note that this is in order to get a very approximate idea of the contents of the text. This will enable students to formulate questions about the text for which they might try to find answers. Students should be discouraged from reading deeply at this point, as they will be able to do this later.

Set for individual work and pairwork discussion. Each pair should agree three questions. Feed back with the whole class. Write some research questions on the board.

Exercise C

Set for individual work followed by pairwork discussion. Feed back with the whole class. Ask whether the questions you have put on the board have been answered in the text.

Exercise D

These questions require students to 'infer' information – that is, understand what is not directly stated.

Set for individual work and pairwork checking. Feed back with the whole class, making sure that students understand the answers.

Answers

Model answers:

1 Use company profits; sell assets; reduce stock inventory.
2 Borrowing (from different sources such as friends, family, banks, shareholders).
3 Internal financing methods are usually not sufficient. Therefore the implication is that more substantial amounts of money can be raised from external sources such as loans or share issues.
4 Expand: companies need long-term capital in order to grow.
5 Yes – medium-term 'includes' leasing, implying that there are other types.
6 Location: from inside or outside the company; period of time: long, medium or short periods.

Exercise E

Set for individual work and pairwork checking. Feed back with the whole class. Point out that these phrases are very important in academic writing and will help to determine whether something is a fact or an opinion – an important aspect of reading comprehension. They are also used by writers in developing their arguments for or against a particular point of view.

Answers

Model answers:

It is obvious, therefore, that successful businesses have to be good at finding sources of finance.	C
Many writers seem to agree that a difference should be made between internal and external sources.	T
It appears to be the case, then, that raising finance is one among several problems that small businesses face.	T
… many writers have claimed that banks are very positive in offering help to small entrepreneurs …	T
… the evidence does not support this belief.	C
… a recent survey has found that business start-ups experience considerable difficulty in this area.	C
… much of the data suggests that James Cooper's experience was typical rather than unusual …	T

Exercise F

Set for pairwork. Feed back with whole class. Discuss any differences in students' answers, and whether neutral equivalents are hard to find for some of the words.

Answers

Possible answers:

1 However, even very large companies nearly always start out small, as can be seen in Wal-Mart's astonishing development from an insignificant cut-price chain store business in the southern USA to gigantic global retailer. Ortega (1998) describes how Sam Walton, the founder, and his wife had to scrape the money together themselves for their first Wal-Mart store in the 1960s. Later, Walton could only obtain enough funds to build 15 Wal-Mart stores. By 1970, however, Wal-Mart stock was being offered on the New York Stock Exchange; with the capital raised Walton succeeded in expanding the business to 276 stores. At the end of the 1980s, there were nearly 1,400 stores generating sales of $26 billion (Wal-Mart, n.d.). In 2007, Wal-Mart could boast a turnover of over $300 billion.

2 The choice of words emphasizes the dramatic development of Wal-Mart and gives the impression that the writer is impressed by it.

3

Marked word	Neutral alternative
astonishing	successful, rapid*
insignificant	small
cut-price	cheap
gigantic	large
scrape the money together	find, supply, put up
succeeded (in)	(expanded)**
boast	report, announce, had

*although *rapid* is not as neutral as *fast* or *quick*, it collocates better with *development*

**Walton expanded the business* is probably the most neutral way of stating this

Exercise G

Draw the table from the Answers section (see next page) on the board. Ask students to look at the example sentence and say which box each part of the sentence should go in. Complete the table for the example sentence as shown. Point out how each of the noun phrases is made up of several words. In each case, elicit which words are the core of the noun phrases (shown in bold in the table). Do the same with the verb phrases. Ask students to suggest how the sentence can be rewritten in several short, very simple sentences in which noun phrases and verb phrases are reduced to the core meaning as far as possible. Demonstrate with these examples if necessary:

Trade credit is short-term.

An overdraft is short-term.

Medium-term borrowing includes leasing.

Medium-term borrowing includes hire purchase.

(Or: *Leasing is medium-term borrowing; Hire purchase is medium-term borrowing.*)

Point out how in the actual sentences the noun phrases have been expanded so that there is:

trade credit + *from suppliers* + *or* + *an overdraft*

the leasing + *or* + *hire purchase* + *of equipment*

Set questions 1–4 (relating to sentences A and B) for individual work and pairwork checking. Feed back with the whole class.

Answers

Model answers:

1/2 A Short-term capital | needs to be repaid | over a short period, | whereas | long-term capital, | which | a company | needs | in order to expand, | will normally be paid back | over a number of years.

B Thus, much of the data | suggests | that | James Cooper's experience | was | typical rather than unusual, | and | the suspicion | that | high street banks | are | often cautious in lending money to small businesses | appears to be borne out | in reality.

Example	Subject noun phrases	Verb phrases	Object/complement noun phrases	Adverbial phrases	Notes
	Trade credit from suppliers or **an overdraft**	**are** usually thought (of)	as **short-term**,		*or* is a joining word (or conjunction). It can join two noun phrases as here, or two clauses.
	medium-term **borrowing**	**includes**	the **leasing** or **hire** purchase of equipment.		
A	short-term **capital**	needs to be **repaid**	over a short period,		
	long-term **capital**	will ... be **paid back**		over a number of years.	*long-term capital* is the object of the relative clause which follows
	a **company**	needs	which (= **long-term capital**)	in order to expand	the phrase with *in order to* has been designated as adverbial rather than having to explain non-finite clauses
B	much of the **data**	**suggests**	James Cooper's experience was typical rather than unusual,		the clause beginning *James ...* is the object of *suggests*
	James Cooper's **experience**	**was**	**typical** rather than unusual,		*rather than* is a conjunction used here in the sense of *not*
	the **suspicion**	appears to **be borne out**		in reality.	
	banks	**are**	often **cautious** in lending money to small businesses		the complement here is made up of an adjective plus gerund
	banks	**lend**(ing)	money to small businesses		the subject is not directly stated in this clause because the verb is in a gerund form / there are two objects: a direct (*money*) and an indirect (*to small businesses*)

4 Possible sentences:

A Capital needs to be repaid.

Short-term capital needs to be repaid over a short period.

A company needs long-term capital in order to expand.

Long-term capital will normally be paid back over a number of years.

B James Cooper's experience was typical.

The data suggests something.

The data suggests that James Cooper's experience was typical.

There is a suspicion.

This suspicion is borne out in reality.

Banks are cautious.

Banks lend money to businesses.

Banks are cautious in lending money.

Banks are cautious in lending money to small businesses.

Language note

1 There are several types of conjunction in English.

Coordinating conjunctions such as *and*, *or*, *but* link elements of equal grammatical status.

Correlative conjunctions have two items: *either ... or ...*; *both ... and ...*.

Subordinating conjunctions relate clauses to each other using single words (e.g., *that* with verbs of saying, thinking, etc., *after*, *as*, *before*, *if*, *although*, *while*) or phrases (e.g., *as soon as*, *in order to*, *provided that ...*).

See a good grammar reference book for full explanations.

2 Adverbial phrases add information about the actions or processes described by the verb phrase.

Closure

Here is some advertising language from the website of a company that sells furniture and household goods. Ask students to identify any marked vocabulary items in each sentence and to suggest more neutral words. Feed back, comparing answers and discussing any differences of opinion.

Brilliant tips for a fun evening with friends!

Stylish solutions to make your house a dream home!

Innovative ideas for children's bedrooms!

Super-fancy quality for everyone!

Pay back your loan in bite-sized pieces!

Buy our exclusive kitchen in a robust yet alluring design!

Do you need some inspiration? We have some great ways of de-cluttering your office!

Possible changes:

(*Brilliant tips*) <u>Good ideas</u> for a (*fun*) <u>pleasant/enjoyable</u> evening with friends!

(*Stylish solutions*) <u>Fashionable ideas</u>/<u>items</u> to make your house a (*dream*) <u>nice</u>/<u>pleasant</u> home!

(*Innovative*) <u>New</u> ideas for children's bedrooms!

(*Super-fancy*) <u>Good</u> quality for everyone!

Pay back your loan in (*bite-sized pieces*) <u>small amounts</u>!

Buy our (*exclusive*) <u>special</u> kitchen in a (robust yet alluring) <u>strong but attractive</u> design!

Do you need some (*inspiration*) <u>ideas</u>? We have some (*great*) <u>good</u> ways of (*de-cluttering*) <u>tidying up</u> your office!

10.3 Extending skills

10.3 Extending skills · essay types • situation–problem–solution–evaluation essays

A Read the three essay questions. What types of essay are they?

B Look at text A on the opposite page. Copy and complete Table 1.

C Look at text B on the opposite page. Copy and complete Table 2.

D Look again at the solutions in Exercise B (Table 1). What are their possible advantages and disadvantages?

E Read the title of essay 3 again.
1 Make a plan for this essay.
2 Write a topic sentence for each paragraph in the body of the essay.
3 Write a concluding paragraph.

1 Compare the methods a company might use to raise short- and long-term finance.

2 Explain from a financial viewpoint how some of the main sources of income and funding might help a company to achieve its goals.

3 Describe, with some actual examples, the financial problems faced by small business start-ups. Consider how small businesses can best solve these difficulties.

Table 1
Situation	
Problem	
Solutions	

Table 2
Solution	
Argument for	
Argument against	

10.4 Extending skills · writing complex sentences • references • quotations

A Expand these simple sentences. Add extra information. Use the ideas in Lesson 3.
1 High street banks do not often give loans to new small businesses.
2 Small entrepreneurs cannot issue shares to the public.
3 The first four types of funds are fairly easy to obtain.
4 Borrowing from the family has certain risks.
5 Private investors will take some of the profits.

B Look at text C on the opposite page. Copy and complete Tables 1–3.

Table 1: Referencing books
Author(s)	Place	Date	Publisher

C Look at text D on the opposite page.
1 Complete a further row of Table 1.
2 How could you write this as a reference?

Table 2: Referencing journals
Name of journal	Volume	Pages

D What do the abbreviations in the blue box mean?

Table 3: Referencing websites
Retrieval date	URL

E Look at the direct quotes in the text on page 81
1 Find all the research sources (e.g., Grange 2005, p. 79).
2 Mark the page numbers next to the correct reference on the opposite page.
3 What punctuation is used before and within each direct quote? Why?
4 What words are used to introduce each direct quote? Why does the writer choose each word?

&	©	cf.	edn.	ed(s).	et al.
ibid.	n.d.	op. cit.	p.	pp.	vol.

Case Study 1

In 2000, Sarah Stoppard left her nine-to-five job and set up a company called Three Bears Furniture which designed and sold children's furniture (such as child-sized chairs in the shape of a flower, and toy-boxes which looked like pirate ships). Her high street bank refused her a loan, but agreed to an overdraft of £4,000. With this and a government Small Business Start-up loan of £5,000, Sarah was able to lease a stall in a craft market in her local town and also set up a website through which she could sell her furniture. When, in 2002, she wanted to expand her retail outlets to a shop on the high street, her bank again refused her a loan, despite the fact that she was now beginning to make a profit. Eventually, Sarah borrowed the money for the shop lease from her mother and brother.

Source: Venture, 2005

It is clear that small businesses cannot rely on banks for financial help. Another alternative which may be considered by small entrepreneurs is to raise finance through the sale of equity in the business to a venture capitalist (Brookes, 2003, p. 231). Grange (2005, p. 84) argues that this represents 'a sound option' since these investors are often experienced business people and the small business owner may benefit from their business advice. However, Grange (ibid.) also points out that 'The disadvantage is that the small entrepreneur is no longer the sole owner, and more importantly perhaps, may well see their hard earned profits go to someone else.'

References

Brookes, S. P. (2003). *Introduction to the sources of finance*. London: Howe & Pole.

Grange, R. (2005). Low margins: A review of some successful small business enterprises. *Journal of Business and Entrepreneurship*, 4, 75–89.

Ortega, B. (1998). *In Sam we trust*. New York: Times Books.

Palmerstone, P. J., Jackson, C., Webbings, S., & Burns, R. (1999). *How companies manage their finances*. New York: Mole & Rain.

Wal-Mart. (n.d.) *The Wal-Mart story*. Retrieved March 7, 2007, from http://www.walmartstores.com/GlobalWMStoresWeb/navigate.do?catg=5

Case Studies in Small Businesses

Brian Venture

Wentworth & Bourne

First published in 2005 by Wentworth & Bourne Ltd. 11 Vine Lane, London EC4P 5EI © 2005 Brian Venture Reprinted 2007

All rights reserved. No part of this publication may be reproduced, stored in a retrieval system, or transmitted in any form or by any means, electronic, mechanical, photocopying, recording or otherwise without the prior written permission of the Publishers.

British Library Cataloguing-in-Publication Data A catalogue record for this book is available from the British Library

Typeset by Glenda Graphics, Barnstaple, Devon, UK Printed and bound by PW Enterprises, Bude, Cornwall, UK

ISBN 0-321-09487-3

82   83

Lesson aims

- understand situation–problem–solution–evaluation structure in essays
- understand the use of information in this type of essay structure to:
  describe
  give cause and effect
  compare
  evaluate
  argue for

Further practice in:

- identifying required essay types
- producing an outline
- writing key sentences – which can be expanded in the next lesson into longer sentences

Introduction

Revise the different types of essay that were examined in Unit 8. Say or write on the board some key words or phrases from essay titles such as the following:

State …

Outline …

Describe …

Compare …

Evaluate …

Discuss …

Why …?

How …?

To what extent …?

How far …?

Ask students to say

- what type of essay is required
- what type of organizational structure should be used

If students find this difficult, refer them to the *Skills bank* for Unit 8.

Exercise A

Set for individual work and pairwork checking. Feed back with the whole class. Point out that in real life, essays given by lecturers often involve several types of writing in one essay. This is the case with essay 3. Tell students that in fact a possible structure for essay 3 would be the following, which is commonly found in many types of writing (including newspapers and academic writing).

Situation: description of a state of affairs, usually giving reasons and background information	description
Problem(s): the problems which are caused by the state of affairs; plus the effects of these problems	description (cause and effect)
Solution(s): ways of dealing with the problems (i) which may have been tried in the past or are being tried now; (ii) which will, may or could be tried in the future; suggestions for further solutions	description (+ possibly suggestion)
Evaluation of solution(s): comparison of solutions; opinion on how successful the solutions are or could be + justification; an opinion on which is the best option + justification	comparison and argument

Tell students they will plan (and possibly write) this essay.

Answers

Model answers:

1 Comparison, plus some evaluation.
2 Analysis.
3 Description, then comparison and evaluation/argument/opinion, plus support (see table above).

Exercise B

Set for individual work and pairwork checking. Feed back with the whole class.

Answers

Model answers:

Situation	Sarah Stoppard started a small business in 2002 (note that she needed finance, once at the start + again when she wanted to expand)
Problem	her bank would not give her a loan (both when she started her business and when she wanted to expand)
Solutions	overdraft arrangement government start-up loan borrowing from family

Exercise C

Set for individual work and pairwork checking. Feed back with the whole class.

Answers

Model answers:

Solution	sell equity to a venture capitalist
Argument for	the investor may give useful advice
Argument against	the business owner will lose some of the profit

Exercise D

Set for pairwork discussion. Feed back with the whole class. Accept any reasonable suggestions. Common-sense answers are also suitable here.

Answers

Possible answers:

	Advantages	Disadvantages
Overdraft arrangement	easy access flexible for day-to-day payments negotiable	short-term small amounts expensive not possible for major capital investment
Government start-up loan	easy access low interest	small amounts filling in forms to get the loan not suitable for long-term or major capital investment
Borrowing from family	easy access informal (no form filling)	small amounts short-term personal: could cause family problems depends on family finance

Exercise E

1 Set for pairwork discussion. Remind students to refer back to the text in Lesson 2 for ideas and information, as well as the texts they have discussed in this lesson. Remind students about the basic structure of an essay (introduction – main body – conclusion).

If you wish, you can give students the first two columns of the table in the Answers section, with the third column empty for them to complete. The table is reproduced in the additional resources section (Resource 10B) for this purpose.

Feed back with the whole class. Build the plan on the board, using the ideas in the Answers section to help.

2 Ask students to write some topic sentences for the four body paragraphs, using the information in the plan. Remind students that topic sentences need to be very general. Set for individual work.

Feed back with the whole class, writing some examples on the board.

3 Set for pairwork, then discussion with the whole class. Or if you prefer, set for individual homework. The ideas should be those of the students. Remind them to introduce their ideas with suitable phrases.

Note: Students will need their essay plans again in Lesson 4.

Answers

1 Possible essay plan:

Introduction		Examples of ideas
introduce the topic area give the outline of the essay		small businesses → many difficulties when starting up *In this essay, I will discuss financial difficulties …* *I will illustrate/describe …* (examples) *I will consider …* (solutions) *Finally, I will suggest …* (best solution)

Body	**Para 1:**
	situation/problems
	(general)
		small businesses → financing problems ∵
		1. high street banks don't often give loans to new small businesses
		   (evidence: a number of surveys)
		2. large public share issues not possible for small entrepreneurs (not the
		   case for large businesses)

	Para 2: problems (specific examples)	examples of cases: James Cooper Sarah Stoppard Sam Walton
	Para 3: solutions	1. overdraft with bank 2. trade credit (suppliers) 3. government small business loan 4. family 5. private investor
	Para 4: evaluations of solutions	first 4 types of funds fairly easy to obtain but (i) short-term, (ii) small amounts of money, (iii) bank overdrafts = expensive family → certain risks (i.e., if business not successful → personal problems) private investor → will take some of the profits but = useful for advice
Conclusion		*In my view/As I see it, the best option is … because …* *Firstly …* *Secondly …* *Thirdly …*

2 Possible topic sentences:

Para 1	One of the most serious areas of difficulty which small businesses face is how to raise enough money to begin the business.
Para 2	There are many example cases which illustrate the financial difficulties faced by business start-ups.
Para 3	There are a number of solutions available to small entrepreneurs.
Para 4	All of these solutions have a number of disadvantages as well as advantages.

3 Students' own concluding paragraphs.

Language note

Although 'situation–problem–solution–evaluation of solution' is often said to be an organizing principle in writing, in practice it is sometimes difficult to distinguish between the situation and the problem: they may sometimes seem to be the same thing. The important thing is to be clear about the main *focus* of the essay – that is, the answer to the question *What am I writing about?* – and to structure the essay around this.

Closure

Set up a Dragon's Den-style role play. Dragon's Den is a TV series in which entrepreneurs try to persuade a panel of investors to invest in their business. The investors are highly successful and experienced businessmen and women. The entrepreneurs are people who have a good idea for a business. The investors try to find out whether the entrepreneurs have really got a good idea, whether they have done the necessary preparation and planning for their business, and whether their plans are financially sound.

Put students in groups of four. Within each group, students work in pairs. Each pair should think of a product or an idea for a business. They should prepare a short (one-minute) presentation on their idea, which should include why it is a good idea, how they plan to put it into operation, how much money they will need and where they plan to get it. They should also decide how much to ask the investors for – bearing in mind that the investors will want a percentage (to be negotiated) of the profits.

When both pairs are ready, they should take in it turns to be the entrepreneurs and the investors. The entrepreneurs should try to persuade the investors to invest in their business for a reasonable return on their investment. The investors will need to be sure that the idea is a good one and that it is financially sound.

10.4 Extending skills

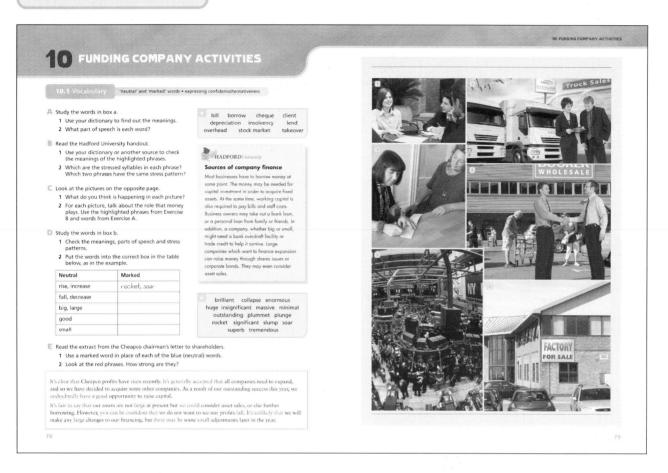

10 FUNDING COMPANY ACTIVITIES

General note

This lesson focuses on writing references for a bibliography according to the APA (American Psychological Association) system. Before the lesson, it would be useful to familiarize yourself with this system. See the *Skills bank*, and for more detailed information, the following website: http://owl.english.purdue.edu/owl/resource/560/10/

Lesson aims

- use quotations with appropriate punctuation and abbreviations such as ibid.
- write a reference list (APA system)

Further practice in:

- the reverse activity to Lesson 2, i.e., putting extra information into simple sentences in an appropriate way

Introduction

Introduce the idea of using sources in writing. Look back at the text in Lesson 2 and ask students to find all the places where a reference to a source is mentioned.

Ask them to find a quotation and a paraphrase. What are the main differences?

Exercise A

Remind students of the essay plan in Lesson 3. If you wish, you can reproduce the following table for them. They should try to get all the information in each numbered point into one sentence.

Para 1	1. high street banks don't often give loans to new small businesses (evidence: a number of surveys) 2. large public share issues not possible for small entrepreneurs (not the case for large businesses)
Para 4	1. first 4 types of funds fairly easy to obtain but (i) short-term, (ii) small amounts of money, (iii) bank overdrafts = expensive 2. family → certain risks (i.e., if business not successful → personal problems) 3. private investor → will take some of the profits but = useful for advice

Do the first sentence with the whole class as an example on the board. Students should feel free to add words as appropriate to make a coherent sentence; they can also paraphrase (e.g., *don't often give → are reluctant to give*).

Set the remaining sentences for individual work.

Answers

Possible answers:

1 A number of surveys have shown that high street banks are often reluctant to give loans to small businesses in the initial start-up phase.

2 Unlike large businesses, small entrepreneurs cannot raise substantial sums of money through large-scale issues of shares to the public.

3 Although the first four types of funds may be fairly easy to obtain, not only are they are all rather short-term and the amounts of money that can be borrowed rather small, but bank overdrafts in particular are expensive to maintain.

4 Borrowing from family members carries certain risks, because if the business does not do well, this is likely to create personal problems.

5 Although using a private investor has the disadvantage that the small entrepreneur will not get all of the profits from the business, the private investor may be able to give useful business advice.

Exercise B

Tell students that this is a list of references from the text in Lesson 2. Note that it is called 'References' because it lists all the references actually given (it is not a list of all the references the author might have consulted but not referred to – this is a bibliography).

Set for individual work and pairwork checking. Note that these tables are intended to help students identify some key information. For a full set of categories to include in a reference list, see the *Skills bank*. Tell students that when writing a reference list they will need to pay close attention to the detail of the layout which is in the APA style (the American Psychological Association). See the *Skills bank* for relevant websites which give further details. In particular, students should note and will need to practise:

- putting the names of writers and multiple writers in the correct alphabetical order according to family name, with the right spacing and punctuation
- writing all numbers correctly, including dates and page references
- using punctuation including the role and placing of full stops, commas and colons
- laying out the references in the correct style with the correct positions (e.g., of indents and tabs)
- using standard APA style features such as italic and brackets

Answers

Table 1:

Author(s)	Place of publication	Date of publication	Publisher
Brookes, S. P.	London	2003	Howe & Pole
Ortega, B.	New York	1998	Times Books
Palmerstone, P. J., Jackson, C., Webbings S., & Burns, R.	New York	1999	Mole & Rain

Table 2:

Name of journal	Volume	Pages
Journal of Business and Entrepreneurialism	4	75–89

Table 3:

Retrieval date	URL
March 7, 2007	http://www.walmartstores.com/Global WMStoresWeb/navigate.do?catg=5

Language and subject note

In the case of journals, there is an increasing tendency to refer to the volume number only in reference lists, omitting the issue number. Thus, for example, *English for Specific Purposes, 16 (1), 47–60* might become *English for Specific Purposes, 16, 47–60*.

Exercise C

Set for individual work and pairwork checking.

Answers

1

Author(s)	Place of publication	Date of publication	Publisher
Venture, B.	London	2005	Wentworth & Bourne

2 Venture, B. (2005). *Case studies in small businesses*. London: Wentworth & Bourne.

Language and subject note

In the APA system, titles of books (but not articles or journal titles) are in italics, sentence case – that is, initial capital letter only, unless the title contains a proper noun. If the title contains a colon, the first word after the colon is also capitalized.

Journal *titles* are in italics and 'headline' or 'title' style – that is, all key words are capitalized but not conjunctions and prepositions. For example: *Journal of Small Business Management*.

Journal articles are sentence case, no italics.

Exercise D

Many of these were covered in Unit 5, so ask students to check back if they are not sure, or they can refer to the list at the back of their books; they can also check online at the APA site and/or the other sites given in the *Skills bank*.

Set for individual work and pairwork checking.

Answers

Model answers:

&	and
©	copyright
cf.	compare
edn.	edition
ed(s).	editor(s)
et al.	and other authors
ibid.	same place in a work already referred to
n.d.	no date (used in a reference list if there is no date – as is often the case with web articles)
op. cit.	the work already referred to
p.	page
pp.	pages
vol.	volume

Exercise E

Remind students (if you have not done so already) of the two main ways in which students can use sources (i.e., references to other writers' work) in their writing:

- by giving the exact words used by another writer
- by paraphrasing another writer's ideas, i.e., rewriting the ideas using their own, different words but retaining the meaning

The first method is referred to as quotation or direct quotation. Direct quotations are in quotation marks.

The second method is referred to as paraphrase, summary or indirect quotation. Note that around 90% of the paraphrase should be new words.

1/2 Draw the table from the Answers section on the boards. Set for individual work. Tell students to look for all the direct quotations and to identify the research sources. They should then locate the source in the reference list on page 83 of the Course Book. Writing the page numbers on the reference list may seem a mechanical exercise, but it is useful for students to get into the habit of doing this. It will enable them to find an original source book, refer to the relevant part of the book, and read more about the subject.

3/4 Students should identify the punctuation and introducing phrases used.
Feed back with the whole class. Make sure that students understand why the different introducing verbs were chosen.

Answers

Model answers:

Lesson 2: See table below. Lessons 3/4: see table on next page.

Quote	Source	Punctuation around the quote	Introducing phrase + reason for choice
'Short-term refers to day-to-day requirements, medium-term is usually one to five years, long-term is more than five years'	page 26 of Palmerstone, P. J., Jackson, C., Webbings, S., & Burns, R. (1999). *How companies manage their finances.* New York: Mole & Rain.	colon + 'Xxx'	Palmerstone et al. (date) <u>define</u> (these) as follows: … reason: what follows is a definition
'… for small businesses trying to get started, use of family resources is quite common'	page 79 of Grange, R. (2005). Low margins: a a review of some successful small business enterprises. *Journal of Business and Entrepreneurialism*, volume 4, pages 75–89.	'… xxx'	Grange (date,) <u>asserts</u> that … reason: this is Grange's opinion

Language and subject note

If the quotation is a full sentence, it begins with a capital letter inside the opening quotation mark and ends with a full stop inside the closing quotation mark.

If there are some words missing from the original quotation that were at the start of the original sentence, the quotation does not begin a capital letter.

Quote	Source	Punctuation around the quote	Introducing phrase reason for choice
'a sound option'	page 84 of Grange, R. (2005). Low margins: a review of some successful small business enterprises. *Journal of Business and Entrepreneurialism*, volume 4, pages 75–89.	'xxx'	Grange (date) <u>argues</u> that this represents … reason: this again is Grange's opinion and part of an argument
'The disadvantage is that the small entrepreneur is no longer the sole owner, and more importantly perhaps, may well see their hard earned profits go to someone else.'	the same as above	'Xxx.'	Grange (ibid.) also <u>points out</u> that … reason: this again is Grange's opinion and part of an argument

Closure

Refer students to the *Skills bank* for a summary of writing references. Study how the following are used:

- names (order)
- punctuation (capital letters, full stops, commas, colons)
- layout (indentation, spacing)
- style features (italics, brackets)

For further practice, use Resource 10C from the additional resources section. Ask students to check the references on a library database or on the Internet (discuss which sources are likely to be the most accurate and give them all the information they need – often the best way to check bibliographical details is to use a university library catalogue, as information found on the Internet is frequently inaccurate or incomplete). They should also make any necessary changes to ensure the references fit the APA models used in this unit. If possible, they should use the online website references (see *Skills bank*) to help them. Remind students that they will also need to put the references in the right alphabetical order.

Correct versions are:

Atrill, P., & McLaney, E. (2006). *Accounting and finance for non-specialists* (5th Ed.). New York: Prentice Hall.

Carrell, P. L., & Carson, J. G. (1997). Extensive and intensive reading in an EAP setting. *English for Specific Purposes, 16,* 47–60.

Howells, P. G. A., & Bain, K. B. (1990). *Financial markets and institutions*. London: Longman.

Kotler, P., & Armstrong, G. (2003). *Principles of marketing* (10th Ed.). London: Pearson/Prentice Hall.

Ortega, B. (1998). *In Sam we trust*. New York: Times Books.

Slack, N., & Chambers, S. (2004). *Operations management* (4th Ed.). Harlow: Prentice Hall Financial Times.

Language and subject note

An ampersand (&) is used with multiple authors, preceded by a comma.

The full stop at the end of the reference is omitted in the case of URLs.

Dates are (for example) April 7 not April 7th.

Extra activities

1 Work through the *Skills bank* and *Vocabulary bank* if you have not already done so, or as revision of previous study.

2 Use the *Activity bank* (Teacher's Book additional resources section, Resource 10A).

A As in the previous unit, students will need lots of practice with the technical and semi-technical finance terms. Set for individual work (including homework) or pairwork. Tell students to focus on the main meanings of the words in business.

Answers

Word/ phrase	Part of speech	Noun – countable or uncountable?	Verb – transitive or intransitive?
account*	n	C	
bankruptcy	n	C, U	
bill	n, v	C	T
borrow	v		T, I
cheque	n	C	
client	n	C	
depreciation	n	U	
insolvency	n	C, U	
lend	v		T
merger	n	C	
overhead	n	C	
stock exchange	n	C	
stock market	n	C	
stocks	pl n	C	
takeover**	n, (v)	C	(T)

* there is also a verb: *account for*

** the verb is normally two words: *take over*

B Set for individual work (including homework) or pairwork. Accept all reasonable answers. Students should be able to explain the meaning.

Answers

Possible answers:

asset	sale(s)
bank	loan, account
bank overdraft	facility
capital	investment
corporate	bond(s)
fixed	asset(s), cost(s)
personal	loan
shares	issues
trade	credit
working	capital

3 Ask students to choose one of the other essays in Lesson 3 and make a plan. They can also write topic sentences for each paragraph in the essay.

11 EXTERNAL INFLUENCES

This unit looks in more detail at the external factors which can affect businesses, with a focus on political, economic and environmental factors, and some brief mention of other factors. The concept of PEST was introduced in Unit 1 and technological factors were examined in Unit 4.

Skills focus

🎧 Listening
- recognizing the speaker's stance
- writing up notes in full

Speaking
- building an argument in a seminar
- agreeing/disagreeing

Vocabulary focus
- words/phrases used to link ideas (*moreover*, *as a result*, etc.)
- stress patterns in noun phrases and compounds
- fixed phrases from academic English
- words/phrases related to environmental issues

Key vocabulary

See also the list of fixed phrases from academic English in the *Vocabulary bank* (Course Book page 92).

boom (n)	pension	
business opportunity	policy	
consultant	population	
demographic	pressure group	
diversify	privatization	
full-time	quota	
immigrant	regulation	
import (n)	retired	
industrialization	shrink	
lean production	tariff	
levy (n)	temporary	
part-timer	textiles	

Environmental terms

biodegradable	greenhouse gas
biofuel	hazardous substance
carbon footprint	landfill
carbon offset	packaging
carbon trading scheme	pollution
emissions	recycling
energy-saving	renewable energy
environmental audit	solar power
environmentally friendly	toxic
fossil fuel	waste disposal
global warming	zero waste

11.1 Vocabulary

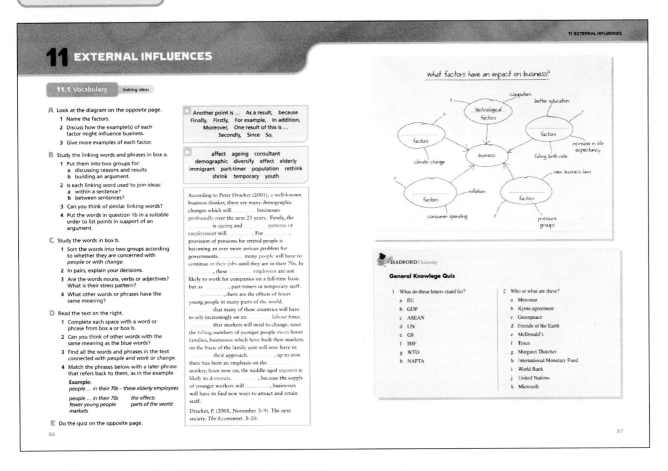

General note

Read the *Vocabulary bank* at the end of the Course Book unit. Decide when, if at all, to refer your students to it. The best time is probably at the very end of the lesson or the beginning of the next lesson, as a summary/revision

Lesson aims

- use rhetorical markers: to add points in an argument; to signal cause and effect (between- and within-sentence linking)
- further understand lexical cohesion: the use of superordinates/synonyms to refer back to something already mentioned; building lexical chains

Further practice in:

- synonyms, antonyms and word sets from business studies
- abbreviations and acronyms

Introduction

1 Revise some vocabulary from previous units. Give students some key words from the previous unit (in italics below) and ask them to think of terms connected with these words (for example, some key phrases from finance).

   bank loan, personal *loan*, working *capital*, bank *overdraft* facility, trade *credit*, *shares* issues, corporate *bonds*, *asset* sales, long *term*, short *term*, medium *term*, hire *purchase*, *venture* capitalist, low/high *margin*, *stock* market, *stock* exchange, business *start-up*

2 Introduce the topic: before asking students to open their books, ask students in general what kinds of thing businesses need to pay attention to outside their own organizations. Accept any reasonable suggestions. Tell the students that they first met some of these concepts in Unit 1 and later Unit 4, but here they are going to consider these topics in more detail.

Exercise A

Ask students to open their books and look at the diagram on page 87.

Check the meaning of the words in the diagram. If necessary give some examples of pressure groups such as animal rights groups, anti-globalization groups, Greenpeace, etc.

1 Set for pairwork. Feed back with the class. Ask the students if they can remember the acronym PEST – which is often used in business for analysis and strategy decision purposes. What additional factor is here? (*Environment* – sometimes added to the PEST acronym as EV – PEST EV.)

2/3 With the whole class, discuss the technology section. What can they remember about technology in Unit 4? Ask students to explain how exactly computers affect businesses. Discuss with the class other possible future technological developments and how they might affect businesses: for example,

what effect might the development of efficient and cheap non-carbon fuels have on businesses? Answer: changing the way their machinery is powered would initially be a major expense, but might save money ultimately.

Next look at the social factors. Discuss with the class the likely effects of the changing age structure and improved education of the workforce on business (note that the topic of the changing age structure and its effect on business is considered further in the text in this lesson). Ask the class to suggest more social factors which might affect business. Accept any reasonable suggestions.

Set the remaining factors (political, economic and environmental) and their effects on business for pairwork discussion. It would be a good idea to ask each pair to think about a different factor. Ask a few pairs to feed back to the class. Accept any reasonable suggestions.

Answers

Possible answers:

1 See diagram.

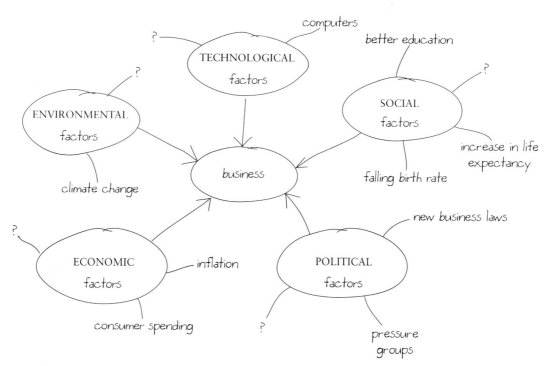

What factors have an impact on business?

2 Answers depend on the students.

3 For the question marks, some more examples of factors are:

Technological factors

   new communications technology

   new industrial materials

   inventions for industrial or domestic use

Social factors

   new fashions such as in entertainment, food, clothes

   changes in attitudes to, for example, child labour, the way food is produced, what makes a family

Political factors

   the impact of government

   deregulation

   privatization

   change in government

   trading standards

   (for big companies) monopoly and competition control by governments

   employment laws

   local trading organizations

   regional trade groups such as EU, Mercosur, NAFTA with protectionist policies

   global organizations such as WTO, World Bank, G8, United Nations

   international conventions and agreements such as Kyoto

Economic factors

   economic/business cycle

   depression

   money markets

   taxes

   changes in main type of wealth-producing activity (e.g., change from farming to manufacturing to service industries)

   growth of new economically powerful countries (China, India, etc)

   development of new or changing markets

   changes in the fortunes of the large economies, e.g., the US

   developing wealth

Environmental factors

   Some of these are covered in detail in Lesson 4. Here students should be thinking about aspects such as:

   global warming

   pollution

   industrialization

   development

   green issues

   areas of special interest or beauty

   waste disposal

   new laws on emissions

   planning permissions

Add some of these to the diagram, as appropriate and as students suggest them. It would be a good idea to make a large poster-sized copy of the diagram or put it on an OHT or other visual medium to which you can add more examples as the unit progresses.

Exercise B

1 Set for individual work and pairwork checking. Feed back with the whole class, building the table in the Answers section on the next page.

2 Explain what is meant by 'within' and 'between' sentences: 'within-sentence linking words' join clauses in a sentence; 'between-sentence linking words' connect two sentences. Demonstrate with the following:

Within-sentence linking words:

Workforces have become highly skilled in many countries <u>because</u> they have improved education standards.

Make sure the students can see that within-sentence linking words precede dependent clauses.

Between-sentence linking words:

Many countries have improved education standards. <u>As a result</u>, the workforce has become highly skilled.

Point out that between-sentence linking words usually have a comma before the rest of the sentence.

Ask students to say which of the other words in box a are 'between' and which are 'within'.

3 Ask for suggestions for synonyms and add to the table.

4 First make sure that students understand the basic principle of an argument, which is:

> Statement
>
> +
>
> one or more support(s) for statement
> (= more facts, reasons, results, examples, evidence, etc.)

Constructing a complex argument will usually entail a statement plus several supports.

With the whole class, elicit suggestions for how to use the linkers when constructing an argument. Build the table in the Answers section on the board.

Answers

Possible answers:

1/2/3

	Use for	Within or between sentence linker	Other similar words/phrases
Another point is ...	building an argument	between	And another thing,
As a result,	reasons and results	between	Consequently,
because	reasons and results	within	as
Finally,	building an argument	between	Lastly,
Firstly,	building an argument	between	To begin with/To start with; For one thing,
For example,	building an argument	between	For instance,
In addition,	building an argument	between	Also,
Moreover,	building an argument	between	Furthermore,
One result of this is ...	reasons and results	between	One consequence of this is ...; Because of this,
Secondly,	building an argument	between	Next, Then,
Since	reasons and results	within	as
So,	reasons and results	between	Therefore, Thus, Hence,

4 A typical argument is constructed like this:

Firstly,	making the major support point
For example,	supporting the point with a specific example
In addition,	adding another related point in support
Secondly,	making the second major support point
Another point is ...	adding another related point in support
Moreover,	adding more information to the point above
Finally,	making the last point

Language note

1 Note that within-sentence linking words may be placed at the beginning of the sentence with a comma after the first clause, as in:

Because many countries have improved education standards, their workforces have become highly skilled.

2 Although the between-sentence linking words are described above as joining two sentences, they can of course link two independent clauses joined by coordinating linking words *and* or *but*, as in:

Many countries have improved education standards and, as a result, the workforce has become highly skilled.

Exercise C

1 Set for individual work. Note that students should try to put each word into one of the two categories, even if it is not immediately clear how it could be relevant. If they are not sure which category to use, they should try to think of a phrase containing the word and imagine how it could be relevant to one of the categories.

2 Ask students to compare their answers and to justify their choices. Feed back with the whole class, discussing the words for which students feel the category is not obvious. If no decision can be reached, say you will come back to the words a little later.

3/4 Set for pairwork. Feed back with the whole class if you wish.

Answers

Possible answers:

	Suggested categories	Part of speech	Other words/phrases
a'ffect	change	v (T)	influence
'ageing	people/change	v (I), adj	getting/becoming older
con'sultant	people	n (C)	(visiting) expert
demo'graphic	people	adj, n (C)	in/of population
di'versify	change	v (I)	change, become more varied
e'ffect	change	n (C)	consequence, outcome, result
'elderly	people	adj	old, older
'immigrant	people	n (C), adj	migrant
part-'timer	people	n (C)	fractional staff
popu'lation	people	n (C, U)	people
re'think	change	v (T)	alter, change
shrink	change	v (I,T)	(I) become smaller/fewer (T) make something smaller
'temporary	change	adj	not permanent
youth	people	n (U, C)	young people

Exercise D

Students should first read through the text to get an idea of the topic.

1/2 Set for individual work and pairwork checking. Feed back with the whole class.

Point out that having done these questions, it should now be possible to say whether the words in box b can be put into a 'change' or a 'people' group. (In the case of *ageing* a case can be made for both groups.) The point here is that the context will make clear what the meaning of a word should be. This is important when it comes to making a guess at the meaning of a word whose meaning one is not sure of initially.

3 Since the text is about people in the context of work, ask students to identify all the words first about *people and work*, and then about *change*. Set for individual work and pairwork checking. Feed back with the whole class, if you wish using an OHT and two coloured pens, or other visual medium. Point out how the two themes of *change* and *people in the context of work* run through the text.

Tell students that a particular topic will have groups of words which are connected to or associated with it – known as 'lexical chains'. These lexical chains show us the themes that run through the text and which help 'glue' the ideas together to make a coherent piece of text. It is a good idea, therefore, to learn vocabulary according to topic areas.

4 It is also common to use synonymous words and phrases to refer back to something already mentioned. Ideally, use an OHT or other visual medium of the text (Resource 11B additional resources section), and with a coloured pen draw a line to show how *people ... in their 70s* is referred to later in the text by *these elderly employees*. Set for individual work and pairwork checking. Feed back with the class (linking the phrases with coloured pens if using Resource 11B).

Answers

Model answers:

1 According to Peter Drucker (2001), a well-known business thinker, there are many demographic changes which will <u>affect</u> businesses profoundly over the next 25 years. Firstly, the <u>population</u> is ageing and <u>so/as a result</u>, patterns of employment will <u>diversify</u>. For <u>example</u>, provision of pensions for retired people is becoming an ever more serious problem for governments. <u>As a result,/So</u> many people will have to continue in their jobs until they are in their 70s. In <u>addition</u>, these <u>elderly</u> employees are not likely to work for companies on a full-time basis but as <u>consultants</u>, part-timers or temporary staff.

<u>Secondly</u>, there are the effects of fewer young people in many parts of the world. <u>One result of this is</u> that many countries will have to rely increasingly on an <u>immigrant</u> labour force. <u>Another point is</u> that markets will need to change: since the falling numbers of young people mean fewer families, businesses which have built their markets on the basis of the family unit will now have to <u>rethink</u> their approach. <u>Moreover,</u> up to now there has been an emphasis on the <u>youth</u> market; from now on, the middle-aged segment is likely to dominate. <u>Finally,</u> because the supply of younger workers will <u>shrink</u>, businesses will have to find new and different ways to attract and retain staff.

191

2

Word	Synomym
profoundly	deeply/greatly
ageing	getting older
patterns of employment	ways of working
people	workers/employees
in their jobs	working
employees	workers
labour	work
falling	decreasing
mean	will result in
segment	market
dominate	take over, be more important

3

People and work	Change
demographic	changes
population	affect
ageing	profoundly
patterns of employment	diversify
pensions	is becoming
retired people	ever more
people	result
in their jobs	effects
in their 70s	fewer
elderly	result
employees	increasingly
to work for	change
on a full-time basis	falling numbers
consultants, part-timers or temporary	fewer
staff	now
young people	rethink
immigrant labour force	up to now
younger people	from now on
families	is likely to
family unit	will shrink
youth	new
middle-aged	
supply	
younger workers	
attract and retain staff	

4

Word	Second phrase
people … in their 70s	these elderly employees
the effects	one result of this
fewer young people people	the falling numbers of younger people
parts of the world	these countries
markets	the youth market; the middle-aged segment

Exercise E

Time this general knowledge quiz if you wish. Alternatively, set it for homework for students to research the answers. Make sure that students understand they need to say what the initials stand for and also what the organization/body does.

In order to be able to follow the lecture in Lesson 2, students will need to be familiar with these organizations and bodies.

Answers

Model answers:

1. **EU** – European Union

   GDP – Gross Domestic Product

   ASEAN – Association of Southeast Asian Nations

   UN – United Nations

   G8 – Group of 8 major industrial nations (France, UK, USA, Germany, Japan, Italy, Russia, Canada)

   IMF – International Monetary Fund

   WTO – World Trade Organisation

   NAFTA – North American Free Trade Association (Canada, USA, Mexico)

2. **Mercosur** – Latin American regional trade agreement

   Kyoto agreement – international protocol, backed by the UN, to reduce carbon emissions

   Greenpeace – independent global organization concerned with conserving the environment

   Friends of the Earth – organization which campaigns for solutions to environmental problems

   McDonald's – US-based and now global fast-food chain

   Tesco – most successful UK supermarket chain

   Margaret Thatcher – former Conservative British Prime Minister, 1979–90

   International Monetary Fund – oversees financial systems on an international scale and offers financial assistance

   World Bank – group of five international organizations providing finance advice to developing countries

   United Nations – international organization of 192 states, founded 1945

   Microsoft – leading US computer software company

Closure

Ask students to review the lesson and list ten of the factors mentioned which affect business. Then divide the class into groups and tell the groups to discuss the factors and try to rank them in order of importance. They will need to think of specific countries if possible and the effects the factors may have on these countries. They should give reasons for their ranking.

Introduction

1 Review phrases indicating a speaker's view of the truth value of a statement. Write a sentence such as the following on the board (i.e., a 'fact' about which there may be differences of opinion): *Privatization of state industries has a beneficial effect on the generation of wealth.*

Ask students to say whether they think this is true or not. Elicit phrases they can use before the sentence to show how certain they are about their opinion.

Dictate or write on the board the following phrases. Ask students to say what the effect of each phrase is when put before the sentence on the board. In each case, does it make the writer sound confident or tentative?

The research shows that …

A survey found that …

The evidence does not support the idea that …

It appears to be the case that …

The evidence suggests that …

The evidence shows that …

It is clear that …

It is possible that …

2 Revise the Cornell note-taking system. Elicit the R words. Ask students to describe how to divide up the page (refer to Unit 9). Revise the other ways to take notes (see Units 1 and 3).

3 Revise note-taking symbols and abbreviations (see Units 5 and 9, and Unit 9 extra activity 4).

General note

Read the *Skills bank – Writing out notes in full* at the end of the Course Book unit. Decide when, if at all, to refer your students to it. The best time, as before, is probably at the very end of the lesson or the beginning of the next lesson, as a summary/revision.

Lesson aims

- recognize and understand phrases that identify the speaker's point of view
- use background knowledge in listening comprehension
- convert notes into full sentences and paragraphs

Further practice in:

- making notes (use of heading systems and abbreviations)
- referring to sources
- general academic words and phrases

Exercise A

Refer students to the Hadford University lecture announcement. Tell them to look at the title and the summary of the talk.

Check that they know the meaning of 'checks and balances' (factors which may have a limiting or controlling effect on business practice).

Set the questions for pairwork discussion. Feed back with the whole class.

Answers

Possible answers:

1 Accept any reasonable suggestions.

2 The lecturer is clearly going to list causes and effects. This suggests that possibly a flowchart or spidergram might be a suitable form of notes (as in Unit 1), as well as the Cornell system (which is used here) or the more conventional numbered points system.

🎧 Exercise B

Play Part 1 once through *without* allowing students time to focus on the questions.

Put students in pairs to answer the questions by referring to their notes. Feed back with the whole class, building a set of notes on the board if you wish. Note that 4 is a general knowledge question – which students should be able to answer from their background general knowledge.

Add the examples to your spidergram from Lesson 1 if you have not already done so.

Ask students which method they are going to use to make notes, now that they have listened to the introduction. They should now make any adjustments necessary to the page they have prepared in their notebooks.

Answers

Model answers:

1 External influences on business.
2 Political and economic factors.
3 Inflation, interest rates, demand, competition, government policies.
4 Economic: inflation, interest rates, demand, competition; political: government policies.

Transcript 🎧 2.8

Part 1

Good morning. My name is Dr William Mitchell and I'm a business consultant. It's a pleasure to be here today. I am going to try and explain some of the major factors which exert pressure on companies from the outside, that is to say, I shall mainly be looking at some different types of external influences which affect the way business operates.

Don't misunderstand me, I don't want to imply that there are no *internal* questions for a company – as we all know, companies have to think about how they manage their operations and their finance and so on. But there are also matters at a national and an international level which greatly influence business decisions. To some degree, individual companies will be affected differently but it is fair to say that they will all have to keep an eye on which way inflation or interest rates are going, or demand and competition in a particular location. Not only that, but the government policies of the country or countries where they operate. So in an attempt to try and keep the discussion of *external* pressures on business reasonably simple, I'm going to summarize a few of the more interesting points to do with political and economic factors.

🎧 Exercise C

Play the whole of the rest of lecture through *once* without stopping. Students should take notes as they listen.

Answers

See *Notes* section of the table in Answers to Exercise E.

Exercise D

Put students in pairs to answer the questions by referring to their notes. Feed back with the class to see how much they have been able to get from the lecture. If they can't answer something, do not supply the answer.

Answers

Model answers:

1 political
2 taxation policies, pressure groups, election results, regional trading groups and protection through tariffs or quotas, encouragement for foreign companies
3 Margaret Thatcher's conservative government came to power in the UK.
4 The privatization process was in place by the mid-1980s; many new business opportunities were created with privatization, especially in service industries; manufacturing declined; business benefited.
5 a Greenpeace; Friends of the Earth
   b McDonald's
   c Pure Food Movement
   d World Bank
6 farming/agriculture
7 service industries
8 manufacturing
9 These countries may become more economically powerful than the US.

Transcript 🎧 2.9

Part 2

To start with, then: the political influences on business. Whether it is taxation policies, election results or pressure groups, politics has a crucial role to play. Will a particular government try to protect its country's businesses by signing up to a regional trading group which imposes tariffs or quotas? Will the government encourage foreign companies to come into the country and set up new business operations? These questions and many more demonstrate the political dimension of business.

The answers will affect business for the good or for the bad.

Well, let's take the example of election results. The UK is a good example of how a new government can bring about a major change affecting the business world. When Margaret Thatcher's Conservative government came to power in 1979, they started to address some of the difficulties of state-owned industries in both manufacturing and service sectors. By the mid-1980s the process of privatization of state industries had begun to change the business landscape for ever. Many new business opportunities were created, particularly in the service sector, and while manufacturing declined overall, it is clear that the business world benefited greatly. These politically driven policies have since been copied all over the world, and notably in the former communist countries.

Another area which we can include in the political domain is the effect of pressure groups. Governments and businesses have to deal with the political influence and public protests of these groups. There is Greenpeace, for instance, who campaign on environmental issues: in 1995 their protests made the company Royal Dutch Shell seem so morally wrong that the company lost about 50% of their sales. Another environmental organization is Friends of the Earth, who as well as campaigning for the environment, also try to control the immense power of big businesses, such as Tesco, the largest UK supermarket chain. A good example of the damage that can be caused by protesters is the famous law case involving McDonald's. Two environmental protesters were taken to court by McDonald's for writing bad things about the company's business practices. In fact, during the trial, the company's allegedly poor business practices were discussed and McDonald's has since found it hard to recover from the negative image that was generated.

There are many other pressure groups which have been able to bring about major changes in public awareness of issues with serious consequences for business. In the US, for example, in 1906, a campaign by the Pure Food Movement forced the government to bring in laws which controlled food additives and food safety.

An important aspect of the political landscape is, of course, the regional trade organizations – such as the EU or Mercosur, or ASEAN – which governments may elect to belong to. These groups provide a highly advantageous internal market and often protect their members from competition from businesses from outside the group. A good example of this is the situation in 2005 involving the flood of Chinese textile imports into the EU. Too many Chinese clothing products came into Europe, breaching the quota limits allowed. European manufacturers were afraid that European jobs would suffer and the clothes were kept locked in warehouses until an agreement was reached.

There are also other organizations – such as the World Bank or the World Trade Organization – which can have a strong influence on how countries organize their business. The WTO deals with the rules of trade between nations. The main structure of the WTO is a set of trading agreements, which are negotiated and then signed up to by the governments of the world's trading nations. There is a clear overlap here between business and politics, to the extent that it is the government of a country that takes the decision on whether to be a member of an international trading group.

However, some people say that these types of organization are mainly concerned with the interests of big business. The evidence shows that this is especially true with respect to under-developed countries. In my view, the World Bank is a case in point. The influence of the World Bank, for example, on the economies of these countries has been very harmful. A very good book by John Perkins called *Confessions of an Economic Hit Man* published in 2004 gives an interesting explanation of how the World Bank actually benefits big business rather than a country's own people.

So, as we can see, the effect of politics on the way businesses develop is very important, particularly in the context of today's multinational and global environment.

Now, let's turn to economic influences on the business world. An important economic dimension is the history of the changing importance of the different industrial sectors. Peter Drucker, who was a major business thinker, gives a good description of this in his article entitled 'The New Society' published in *The Economist* in 2001. By the way, if you don't know anything about Drucker, a good introduction to his work can be found on a website at the University of Pennsylvania (I'll give you the URL later). Briefly, in *The Economist* article, Drucker explains how at the beginning of the 20th century (in 1913) farm products accounted for 70% of world trade, but farming has now fallen to less than one fifth of the world's economic activity. In many developed countries, the contribution by agriculture to their GDP has reduced dramatically. More recently also, manufacturing has seen a substantial decline in many of the developed nations. Manufacturing as an economic activity in many developed countries has given way to a major increase in service industries, with a consequent rise in the importance of finance and the money markets. These changes in the nature of economic output are, of course, reflected in the types of business which we find in these countries.

At the same time, in the newly emerging boom economies, the governments are trying hard to reduce the reliance on subsistence farming in favour of new manufacturing. India is an example of this; and China, too, of course, is another country which has seen a boom in manufacturing. These new boom economies are offering stiff competition in the manufacturing domain to companies in the older established developed countries.

And a thought to finish with is the question of to what extent these booming economies will become the main drivers of the global economy. One writer in *Money Management* magazine has no doubt that, and I quote, 'China will continue to be a dominant player driving world growth, which will have flow through to other economies.' This means that we may see the older economies such as the United States losing out increasingly to China and India. Now, I'm going to stop at this point …

Note

Source references for lecture:

Dowling, J. (2006). Fluctuating global fortunes. *Money Management*, 20 (21),12-15. Retrieved May 25, 2007 from www.moneymanagement.com.au

Drucker, P. (2001, November 3-9). The next society. *The Economist*, p.3-20 Retrieved January 2, 2005, from www.economist.com/surveys/display story.cfm? story_id=770819

Knowledge@Wharton. (2005). Farewell, Peter Drucker: A tribute to an intellectual giant. Retrieved May 25, 2007 from: http://knowledge. wharton.upenn.edu/article.cfm?articleid=1326

Perkins, J. (2004). *Confessions of an economic hit man*. San Francisco: Berrett Koehler.

Exercise E

1 Set for individual work.
2 Set for individual work and pairwork checking. Feed back with the whole class.

Answers

Possible answer: See next page.

◖ Exercise F

Discuss the question with the whole class. Ask them if they can remember any phrases which signal whether the comments are true or just opinion.

Play the extract. Ask students to tell you to stop the recording when they hear key phrases. Write the phrases on the board.

Remind the students that it is important to recognize when someone is giving only their opinion, which others might well disagree with.

Transcript ◖ 2.10

However, some people say that these types of organization are mainly concerned with the interests of big business. The evidence shows that this is especially true with respect to under-developed countries. In my view, the World Bank is a case in point. The influence of the World Bank, for example, on the economies of these countries has been very harmful. A very good book by John Perkins called *Confessions of an Economic Hit Man* published in 2004 gives an interesting explanation of how the World Bank actually benefits big business rather than a country's own people.

Answers

Model answers:

Some people say that (these types of organization are mainly concerned with the interests of big business.)	This phrase can be used to give both a speaker's own opinion as well as an opposing view.
The evidence shows that this is especially true (with respect to underdeveloped countries.)	Sometimes, to put their case strongly, people will present opinions as facts, very strongly stated, with no tentativeness.
In my view, (the World Bank is a case in point.)	This is clearly the lecturer's opinion.
(The influence of the World Bank … has been) *very harmful*.	This is a continuation of 'In my view'.
A very good book … gives an interesting explanation (of how the World Bank …)	Whether something is 'good' or 'interesting' is always a matter of opinion.
… *actually* (benefits big business rather than a country's own people)	The lecturer means 'contrary to what most people think'. Again the lecturer is stating the case very strongly to persuade the listener.

Answers (for Exercise E)

Possible answer:

Review	Notes
Types of political influence are …?	1 <u>Political factors</u>: e.g., taxation policies, pressure groups, election results, protection thro' tariffs or quotas; foreign companies coming into country
Example of a political influence on business …?	a) election results, e.g., Margaret Thatcher's new government 1979 UK ➜ mid-1980s privatization ➜ new business opportunities esp. service sector ➜ manufacturing declined ➜ policy copied by other countries
Examples of pressure groups …?	b) pressure groups, e.g., i) Greenpeace: environment ➜ Shell lost 50% sales ii) Friends of the Earth: also environment; tries to control big businesses (e.g.,Tesco) iii) McDonald's law case ➜ negative image iv) Pure Food Movement (US 1906) ➜ new food laws
Some regional trade organizations are …? What happened in the EU …?	c) regional trade organizations, e.g., EU or Mercosur, or ASEAN: internal markets & protect members from competition: ➜ e.g., in 2005 Chinese textile imports into the EU ➜ clothes locked up until agreement reached ∴ fear for European jobs
Other political organizations which affect business …? Problem with World Bank …?	d) other organizations (signed up to by governments), e.g., World Bank, World Trade Organization • WTO ➜ the rules of trade between countries BUT • World Bank ➜ benefits big business not country's people
Economic influence on business …?	2 <u>Economic factors</u>: e.g., changing importance of different industrial sectors. Drucker ('The New Society' 2001):
Developed countries: decline in …?	• 1913: farm products = 70% of world trade. Now < ⅕ of economic activity
Growth in …?	• developed countries: = big ⬇ in contribution by agriculture to GDP = also manufacturing decline ➜ ⬆ in service industries
'New' economies: increase in …?	• 'new' economies: reduce farming ➜ ⬆ manufacturing (e.g., India & China) ➜ competition with developed countries
In future …?	• ? will China/ India, etc. ➜ dominate world economy instead of US?

Summary

There are many political influences on business. They include new governments, pressure groups and regional or other global organizations. Economic influences on business can be seen in the way economic activity has changed. In developed countries there is now an emphasis on service industries, while the new boom economies are increasing their manufacturing output. It's possible that these new economies will become more economically powerful than older developed economies such as the US.

🎧 Exercise G

Allow students time to read the phrases and the types of information, making sure that they understand any difficult words. Remind students that 'type' of information tells you what the speaker intends to do with the words. The words themselves are something different.

Ask students to try to match the phrases and types of information as far as they can. Note that it is not always possible to say what the function of a phrase is outside its context, so they may not be able to match all the phrases and information types before hearing the extracts. Note that some types of information are needed more than once.

When they have done as much as they can, play the extracts one at a time, allowing time for students to identify the type of information which follows. Check answers after each extract, making sure that students understand the information that actually follows the phrase. If possible students should also give the actual words.

Answers

Model answer:

	Fixed phrase	Type of information which follows the phrase
1	that is to say	restatement
2	Don't misunderstand me.	clarification
3	To some degree,	tentative point
4	it is fair to say that …	tentative point
5	Not only that, but …	another point
6	in an attempt to …	a purpose for speaking
7	to the extent that …	clarification
8	with respect to …	statement of a topic
9	… is a case in point	an example
10	… gives a good description of … in …	summary of a source
11	Briefly, (he) explains how …	summary of a source
12	(She) has no doubt that …	definite point

Transcript 🎧 2.11

Extract 1

I am going to try and explain some of the major factors which exert pressure on companies from the outside, that is to say, I shall mainly be looking at some different types of external influences which affect the way business operates.

Extract 2

Don't misunderstand me. I don't want to imply that there are no *internal* questions for a company.

Extract 3

To some degree, individual companies will be affected differently.

Extract 4

But it is fair to say that they will all have to keep an eye on which way inflation or interest rates are going.

Extract 5

Not only that, but the government policies of the country or countries where they operate.

Extract 6

So, in an attempt to try and keep the discussion of *external* pressures on business reasonably simple, I'm going to …

Extract 7

There is a clear overlap here between business and politics, to the extent that it is the government of a country that takes the decision on whether to be a member of an international trading group.

Extract 8

The evidence shows that this is especially true with respect to underdeveloped countries.

Extract 9

… the World Bank is a case in point.

Extract 10

Peter Drucker, … gives a good description of this in his article entitled 'The New Society' published in *The Economist* in 2001.

Extract 11

Briefly, in *The Economist* article, Drucker explains how at the beginning of the 20th century (in 1913) farm products accounted for 70% of world trade.

Extract 12

One writer in *Money Management* magazine has no doubt that, and I quote, 'China will continue to be a dominant player driving world growth, which will have flow through to other economies.'

Note

In Extract 9 the information *precedes* the phrase.

Exercise H

Use this section from the Cornell notes to demonstrate what to do:

Notes

<u>1 Political factors</u>: e.g., taxation policies, pressure groups, election results, protection thro' tariffs or quotas; foreign companies coming into country

(a) election results, e.g., Margaret Thatcher's new government 1979 UK

→   mid-1980s privatization

→   new business opportunities esp. service sector

→   manufacturing declined

→   policy copied by other countries

Elicit from the students suggestions on how to write up the notes in complete sentences. Write the suggestions on the board.

Ask students to say what they need to add in to the notes to make a good piece of writing: e.g.,

Grammar: relative pronouns, articles and determiners, prepositions, auxiliary verbs, linking words, 'there was/were' clauses (in italics in the model notes below).

Vocabulary: some vocabulary may need to be added, particularly where symbols are used in the notes, or where extra words are needed to make sense of the information or give a good sense of flow in the writing (in bold below).

Note that this of course works the other way: when making notes, these elements can be excluded from the notes.

Possible rewrite of the notes:

Political factors *which* **affect business include,** *for example,* taxation policies, pressure groups, election results, protection through tariffs or quotas and foreign companies coming into the country.

One **example** *of the* **effect** *of* election results *on* **business can be seen** *when* Margaret Thatcher's new government **came to power** *in* 1979 *in the* UK. *By the* mid 1980s *the* **process** *of* privatization *had* **begun.** *There were several* **results** *of this* **process.** *Firstly, there were many* new opportunities *for* business, *especially in the* service sector. *Secondly, the* manufacturing sector declined. *Also this* **new** policy *was* copied by other countries **around the world.**

Set another section for individual writing in class or for homework. Either ask students to refer to their own notes, or to the Cornell notes on page 104 of the Course Book.

Closure

1   Tell students to review and make a list of the main topics and arguments presented in this lesson. Then ask them to try and summarize the viewpoints, using some of the language they have practised.

2   They could also give a two-or three-sentence summary of anything that they themselves have read, e.g., *I read a useful article on X by Y. It said that …*

3   Ask students to do some research and to make a list of useful or interesting books/articles/websites on the topics in this lesson. They should draw up a list, including correct referencing, and share their sources with other students.

11.3 Extending skills

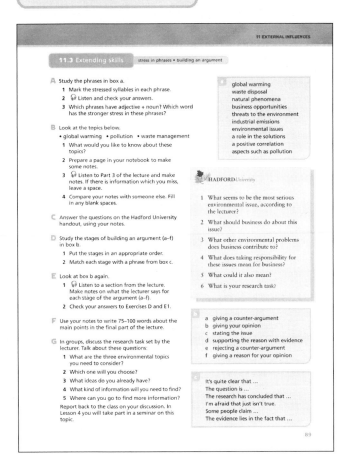

There is no question that (= certain)

We have to accept the evidence (= certain)

Some people claim that (= tentative)

What seems obvious is that (= certain)

As everyone is aware (= certain)

To some degree (= tentative)

This means ultimately that (= certain)

It's quite clear that (= certain)

We could argue that (= tentative)

🎧 Exercise A

1/2 Set for individual work and pairwork checking. This is an exercise in perceiving rhythm. At this point there is no need to distinguish between different levels of stress. Students can underline all the stressed syllables. They will also need to count all the syllables.

Feed back with the whole class, checking pronunciation of the phrases and meanings.

3 Discuss this with the class first. Demonstrate with ˌglobal ˈwarming, showing how if you say ˈglobal ˌwarming, it appears that a contrast is being made with another type of warming. Tell students that the usual pattern for the adjective + noun phrase is for a heavier stress to go on the noun. *Waste disposal* is, however, different: it is a compound made from a noun + noun, and the stress is: ˈwaste disˌposal – i.e., the heavier stress goes on the first noun. Set students to pick out the other adjective plus noun patterns, writing each one on the board. Elicit the stress patterns and give students time to practise the phrases.

Answers

Model answers:

1/2 ˌglobal ˈwarming

ˈwaste disˌposal

ˌnatural pheˈnomena

ˈbusiness opporˌtunities

ˈthreats to the enˈvironment

inˌdustrial eˈmissions

enˌvironmental ˈissues

a ˈrole in the soˈlutions

a ˌpositive correˈlation

ˈaspects such as polˈlution

3 Adjective + noun (second word has stronger stress): global warming, natural phenomena, industrial emissions, environmental issues, a positive correlation

Lesson aims

- recognize stress patterns in noun phrases
- understand how to develop an argument
  stating the issue
  giving a counter-argument
  rejecting a counter-argument
  giving opinions, supporting opinions
- use more general academic words and phrases mainly used in speaking

Further practice in:

- expressing degrees of confidence/tentativeness
- reporting back

Introduction

1 Revise the lecture in Lesson 2. Ask students to use the model Cornell notes. They should cover up the notes section and use the review and summary sections (which they completed in Lesson 2) to help recall the contents of the lecture. They could work in pairs to do this.

2 Revise phrases which express degrees of confidence in 'facts'. Dictate these phrases. Do they show that the speaker is certain or tentative?

Transcript 🎧 2.12

global 'warming

'waste dis,posal

,natural phe'nomena

'business oppor,tunities

'threats to the en'vironment

in,dustrial e'missions

en,vironmental 'issues

a 'role in the so'lutions

a ,positive corre'lation

'aspects such as pol'lution

🎧 Exercise B

1 Look at the three topics. Discuss with the class what they know already about these topics and find out what opinions they may have. Put students in pairs and ask each pair to write down one question to which they would like an answer in the lecture.

2 Set for individual work.

3 Play Part 3 straight through; students make notes.

4 Put students in pairs to compare their notes and fill in any gaps they may have.

Transcript 🎧 2.13

Part 3

Turning now to the issue of the effect of environmental issues on business ... of course, a major concern is the problem of global warming. If it's as serious as some people claim, then it is likely to have a great many implications for business.

So how serious a problem is it? First of all, there is no question that the Earth is heating up. We have to accept the evidence, such as the mean rise in temperatures, the melting of the polar ice-caps, the changing patterns in the habits of wildlife, and so on. But the real question is: is global warming the result of human activity? Some people claim, even some scientists have said, that it is nothing to do with humankind; it's the result of natural phenomena such as sunspots or volcano activity. But I'm afraid that just isn't true. It's quite clear that global warming is the direct result of human – especially business – activity. Most of the research into global warming has concluded that the burning of fossil fuels in the processes of industrialization is what is responsible. The evidence for this lies in the fact that there is a clear, positive correlation between the increase in the presence of CO_2 in the atmosphere and the rise in the Earth's temperature.

So if business is the cause, then business will have to be a part of the solution. Although some people may continue to claim that climate change is inevitable, what seems obvious is that business must play a key role trying to improve a dangerous situation – dangerous for the entire human race.

What's more, of course, we can see other threats to the environment from other aspects such as pollution, waste, and so on, many of which derive directly from the effects of the activities of business. As everyone is aware, emissions from industry are often toxic and can damage both human and animal health as well as the environment generally. Waste disposal is becoming an ever more serious problem too. It's just not possible any more to put all our garbage in a hole in the ground. Attitudes to waste – not just from industrial processes but also waste from the service industries – need to change radically.

When we look at environmental concerns such as these, the big question is how are we going to manage these problems? What strategies need to be put into place to help control CO_2 emissions, pollution and waste disposal? To some degree, as I've said, business must take responsibility for what is happening and must do something about it. This means ultimately that business must bear the costs of the changes that are necessary.

On the other hand, rather than being a threat, perhaps we should think about whether environmental issues actually offer business something positive too. Can business actually benefit from the steps which will be needed? We could argue that possible environmental solutions offer many business opportunities. For example, environment consultants can use their knowledge to advise companies; companies can develop environmental initiatives which appeal to consumers and boost sales; some measures, such as recycling, may actually result in lower business costs; and so on.

Now I'm going to set you a task which will involve investigating some of the points I've raised. I want you to do some research into which areas of business might actually be able to benefit from the changes which are going to be necessary for the environment. I want you to focus, firstly, on some of the new plans, methods and technologies for dealing with environmental problems, with respect to the environmental categories I've mentioned. Secondly, I'd like you to think about whether these methods and plans to save the environment could actually benefit business in the future or whether they will mainly affect business in a negative way.

Exercise C

Set for individual work and pairwork checking. Feed back with the class on question 6 to make sure that it is clear.

Answers

Model answers:

1 Global warming.
2 Business should play a key role in trying to solve the problems.
3 Pollution and waste.
4 Bearing the costs.
5 Opportunities for business.
6 Firstly, examine the new plans, methods and technologies which exist for dealing with global warming/pollution/waste; and secondly, decide whether business could benefit from these methods and plans or whether it will be negatively affected.

Exercise D

1 Set for pairwork discussion. Explain that a 'counter-argument' means an opinion which you do not agree with or think is wrong. 'Issue' means a question about which there is some debate.
2 Set for individual work and pairwork checking.

Do not feed back with the class at this point but move on to Exercise E.

🎧 Exercise E

1 Play the extract. Tell students to stop you when they hear each item. Make sure students can say exactly what the words are in each case. Ask them also to paraphrase the words so that it is clear that they understand the meanings.
2 If necessary, play the extract again for students to check that they have the phrases and types of statement correct.

Answers

Model answers for Exercises D and E:

Type of statement	Phrase	Lecturer's words
c stating the issue	The question is …	The real question is: is global warming the result of human activity?
a giving a counter-argument	Some people claim …	Some people claim … it is nothing to do with humankind …
e rejecting a counter-argument	I'm afraid that just isn't true.	I'm afraid that just isn't true.
b giving your opinion	It's quite clear that …	It's quite clear that global warming is the direct result of … business activity.
f giving a reason for your opinion	The research has concluded that …	The research … has concluded that the burning of fossil fuels in the processes of industrialization is what is responsible.
d supporting the reason with evidence	The evidence lies in the fact that …	The evidence lies in the fact that there is a clear positive correlation between the increase in the presence of CO_2 in the atmosphere and the rise in the Earth's temperature.

Language note

A common way in which an argument can be built is to give a counter-argument, then reject the counter-argument with reasons and evidence. There are, of course, other ways to build an argument. For example, the counter-arguments may be given after the writer/speaker's own opinion. Or all the arguments against may be given followed by all the arguments for an issue (or vice versa), concluding with the speaker/writer's own opinion.

Transcript 🎧 2.14

But the real question is: is global warming the result of human activity? Some people claim, even some scientists have said, that it is nothing to do with humankind; it's the result of natural phenomena such as sunspots or volcano activity. But I'm afraid that just isn't true. It's quite clear that global warming is the direct result of human – especially business – activity. Most of the research into global warming has concluded that the burning of fossil fuels in the processes of industrialization is what is responsible. The evidence for this lies in the fact that there is a clear, positive correlation between the increase in the presence of CO_2 in the atmosphere and the rise in the Earth's temperature.

Exercise F

Set for individual work – possibly homework – or else a pair/small group writing task. If the latter, tell students to put their writing on an OHT or other visual medium, so that the whole class can look and comment on what has been written. You can correct language errors on the OHT.

Exercise G

Set students to work in groups of three or four. Make sure they understand that they should choose to focus on one of the three topics: global warming, pollution or waste. Allow each group to choose their topic. Make sure that each topic is covered by at least one, preferably two groups. Ask one person from each group to present the results of the group's discussion.

Tell the class that they should carry out research into their group's topic. You will also need to arrange the date for the feedback and discussion of the information – this is the focus of Exercise G in Lesson 4.

Closure

Arguments, counter-arguments and giving opinions

Before you ask students to look at the statements below, tell them they should think about the methods listed above which can be used to build an argument. Then ask them to think about whether they agree with the statements below. They should prepare a brief summary of their viewpoints on the topics; they should also try and use some of the phrases used in this lesson.

1 Business is responsible for most of the world's pollution – therefore it should pay the bill to clean it up.

2 Space exploration is a waste of money which could be better spent on the environment.

3 Low inflation is the best indicator of economic stability.

4 Politics is not important in business.

5 All businesses should use English because it is an international language.

6 Global warming is inevitable and there is nothing anyone can do about it.

7 Business needs to be involved in all aspects of environmental strategy.

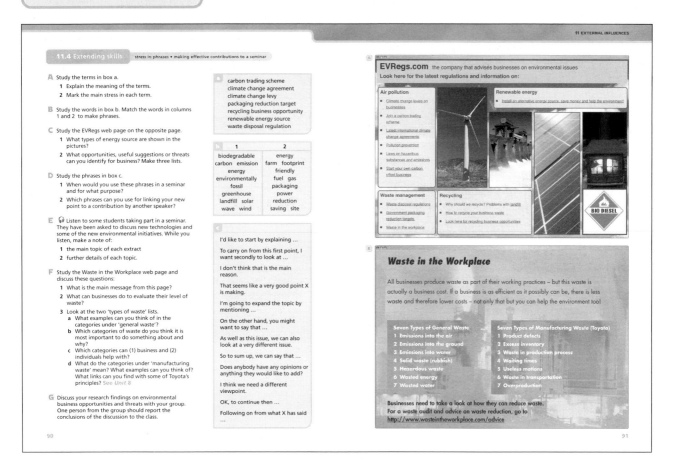

Lesson aims

- recognize stress in compound phrases
- link contribution to previous contributions when speaking in a seminar
- understand vocabulary in the area of environmental issues

Further practice in:

- taking part in seminars:
  introducing, maintaining and concluding a contribution
  agreeing/disagreeing with other speakers

Introduction

1 Remind students that they are going to be presenting their research findings later in this lesson. Check that they can remember the main points from Lesson 3 lecture extracts; key phrases from the lecture could be used as prompts, e.g.,

   So how serious a problem is it? (evidence of human and business activity)

   Business will have to be a part of the solution (i.e., a key role in trying to improve a dangerous situation)

   Other threats to the environment (e.g., pollution, waste, emissions)

   The big question is … (how are we going to manage these problems?)

   But the real question is… (is global warming the result of human activity?)

2 The following activity is a good way to check that students are familiar with the terminology and vocabulary from Lesson 3. Ask students to write down 5–10 words or expressions from the previous lesson relating to the environment and the current problems. Then use two or three students as 'secretaries'. Ask the class to dictate the words so that the secretaries can write the vocabulary on the board. Use this as a brainstorming session.

Exercise A

These are more complex noun phrases than in Lesson 3, since they are made up of three words. In some cases the pattern is noun + noun + noun. In this case, there may be a compound made from the first two nouns, or the last two nouns. In other cases, the pattern is adjective + noun + noun, in which the second and third words make a compound. These patterns should become clear once the meaning is understood.

1 Discuss *climate change levy* with the class as an example. Elicit that it is a levy (or tax) imposed to cover the cost of climate change. Set the remaining phrases for individual work and pairwork discussion. Feed back with the whole class, writing each phrase on the board and underlining the words which make a compound noun.

2 Tell students to try to identify where the main stress should come in each phrase. (Note that it will fall on the first element of the compound in each case. There will, of course, be secondary stresses on the other stressed syllables.) Demonstrate with *climate change levy*: *climate change* is a compound noun. Although it is acting in an adjectival role, the first noun will carry the main stress in the phrase: '*climate change levy*.

Tell students only to identify the syllable on which the heaviest stress in the phrase falls.

Answers

Model answers:

'<u>carbon trading</u> scheme	a plan for trading carbon emissions
'<u>climate change</u> agreement	an agreement between the countries of the world in order to try to prevent climate change
'<u>climate change</u> levy	a tax to cover the cost of climate change
'<u>packaging reduction</u> target	a target for packaging reduction, i.e., to reduce amount of packaging used for goods
recycling '<u>business opportunity</u>	a business opportunity in the field of recycling
renewable '<u>energy source</u>	an energy source that is renewable
'<u>waste disposal</u> regulation	a regulation for waste disposal

Language note

Stress placement, especially in complex compound noun phrases, is notoriously unstable. Stress may often move, depending on the context: for example, *bad-'tempered* – but '*bad-tempered 'teacher*. It's also possible that some native speakers may not agree about some of the phrases above. The main point is to try to notice where the main stresses fall.

Exercise B

Set for individual work and pairwork checking. Tell students that although in some cases it will be possible to make a phrase with more than one option, they must use each word once, and they must use all the words.

Feed back with the whole class. Check that the meaning of the phrases is understood. Check pronunciation.

Answers

Model answers:

biodegradable	packaging
carbon	footprint
emission	reduction
energy	saving
environmentally	friendly
fossil	fuel
greenhouse	gas
landfill	site
solar	energy
wave	power
wind	farm

Language note

Although in most noun–noun compounds the main stress comes on the first element, there are some compounds where this is not true. Definitive pronunciation of compounds can be found in a pronunciation dictionary.

Exercise C

Refer students to web page A. Set for pair or small group discussion. In question 2, students should identify which points can help companies reduce costs or may involve them in more costs.

Answers

1 Wind, hydro, solar, biofuel.

2 Possible answers:

Suggestions (to help companies reduce costs)
- join a carbon trading scheme
- use renewable energy: solar, wind, hydro and biofuel energy sources
- recycle business waste
- reduce waste in the workplace

Opportunities (possibilities to make some money)
- business opportunities in recycling
- start a carbon offset business

Threats (likely to involve extra costs)
- climate change levies on businesses
- latest international climate change agreements
- pollution prevention
- laws on hazardous substances and emissions
- waste disposal regulations
- government packaging reduction targets
- problems with landfill

Exercise D

This is mainly revision. Set for individual work or pairwork discussion. Feed back with the whole class.

Answers

Possible answers:

I'd like to start by explaining …
= beginning

To carry on from this first point, I want secondly to look at …
= maintaining/continuing a point

I don't think that is the main reason.
= disagreeing

That seems like a very good point X is making.
= confirming

I'm going to expand the topic by mentioning …
= adding a new point to someone else's previous contribution

On the other hand, you might want to say that …
= disagreeing

As well as this issue, we can also look at a very different issue.
= adding a new point to someone else's previous contribution

So to sum up, we can say that …
= summarizing/concluding

Does anybody have any opinions or anything they would like to add?
= concluding

I think we need a different viewpoint.
= disagreeing

OK, to continue then …
= maintaining/continuing a point

Following on from what X has said …
= adding a new point to someone else's previous contribution

🎧 Exercise E

Before students listen, tell them to look at the exercise and questions. Check that students understand the topic for the seminar discussion. Ask them what they might expect to hear.

Play each extract one at a time and ask students to identify the main topic and some further details. Feed back with the whole class.

Answers

Model answers:

	Main topic	Further details
Extract 1	new technologies	wind power, wave power, solar power, hydroelectric power, biofuels
Extract 2	new environmental initiative – carbon trading	carbon credits, carbon market
Extract 3	carbon offset	carbon offset credits, carbon footprint
Extract 4	zero waste	get rid of 'Take, Make, Waste'. Instead adopt 'Waste Equals Resource' principle

Transcript 🎧 2.15

Extract 1

MAJED: The lecturer we listened to last week introduced a number of interesting issues. In my part of the seminar, I would like to build on what he said and talk about a number of new technologies which have recently been introduced as alternatives to fossil fuels: these include wind, wave and solar power. It's obvious that these depend to some extent on the climate and on where a country is located but there is a lot of scope for development (although some people dislike the impact on the countryside, for example, of wind-farms). Hydroelectric power is also an important source that has been around for quite a long time in countries such as Norway, where they have a lot of snow and heavy rainfall. And of course, there's also the idea of biofuels, which are anything based on vegetable matter, such as wood, corn, etc., which we can use for heating and to replace petrol.

Extract 2

EVIE: OK, following on from what Majed has said, I'd like to mention some important environmental initiatives. You can see that as a result of global warming and because of worries about the environment a new form of trading between companies has been created. This is usually called 'carbon trading'. Basically, what this means is that companies have an allowance for carbon emissions. If they create pollution beyond these emissions, that is, if they are heavy polluters, then they will have to buy 'carbon credits' from those companies who pollute less than their allowances (if they do not do this they will face heavy penalties). This is what is known as the carbon 'trade'. So, what this means is that one company can be fined for creating pollution, while another may be rewarded if it reduces carbon emissions. The idea is to reduce overall production of greenhouse gases. Several trading systems already exist, the biggest of which is the one in the EU. The 'carbon market' is getting more popular in business circles as a way to manage climate change.

Extract 3

JACK: Right. Thank you, Evie. I'm going to expand the topic by mentioning another important initiative. What is usually called 'carbon offset' is similar in many ways to the concept of carbon trading. Carbon offsetting involves the calculation of your carbon footprint and then depending on the result, the possible purchase of 'carbon offset credits' from emission reduction projects. Let me try and make this clearer with an example. For instance, if you travel a lot by plane then you might need to offset your carbon footprint by some more environmentally friendly green action such as reducing your energy levels in your house or not using your car so much. Several companies already exist to advise on and manage this: for example, carbonfootprint.com.

Extract 4

LEILA: As well as carbon issues we can also look at a very different sort of initiative. Here, I'm going to explain about the concept and philosophy of zero waste. Zero waste has been around for a while; basically, it is a strategy which looks for inefficiencies in the way materials are produced, packaged, used and disposed of. As well as community, home and school programmes, there are business and industrial opportunities, for example in the design of products, maximization of energy use, and improved efficiency methods. The aim is to remove the 'Take, Make, Waste' principle which we have at present and to replace it with the 'Waste Equals Resource' cyclical approach. This would help to remove all waste from the environment. Zero waste aims to promote industrial, social and domestic ecology via a concerted effort (for example, through education in schools and colleges).

Exercise F

1/2 Set for pairwork. Tell students to study the Waste in the Workplace web page (B). Feed back with the whole class.

3 Set for small group discussion. Feed back with the whole class.

   a Students should consider a wide variety of contexts:
      - in the school environment: There is energy waste (heat, light, power) and solid waste (paper, food, containers).
      - in the home and in daily life: How much attention do people pay to waste? What do they throw away and why? How much do they recycle?
      - in businesses: What examples can students give of waste produced by businesses?

   b/c Students should make lists and then try and prioritize their list. For example, types of waste could be household, industrial, dangerous, and so on.

   d Note that Unit 8 dealt with management and managing efficiency. If necessary, students can look back at this unit. Make sure students understand the terminology in the web page. Students should consider the processes involved in producing a car (or any other industry that they are familiar with) and try to give examples of what each of the seven manufacturing waste categories might mean.

Answers

Possible answers:

1 Waste is both an environmental problem and a business expense. Reducing waste will not only help the environment but will reduce business costs.

2 They can have an 'audit' done, i.e., an evaluation of the waste in their business; and they can get advice on how to deal with it.

3 d Product defect: cars don't work well and have to be repaired/replaced (*poka-yoke, jidoka, kaizen*).

      Excess inventory: too much stock held, involving unnecessary expense (*Just in Time, kaizen*).

      Waste in production process: materials are left unused in the manufacturing process, or there are unnecessary processes (lean production).

      Waiting times: not all parts are ready and there on time to keep workers productive; customers waiting a long time for cars to be produced.

      Useless motions: too many movements involved, thus wasting time (lean production).

      Waste in transportation: goods are transported over long distances; transport is inefficient, e.g., old trucks.

      Overproduction: too many cars are made which cannot be sold, and they have to be stored or taken somewhere else.

Exercise G

In their groups students should now present their research findings on the business opportunities or threats of environmental concerns to the rest of the group. Remind them that the task was to:

- investigate the new plans, methods and technologies which exist for dealing with global warming/pollution/waste
- decide whether business could benefit from these methods and plans or whether business would be negatively affected

Encourage students to use the seminar language practised in this unit and earlier. In addition, students can, of course, make use of the information in Lesson 4. They should be looking at, or at least mentioning, some or all of the following:

- explaining the issues: climate change (global warming, CO_2 emissions, etc), waste and pollution, and the rules and regulations that may (or have already) come into force
- mentioning causes: traffic, people, pollution, industry, developed/developing countries
- saying what business needs to think about (the aspects which currently cause problems): transport, packaging, wasteful processes, etc.
- suggesting ways that new businesses might be able to benefit:

  needs analysis

  advice and consultancy: selling advice, producing information, setting up examples of waste management

  zero waste opportunities: zero packaging

  products: e.g., solar, wind, water storage, energy efficiency in households (e.g., lights), energy saving products (e.g., batteries, phones, computers)

  energy monitoring: tracking what you are doing

  awareness raising, education and training: training courses, websites, packs for education

As a group students should try to come to an overall conclusion. This conclusion should be presented to the rest of the class, together with supporting evidence from students' own research.

Closure

Ask students to imagine that they are 10–15 years in the future. What differences do they think there will be in the environment and the way it is treated? How will situations have changed? Ask them to think about the following:

landfill site

coal-fired power station

wind farm on a mountain

wave power in the ocean

crowded airport

traffic jam

domestic rubbish, e.g., wheelie bin

company website

1 Work through the *Vocabulary bank* and *Skills bank* if you have not already done so, or as revision of previous study.

2 Use the *Activity bank* (Teacher's Book additional resources section, Resource 11A).

   A Set the wordsearch for individual work (including homework) or pairwork.

   Answers

   Possible phrases:

carbon offsetting	climate change
energy conservation	environmentally friendly
global warming	industrial pollution
lean production	solar power
wind farm	zero waste

   B Set for individual work (including homework) or pairwork. Check students understand meanings.

   Possible answers

   demographic changes

   elderly employees

   European Union

   immigrant workforce

   labour force

   skilled labour

   United Nations

   youth market

3 Tell students to add other words to each of the words below to make as many two-word phrases as possible. Elicit one or two examples, then set for individual work or pairwork.

- carbon
- environmental
- waste

Possible phrases:

carbon trading, carbon footprint, carbon offset(ting), carbon dioxide, carbon market

environmental issues, environmental concerns, environmental pressure group, environmental action

waste management, waste reduction, business waste, zero waste

4 Use an extended activity to allow students to practise some of the concepts they have studied in this unit. Tell students to work in groups. They are going to design a zero-waste process – the product is a teaspoon. Students need to think about the materials, the sources, the location, transport and so on. Divide the activities into stages as follows:

   a Identify the various stages involved in producing a spoon from the beginning to the end, e.g., the raw materials, the production, the transportation, the marketing, the distribution, the retail selling.

   b The groups should make specific suggestions for:

- the raw materials and where they are going to come from
- the location of the production plant
- how they will transport materials and the finished product
- aspects such as the workforce, packaging, delivery, etc.
- waste systems from the factory (energy, waste disposal, recycling, etc.)
- how they will try and ensure zero-waste systems across the whole process (management strategies)

   c Draw up a flow plan showing the various stages of the product process – make sure that zero-waste factors are included at each stage. (Plans can be put onto A2 sheets, flipcharts or another visual medium and displayed for other groups to compare.)

12 STRATEGY AND CHANGE

This unit provides an opportunity for revision of many of the concepts and vocabulary items used in the book. It features a case study of a transport company that is losing market share; reasons for this are analyzed and possible solutions put forward for discussion.

Skills focus

Reading

- understanding how ideas in a text are linked

Writing

- deciding whether to use direct quotation or paraphrase
- incorporating quotations
- writing research reports
- writing effective introductions/conclusions

Vocabulary focus

- verbs used to introduce ideas from other sources (*X contends/suggests/asserts that ...*)
- linking words/phrases conveying contrast (*whereas*), result (*consequently*), reasons (*due to*), etc.
- words for quantities (*a significant minority*)

Key vocabulary

absenteeism	franchise (n)	questionnaire
annual turnover	interest rates	random sample
bid (v)	internationalization	redundancy
case study	interviewee	respondent
contract (n)	interviewer	sales trend
customer care	joint venture	state-run
cut-price	lease (n and v)	stock inventory
data	market leader	stock market flotation
distribution channel	market size	SWOT analysis
diversification	national operator	transport network
economic cycle	privatization	
findings	product range	

12.1 Vocabulary

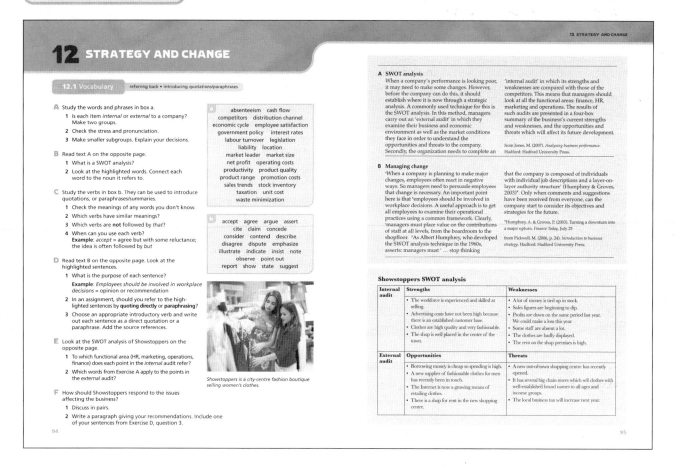

General note

Read the *Vocabulary bank* at the end of the Course Book unit. Decide when, if at all, to refer your students to it. The best time is probably at the very end of the lesson or the beginning of the next lesson, as a summary/revision.

Lesson aims

- understand deictic reference – pronouns and determiners
- refer to sources: the choice of introductory verb and stance of writer towards reference
- choose whether to quote or paraphrase

Further practice in:

- words and phrases from the discipline

Introduction

1 Revise the following words and phrases from the two previous units. Ask students to say which grammar class the words belong to and to provide definitions of them.

insolvency (n C/U)

bankruptcy (n C/U)

plummet (v)

inventory (n C)

insignificant (adj)

equity (n U/C)

demographic (adj, n C)

segment (n C, v)

levy (n C, v)

renewable (adj)

trade (v, n C/U)

2 Introduce the topic of the unit: write the words *strategy* and *change* on the board. Ask students: what do these signify for businesses? What factors do businesses need to take into consideration when they are thinking about strategy and change? What processes will they need to go through in order to decide their plans for the future? Have a class discussion on what businesses need to consider when they are thinking about future development. Accept any reasonable suggestions. Do not elaborate but tell students that this will be the topic of this unit.

Exercise A

1/2 Set for pairwork. Warn students that they may find that some words can be both *internal* and *external*. Ask students to mark the most strongly stressed syllable in compounds.

Feed back with the whole class, checking meanings.

3 Set for individual work and pairwork checking. Feed back with the whole class. Accept any groupings as long as they can be justified. Make sure the groupings below are also understood.

Answers

Model answers:

Internal	'cash flow lia'bility net 'profit 'operating costs 'unit cost	finance
	absen'teeism employee satis'faction labour 'turnover	HR
	lo'cation 'product quality* 'product range* pro'motion costs 'sales trends*	marketing
	produc'tivity 'product quality* 'stock inventory waste minimi'zation	operations
External	economic 'cycle government 'policy 'interest rates legis'lation tax'ation	political and economic factors
	com'petitors distri'bution channel market 'leader market 'size 'product range* 'sales trends*	market conditions

*these can go in more than one category

Exercise B

Introduce the idea of textual cohesion, created by referring back to words or ideas already mentioned with pronouns such as *it* and *this* (pronouns and determiners/deictics). Say that this an important way in which the sentences in a text are 'held together'. In reading and understanding it is important to know what is being referred to by such words.

You can build up the answers to question 2 by copying Resource 12B in the additional resources section onto an OHT or other visual medium.

Set for individual work and pairwork checking. Feed back with the whole class. Establish why a writer might use a particular referring word (see table on next page).

Answers

Model answers:

1 A technique which enables a company to evaluate itself by analysing Strengths, Weaknesses, Opportunities and Threats.

2 **SWOT analysis**

When a company's performance is looking poor, **it** may need to make some changes. However, before **the** company can do **this**, it should establish where it is now through a strategic analysis. A commonly used technique for **this** is the SWOT analysis. In **this** method, managers carry out an 'external audit' in which **they** examine **their** business and economic environment as well as the market conditions **they** face in order to understand the opportunities and threats to the company. Secondly, the organization needs to complete an 'internal audit' in which **its** strengths and weaknesses are compared with **those** of the competitors. **This** means that managers should look at all the functional areas: finance, HR, marketing and operations. The results of **such audits** are presented in a four-box summary of the business's current strengths and weaknesses, and the opportunities and threats which will affect **its** future development.

Word	Refers to	Comments
the + noun	a previously mentioned noun	one of several ways in which choice of article is governed
it, they	a noun	generally refers to the nearest suitable noun previously mentioned or the subject of the previous sentence
its, their	a previously mentioned noun, indicating possession	other possessive pronouns used in text for reference: *his, her, hers, theirs,* etc.
this	an idea in a phrase or a sentence	• often found at the beginning of a sentence or a paragraph; a common mistake is to use 'it' for this purpose • also used with prepositions (e.g., *for this*)
this/these + noun	a previously mentioned noun/ noun phrase	also used with prepositions (e.g., *in this method*)
those	a previously mentioned noun/ noun phrase	• also used with prepositions • In this text 'those of the competitors' means 'the strengths and weaknesses of the competitors'; there is no need to repeat 'strengths and weaknesses'. *Those of* + noun is a useful construction to learn. • *Those* – not *these* – is used to show distance between the writer/speaker and the objects/concepts themselves.
such + plural noun	a previously mentioned noun	Meaning is: 'Xs like this'. Note that when referring to a singular noun, 'such a X' is used (e.g., *in such a situation*).

Language note

Clearly, in this text, there are also relative pronouns which refer back to previously mentioned nouns in relative clauses. However, the grammar of relative pronouns is not covered here.

This is a complex area of written language. The reference words here are commonly found and arguably students should be able to use them in their writing. There are, of course, various other ways to refer back to a word or idea, such as when comparing: *the former ... the latter ...; some ... others ... .*

For more on this, see a good grammar reference book.

Exercise C

1-3 Set for individual work or pairwork. Feed back. Discuss any differences of opinion in question 2 and allow alternative groupings, with reasonable justifications. Establish that not all the verbs have equivalents.

4 Discuss this with the whole class, building the table in the Answers section on the next page. Point out to students that the choice of introductory verb for a direct or indirect quote or a paraphrase or summary will reveal what they think about the sources. This is an important way in which, when writing essays, students can show a degree of criticality about their sources. Critically evaluating other writers' work is an important part of academic assignments, dissertations and theses.

Point out also that some verbs have a degree of markedness, that is, extra meaning or connotation (as in the final column).

Answers

Possible answers:

2 accept, agree, concede
argue, assert, claim, contend, insist
consider, note, observe, point out, state
disagree, dispute
illustrate, indicate, show

3/4 See table on next page.

Answers

Possible answers:

		Used when the writer …
accept	that	reluctantly thinks this idea from someone else is true
agree	that	thinks this idea from someone else is true
argue	that	is giving an opinion that others may not agree with
assert	that	is giving an opinion that others may not agree with
cite	+ noun	is referring to someone else's ideas
claim	that	is giving an opinion that others may not agree with
concede	that	reluctantly thinks this idea from someone else is true
consider	that	is giving his/her opinion
contend	that	is giving an opinion that others may not agree with
describe	how; + noun	is giving a description
disagree	that; with + noun	thinks an idea is wrong
dispute	+ noun	thinks an idea is wrong
emphasize	that	is giving his/ her opinion strongly
illustrate	how; + noun	is explaining, possibly with an example
indicate	that	is explaining, possibly with an example
insist	that	is giving an opinion that others may not agree with
note	that	is giving his/her opinion
observe	that	is giving his/her opinion
point out	that	is giving his/her opinion
report	that	is giving research findings
show	that	is explaining, possibly with an example
state	that	is giving his/her opinion
suggest	that; + gerund	is giving his/her opinion tentatively; or is giving his/her recommendation

Exercise D

Discuss with the students when it is better to paraphrase and when to quote directly. Refer to the *Skills bank* if necessary.

1/2 Set for individual work and pairwork checking. Feed back with the whole class.

3 Set for individual work. Remind students that if they want to quote another source but omit some words, they can use three dots (…) to show some words are missing.

Answers

Possible answers:

See table on next page.

Answers

Possible answers:

1-3

Original sentence	The writer is ...	Direct quote or paraphrase?	Suggested sentence
a When a company is planning to make major changes, employees often react in negative ways.	making a statement of fact	paraphrase	Pickwell (2006) points out that staff may be unhappy about possible changes in their company.
b ... employees should be involved in workplace decisions.	giving an opinion or recommendation	paraphrase	Pickwell (2006) argues that staff need to be consulted about any possible changes.
c ... managers must place value on the contributions of staff at all levels, from the boardroom to the shop floor.	giving a strong opinion	paraphrase with a direct quotation of the last seven words, which make a 'special' phrase.	Pickwell (2006) emphasizes the need to take everyone's views seriously 'from the boardroom to the shop floor' (p. 24).
d As Albert Humphrey ... asserts: managers must '... stop thinking that the company is composed of ... a layer-on-layer authority structure'	quoting from another writer; the other writer is making a strong statement	quote the other writer directly	Pickwell (2006) cites Humphrey, who insists that managers should '... stop thinking that the company is composed of ... a layer-on-layer authority structure' (Humphrey & Groves, 2003 pp.124–126)

Exercise E

This is an exercise in relating the vocabulary discussed in Exercise A to meanings in business. It will help prepare students for work later in the unit. Refer students to the picture and the SWOT analysis. Make sure they understand what Showstoppers is.

Set for pairwork discussion. Feed back with the whole class if necessary.

Answers

Possible answers:

1 Internal Audit

Strengths	Functional area	Weaknesses	Functional area
Workforce is experienced and skilled at selling.	HR	A lot of money is tied up in stock.	finance
Advertising costs have not been high because there is an established customer base.	marketing	Sales figures are beginning to dip.	finance/marketing
Clothes are high quality and very fashionable.	marketing/operations	Profits are down on the same period last year. The shop could make a loss this year.	finance
The shop is well placed in the centre of the town.	marketing	Some staff are absent a lot.	HR
		The clothes are badly displayed.	marketing
		The rent on the shop premises is high.	finance

Opportunities	Words from Exercise A	Threats	Words from Exercise A
Borrowing money is cheap so spending is high.	interest rates economic cycle	A new out-of-town shopping centre has recently opened.	competitors, location
A new supplier of fashionable clothes for men has recently been in touch.	product range	It has several big chain stores which sell clothes with well-established brand names to all ages and income groups.	competitors, market leader, product range
The Internet is now a growing means of retailing clothes.	distribution channel	The local business tax will increase next year.	taxation
There is a shop for rent in the new shopping centre.	location		

Exercise F

1 Set for pairwork discussion, followed by class discussion.

2 Before setting the students to write, tell them they should refer to text B in their answer.

Answers

Possible answers:

1 Accept any reasonable suggestions.

2 It is clear that Showstoppers' profitability is declining. This is probably because of the new shopping centre. But it is also clear that the staff need to have some training to improve their display skills and to increase their motivation to improve the absence problems. There are several possibilities that the business could consider, including moving to new premises, starting a new Internet retail operation, and starting a new line in men's clothes. However, Pickwell (2006) argues that staff need to be consulted about any possible changes. Therefore, I recommend that before any decisions are made, all the staff are asked about what they think should happen.

Closure

Ask students to think about their local high street or shopping centre or online stores. They should do the following (the exercise can be done in groups or pairs):

● List their favourite shops, the ones most used/visited, and so on; specify products, services, reasons for visiting, etc.

● Using this list, add what they like and don't like about the shops, plus any problems they have noticed or encountered with particular stores.

● Use the points they have listed above to create a SWOT framework – allocating each of the points in their list to the appropriate category in the SWOT framework.

● Finally, rank the companies/shops in some sort of order of excellence.

The object of the exercise is to look at SWOT from an informal, consumer viewpoint. It should also help to prime students for the questionnaires and the research reports in Lessons 3 and 4.

12.2 Reading

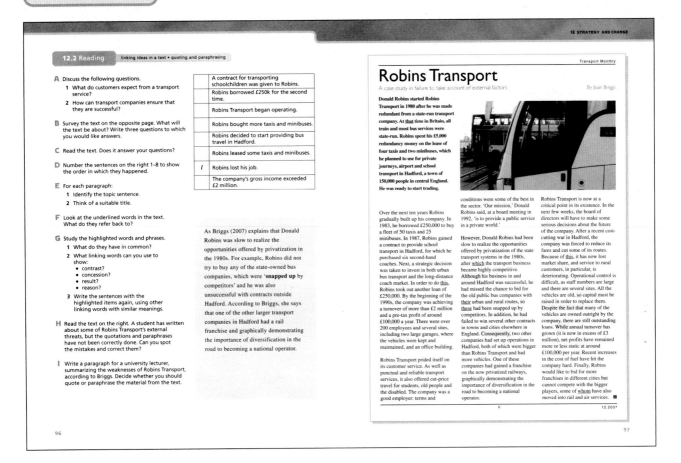

12.2 Reading   linking ideas in a text • quoting and paraphrasing

A Discuss the following questions.

1 What do customers expect from a transport service?

2 How can transport companies ensure that they are successful?

B Survey the text on the opposite page. What will the text be about? Write three questions to which you would like answers.

C Read the text. Does it answer your questions?

D Number the sentences on the right 1–8 to show the order in which they happened.

E For each paragraph:

1 Identify the topic sentence.

2 Think of a suitable title.

F Look at the underlined words in the text. What do they refer back to?

G Study the highlighted words and phrases.

1 What do they have in common?

2 What linking words can you use to show:
- contrast?
- concession?
- result?
- reason?

3 Write the sentences with the highlighted items again, using other linking words with similar meanings.

H Read the text on the right. A student has written about some of Robins Transport's external threats, but the quotations and paraphrases have not been correctly done. Can you spot the mistakes and correct them?

I Write a paragraph for a university lecturer, summarizing the weaknesses of Robins Transport, according to Briggs. Decide whether you should quote or paraphrase the material from the text.

	A contract for transporting schoolchildren was given to Robins.
	Robins borrowed £250k for the second time.
	Robins Transport began operating.
	Robins bought more taxis and minibuses.
	Robins decided to start providing bus travel in Hadford.
	Robins leased some taxis and minibuses.
1	Robins lost his job.
	The company's gross income exceeded £2 million.

As Briggs (2007) explains that Donald Robins was slow to realize the opportunities offered by privatization in the 1980s. For example, Robins did not try to buy any of the state-owned bus companies, which were '**snapped up** by competitors' and he was also unsuccessful with contracts outside Hadford. According to Briggs, she says that one of the other larger transport companies in Hadford had a rail franchise and graphically demonstrating the importance of diversification in the road to becoming a national operator.

Robins Transport

A case study in failure to take account of external factors   By Joan Briggs

Transport Monthly

Donald Robins started Robins Transport in 1980 after he was made redundant from a state-run transport company. At that time in Britain, all train and most bus services were state-run. Robins spent his £5,000 redundancy money on the lease of four taxis and two minibuses, which he planned to use for private journeys, airport and school transport in Hadford, a town of 150,000 people in central England. He was ready to start trading.

Over the next ten years Robins gradually built up his company. In 1983, he borrowed £250,000 to buy a fleet of 50 taxis and 25 minibuses. In 1987, Robins gained a contract to provide school transport in Hadford, for which he purchased six second-hand coaches. Next, a strategic decision was taken to invest in both urban bus transport and the long-distance coach market. In order to do this, Robins took out another loan of £250,000. By the beginning of the 1990s, the company was achieving a turnover of more than £2 million and a pre-tax profit of around £100,000 a year. There were over 200 employees and several sites, including two large garages, where the vehicles were kept and maintained, and an office building.

Robins Transport prided itself on its customer service. As well as punctual and reliable transport services, it also offered cut-price travel for students, old people and the disabled. The company was a good employer: terms and conditions were some of the best in the sector. 'Our mission,' Donald Robins said, at a board meeting in 1992, 'is to provide a public service in a private world.'

However, Donald Robins had been slow to realize the opportunities offered by privatization of the state transport systems in the 1980s. Although his business in and around Hadford was successful, he had missed the chance to bid for the old public bus companies with their urban and rural routes, so these had been snapped up by competitors. In addition, he had failed to win several other contracts in towns and cities elsewhere in England. Consequently, two other companies had set up operations in Hadford, both of which were bigger than Robins Transport and had more vehicles. One of these companies had gained a franchise on the now privatized railways, graphically demonstrating the importance of diversification in the road to becoming a national operator.

Robins Transport is now at a critical point in its existence. In the next few weeks, the board of directors will have to make some serious decisions about the future of the company. After a recent cost-cutting war in Hadford, the company was forced to reduce its fares and cut some of its routes. Because of this, it has now lost market share, and service to rural customers, in particular, is deteriorating. Operational control is difficult, as staff numbers are large and there are several sites. All the vehicles are old, so capital must be raised in order to replace them. Despite the fact that many of the vehicles are owned outright by the company, there are still outstanding loans. While annual turnover has grown (it is now in excess of £3 million), net profits have remained more or less static at around £100,000 per year. Recent increases in the cost of fuel have hit the company hard. Finally, Robins would like to bid for more franchises in different cities but cannot compete with the bigger players, some of whom have also moved into rail and air services. ∎

6   12.2007

General note

Read the *Vocabulary bank* and *Skills bank* at the end of the Course Book unit. Decide when, if at all, to refer students to them. The best time is probably at the very end of the lesson or the beginning of the next lesson, as a summary/revision.

Lesson aims

- understand rhetorical markers in writing (*but* and *so* categories)
- use direct quotations from other writers:

    common mistakes

    missing words

    fitting to the grammar of the sentence

    adding emphasis to a quote

    continuing to quote from the same source

Further practice in:

- indirect quotations/paraphrases/summaries
- summarizing with a series of topic sentences
- rhetorical markers (adding points)
- deictic reference and relative pronouns

Introduction

Revise the main SWOT concepts from Lesson 1. What does each letter stand for?

To prepare students for the lesson's theme, ask them to think of a journey they have made recently and to describe the transport system, the route, cost, value for money, time taken, the good things and the bad things about the journey.

Exercise A

Set for pairwork or class discussion. Accept any reasonable suggestions.

Answers

Possible answers:

1 Customers might expect: value for money; choice of routes and times; punctuality; frequency of service; quality of vehicles; safety; comfort.

2 As with all sectors, companies have to look for growth. They have to decide what their customers want from them; they have to deal with competition; and they have to make the most of the political and economic environment (deregulation/privatization, in particular, offers many opportunities for the private sector).

Exercise B

Remind students about surveying a text (skim-reading to get an approximate idea of the text contents by looking at the title, looking at the beginning few lines and the final few lines of the text, and by looking at the first sentence of each paragraph). Set for individual work and pairwork discussion. Each pair should agree three questions. Feed back with the whole class. Write some questions on the board.

Exercise C

Set for individual work followed by pairwork discussion. Feed back with the whole class. Ask whether the questions you have put on the board have been answered in the text.

Exercise D

Set for individual work and pairwork checking. This activity could also be done using Resource 12C in the additional resources section. Photocopy and cut up the sentences and hand them out in a jumbled order. Tell students to put them in the correct order.

Answers

Model answers:

5	A contract for transporting schoolchildren was given to Robins.
7	Robins borrowed £250k for the second time.
3	Robins Transport began operating.
4	Robins bought more taxis and minibuses.
6	Robins decided to start providing bus travel in Hadford.
2	Robins leased some taxis and minibuses.
1	Robins lost his job.
8	The company's gross income exceeded £2 million.

Exercise E

1/2 Set for individual work and pairwork discussion. The topic sentences should suggest a suitable title.

Answers

Possible answers:

	Topic sentence	Para title
Para 1	Donald Robins started Robins Transport in 1980 …	The beginning of Robins Transport
Para 2	Over the next ten years Robins gradually built up his company.	The development of Robins Transport
Para 3	Robins Transport prided itself on its customer service.	The company's mission
Para 4	However, Donald Robins had been slow to realize the opportunities offered by privatization of state transport systems in the 1980s …	Privatization and competition in the transport industry
Para 5	Robins Transport is now at a critical point in its existence.	Robins Transport's problems

Exercise F

Set for individual work and pairwork checking.

Answers

Model answers:

Word	Refers to
that	1980
this	investing in both urban bus transport and the long-distance coach market
which	the privatization of the state transport systems
their	the old public bus companies
these	the old public bus companies' urban and rural routes
this	the cost-cutting war in Hadford and the reduction in fares/routes
whom	the bigger players

Exercise G

1 Refer students to the highlighted words. Elicit that they are all linking words or phrases.

2 With the whole class, elicit from the students some linking words that can be used for:

- contrast and concession (i.e., words which have a *but* meaning)
- result and reason (i.e., words which have a *so* or *for* meaning)

Build the table at the bottom of this page on the board, reminding students of the difference between within- and between-sentence linkers (refer to Unit 11 *Vocabulary bank)*.

3 Set for individual work. Encourage students to rewrite the sentences using a different type of linking word from the original (i.e., swapping between- and within-sentence linkers).

Answers

Possible answers:

2 See table below.

3 *Nevertheless/At the same time/Despite this*, Donald Robins had been slow to realize the opportunities offered by privatization of the state transport systems in the 1980s, after which the transport business became highly competitive.

His business in and around Hadford was successful. *However*, he had missed the chance to bid for the old public bus companies with their urban and rural routes. *As a result*, these had been snapped up by competitors.

In addition, he had failed to win several other contracts in towns and cities elsewhere in England *so (that)/with the result that* two other companies had set up operations in Hadford, both of which were bigger than Robins Transport and had more vehicles.

OR

In addition, *as* he had failed to win several other contracts in towns and cities elsewhere in England, two other companies had set up operations in Hadford, both of which were bigger than Robins Transport and had more vehicles.

All the vehicles are old. *Therefore*, capital must be raised in order to replace them.

OR

All the vehicles are old. *Because of this*, capital must be raised in order to replace them.

Many of the vehicles are owned outright by the company. *Nevertheless*, there are still outstanding loans.

Annual turnover has grown (it is now in excess of £3 million). *On the other hand*, net profits have remained more or less static at around £100,000 per year.

Although Robins would like to bid for more franchises in different cities, he cannot compete with the bigger players, some of whom have also moved into rail and air services.

	Within-sentence linkers	Between-sentence linkers
Contrast (*but*) used when comparing	... but ... ... whereas ... ... while ...	However, ... In/By contrast, ... On the other hand, ...
Concession (*but*) used to concede/accept a point which simultaneously contrasts with the main point of a sentence or paragraph	... although ... ... despite/in spite of the fact that ...	However, ... At the same time ... Nevertheless, ... Despite/In spite of (this/noun), ... Yet ...
Result (*so*)	... , so ... ... so that ... ... with the result that ...	So, ... As a result, ... Consequently, ... Therefore, ...
Reason (*for*)	... because ... ... since ... ... as ... ... due to/owing to the fact that ...	Because of (this/noun), ... Owing to (this/noun), ... Due to (this/noun), ...

Language note

The first of these sentences is the beginning of a paragraph and the linker links to the previous paragraph. Therefore, a between-sentence linking word must be used.

Exercise H

Set for individual work and pairwork checking. Feed back with the whole class.

Answers

Model answers:

Corrected version	Comments
As Briggs (2007) explains,	Note the grammar here: either *As Briggs explains* or *Briggs explains that* but not both. This is a common mistake.
Donald Robins was 'slow to realize the opportunities offered by privatization … in the 1980s.'	1. The words which are the same as the original need quotation marks. 2. Some words have been left out. Where this happens three dots are used to signify an omission. It is important that a quote is exactly the same as the original. Any changes (such as omitting words) need to be clearly shown.
For example, Robins did not try to buy any of the state owned bus companies, which were '*snapped up* by competitors' [italics added] and he was also unsuccessful with contracts outside Hadford.	1. Note that much of the information here has been paraphrased – which is the better option for information. 2. If you want to emphasize a part of a quote, use italics and then put [italics added] after the quote.
Briggs (ibid.) further points out that	1. When continuing to refer to a source you can use *further* or *also* or other similar words; *says* is not a good choice of introductory verb since it is too informal. You do not need *according to* as well as a verb of saying. 2. When referring to the same place in the same source, use *ibid.* instead of the full source reference. If it is the same publication (but not the same place in the text), use *op. cit.*
one of the other larger transport companies in Hadford had a rail franchise, 'graphically demonstrating the importance of diversification in the road to becoming a national operator.'	1. It is important to make a quotation fit the grammar of a sentence. Failing to do this properly is a common mistake. 2. The quotation marks must be added to the words which are the same as the source.

Exercise I

Set for individual work, possibly for homework. Alternatively, set for pair or small group work. Students can write the paragraph on an OHT or other visual medium, which you can display and give feedback on with the whole class.

Answers

Possible answers:

It seems that Robins Transport has some serious weaknesses in its operation. For example, Briggs (2007) lists a number of problems facing the company. Firstly, as a result of pressure from competitors in Hadford, the company has lowered its prices and stopped some services. Consequently, the standard of service has become worse and its market share has gone down. Secondly, the operations management is experiencing problems because of the size of its staff and its location in several places. Another difficulty is that the vehicles need replacing. Briggs (ibid.) further points out that one of the main problems is finance: the company cannot expand as it would like to since profits have not grown with turnover. Briggs suggests that one reason for this might be petrol price increases. As Briggs puts it, Robins Transport is 'at a critical point in its existence' (p. 6) and its future is at stake.

Closure

Ask students to discuss these questions.

1 What other kinds of services or business activities can transport companies undertake if they want to expand or diversify?

2 Imagine you work for Robins Transport's marketing department and you want to find out what customers think about the company. What aspects of your service provision should you try to find out about?

Accept any reasonable suggestions.

12.3 Extending skills

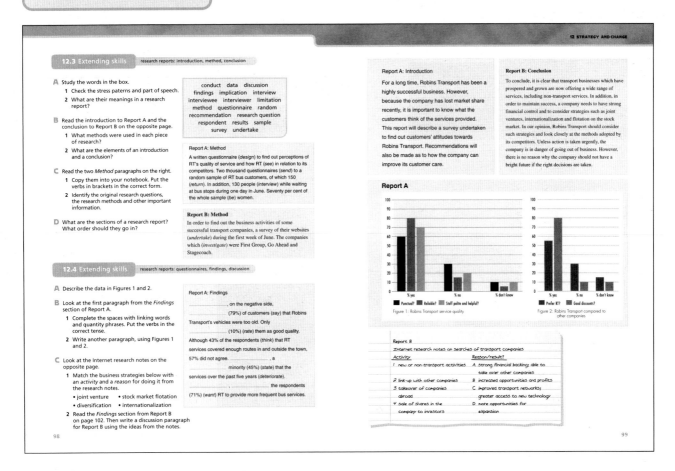

Lesson aims

- structure a research report:

  introduction

  method

  conclusion

Further practice in:

- essay structure
- research methods

Introduction

In preparation for looking at the structure of a research report, revise the sections for an essay: introduction, body, conclusion.

Ask students what should go in each section. Elicit ideas for introductions and conclusions. Do not correct at this point.

Remind students about the methods for doing research (see Unit 5). Ask students what kinds of research would be appropriate if you want to find out what customers think of a company's products or services. (Primary sources are best: survey, questionnaire, interview, quantitative and qualitative methods.)

Ask what sort of research would be appropriate if you

want to find out what business activities companies in a particular sector are involved in. (Secondary sources are the easiest, e.g., Internet research, company reports, trade magazines.)

Tell students that the next two lessons will focus on writing up research in reports. Ask for suggestions for suitable sections of a research report. Do not correct at this point.

Subject note

In the models presented here, the report is executed at a very simple level. For instance, in a real academic research report, there will be a literature review section before the methods section, and the research questions will be linked with this review. There are also different models for reports. For example, a business report (as opposed to an academic research report) may put conclusions and recommendations near the beginning and the findings as the final section.

Exercise A

Set for individual work and pairwork checking. Feed back with the whole class.

Answers

Model answers:

	Notes on stress patterns and parts of speech	Meaning in a research report
con'duct	v (noun is pronounced: 'conduct)	do (some research, a survey, an experiment)
'data	pl n	information; can be numerical (quantitative) or verbal (qualitative)
dis'cussion	n(U/C)	the title of the section in a research report which discusses the findings. Sometimes the discussion is included in the *Findings/Results* section
'findings	pl n	the title of the section in a research report which details what has been found out; each finding should be linked with a research question. The title *Results* can also be used for this section
impli'cation	n(C)	possible effect or result of the findings
'interview	n(C),v	noun: when someone is asked questions in a survey; verb: to ask someone questions in a survey
interview'ee	n(C)	the person being questioned
'interviewer	n(C)	the person asking the questions
limi'tation	n(C)	a problem with the research methods; an aspect which the research could not address
'method	n(C) methods used	title of the section in a research report which explains how the research was carried out. In the plural it refers to the research
questionn'aire	n(C)	a written set of questions
'random	adj	in no fixed order; with no organizing principle
recommen'dation	n(C)	suggestion for action as a result of the findings of the research
re'search ,question	n(C)	what the researcher wants to find out
re'spondent	n(C)	a person taking part in a questionnaire survey
re'sults	pl n	same as *Findings*. Used more or less interchangeably
'sample	n(C),v	the group of people taking part in the research
'survey	n(C),v documents or asking people questions	a type of research in which the researcher sets out to describe a situation or set of ideas or behaviours, by reading a variety of
under'take	v	do (some research, a survey)

Exercise B

Explain to the students that these are examples of a typical introduction and conclusion.

Set for pairwork discussion. Feed back with the whole class. Bring the class's attention to the tenses that are used here (present perfect, present simple, future) as well as the use of the passive.

Answers

Model answers:

1 Report A: Primary research. Probably questionnaire methods; perhaps interviews.

Report B: Probably secondary research, involving Internet searches or possibly company reports.

2 See table on next page.

Good introduction	Example sentences
Introduce the topic. Give some background information.	For a long time, Robins Transport has been a highly successful business.
Say why the topic is important.	However, because the company has lost market share recently, it is important to know what the customers think of the services provided.
Say what you will do in the report. Give a general statement of the purpose of the research.	This report will describe a survey undertaken to find out customers' attitudes towards Robins Transport. Recommendations will also be made as to how the company can improve its customer care.

Good conclusion	Example sentences
Give a general summary/restatement of findings.	To conclude, it is clear that transport businesses which have prospered and grown are now offering a wide range of services, including non-transport services. In addition, in order to maintain success, a company needs to have strong financial control and to consider strategies such as joint ventures, internationalization and flotation on the stock market.
Say what your recommendations are.	In our opinion, Robins Transport should consider such strategies and look closely at the methods adopted by its competitors.
Set out the implications of not taking action.	Unless action is taken urgently, the company is in danger of going out of business.
Comment on future possibilities if action is taken.	However, there is no reason why the company should not have a bright future if the right decisions are taken.

Language note

The impersonal use of the passive for research reports is not absolutely required. It is often possible to find students' work (assignments, dissertations) which contains the use of the first person singular. However, in more formal writing, such as in journal articles, the passive is usually used.

Exercise C

Explain to the students that these paragraphs are examples of the *Method* section of a research report.

1 Set for individual work. Ask students to copy the text into their notebooks and put the verbs into the correct form. Feed back with the whole class, drawing students' attention to the use of the past tense when reporting methods of research, as well as the use of the passive.

2 Set for individual work and pairwork checking. Tell students that they should transform the research questions into real, direct questions. Feed back with the whole group, pointing out that the information given in the *Method* section should include these types of details.

Answers
Possible answers:
See table on next page.

	Research questions	Research method	Other important information
Method (A) A written questionnaire (*design*) <u>was designed</u> to find out perceptions of RT's quality of service and how RT (*see*) <u>was seen</u> in relation to its competitors. Two thousand questionnaires (*send*) <u>were sent</u> to a random sample of RT bus customers, of which 150 (*return*) <u>were returned</u>. In addition, 130 people (*interview*) <u>were interviewed</u> while waiting at bus stops during one day in June. Seventy per cent of the whole sample (*be*) <u>were</u> women.	1. What are customers' perceptions of RT's quality of service? 2. How do customers see RT in relation to its competitors?	written questionnaire	2,000 questionnaires random sample of RT customers 150 returned
		interview	130 people interviewed in one day in June
			70% of whole sample = women
Method (B) In order to find out the business activities of some successful transport companies, a survey of their websites (*undertake*) <u>was undertaken</u> during the first week of June. The companies which (*investigate*) <u>were investigated</u> were First Group, Go Ahead and Stagecoach.	What business activities are successful transport companies engaged in?	Internet survey	done in first week of June 3 companies = First Group, Go Ahead and Stagecoach

Exercise D

Use this to confirm that students understand the organization of a research report. Elicit the answers from the whole class.

Answers

Model answers:

Section	Order in a research report
introduction	1
method	2
findings/results	3
discussion	4
conclusion	5

Sybject note

Different disciplines and reports for varying purposes may have different section names or organization. The model suggested here is a rather general one, and is a pattern commonly adopted in an academic context, though there are variations depending on the level of the writing (whether, for example, it is a master's or PhD dissertation). If students are going to write about 500 words only, you may wish to include *Discussion* with *Findings/Results* or with the *Conclusion*.

Closure

1 Refer students to the *Skills bank* to consolidate their understanding of the sections of a research report and their contents.

2 Ask students to choose a company into which they would like to carry out some customer research. They should think about aspects such as quality, service, reliability, customer perceptions, etc. What topics would they ask customers about in a questionnaire?

12.4 Extending skills

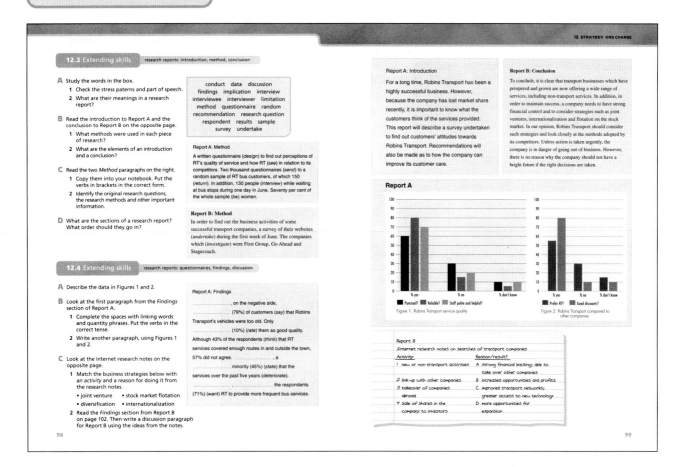

12.3 Extending skills — research reports: introduction, method, conclusion

A Study the words in the box.
1 Check the stress paterns and part of speech.
2 What are their meanings in a research report?

conduct   data   discussion
findings   implication   interview
interviewee   interviewer   limitation
method   questionnaire   random
recommendation   research question
respondent   results   sample
survey   undertake

B Read the introduction to Report A and the conclusion to Report B on the opposite page.
1 What methods were used in each piece of research?
2 What are the elements of an introduction and a conclusion?

C Read the two *Method* paragraphs on the right.
1 Copy them into your notebook. Put the verbs in brackets in the correct form.
2 Identify the original research questions, the research methods and other important information.

D What are the sections of a research report? What order should they go in?

Report A: Method

A written questionnaire (*design*) to find out perceptions of RT's quality of service and how RT (*see*) in relation to its competitors. Two thousand questionnaires (*send*) to a random sample of RT bus customers, of which 150 (*return*). In addition, 130 people (*interview*) while waiting at bus stops during one day in June. Seventy per cent of the whole sample (*be*) women.

Report B: Method

In order to find out the business activities of some successful transport companies, a survey of their websites (*undertake*) during the first week of June. The companies which (*investigate*) were First Group, Go Ahead and Stagecoach.

12.4 Extending skills — research reports: questionnaires, findings, discussion

A Describe the data in Figures 1 and 2.

B Look at the first paragraph from the *Findings* section of Report A.
1 Complete the spaces with linking words and quantity phrases. Put the verbs in the correct tense.
2 Write another paragraph, using Figures 1 and 2.

C Look at the Internet research notes on the opposite page.
1 Match the business strategies below with an *activity* and a reason for doing it from the research notes.
• joint venture   • stock market flotation
• diversification   • internationalization
2 Read the *Findings* section from Report B on page 102. Then write a discussion paragraph for Report B using the ideas from the notes.

Report A: Findings

_____, on the negative side, _____ (79%) of customers (*say*) that Robins Transport's vehicles were too old. Only _____ (10%) (*rate*) them as good quality. Although 43% of the respondents (*think*) that RT services covered enough routes in and outside the town, 57% did not agree. _____, a _____ minority (45%) (*state*) that the services over the past five years (*deteriorate*). _____, the respondents (71%) (*want*) RT to provide more frequent bus services.

Report A: Introduction

For a long time, Robins Transport has been a highly successful business. However, because the company has lost market share recently, it is important to know what the customers think of the services provided. This report will describe a survey undertaken to find out customers' attitudes towards Robins Transport. Recommendations will also be made as to how the company can improve its customer care.

Report B: Conclusion

To conclude, it is clear that transport businesses which have prospered and grown are now offering a wide range of services, including non-transport services. In addition, in order to maintain success, a company needs to have strong financial control and to consider strategies such as joint ventures, internationalization and flotation on the stock market. In our opinion, Robins Transport should consider such strategies and look closely at the methods adopted by its competitors. Unless action is taken urgently, the company is in danger of going out of business. However, there is no reason why the company should not have a bright future if the right decisions are taken.

Report A

Figure 1: Robins Transport service quality

Figure 2: Robins Transport compared to other companies

Report B
Internet research notes on searches of transport companies

Activity	Reason/result?
1 new or non-transport activities	A strong financial backing; able to take over other companies
2 link-up with other companies	B increased opportunities and profits
3 takeover of companies abroad	C improved transport networks; greater access to new technology
4 Sale of shares in the company to investors	D more opportunities for expansion

98

99

Lesson aims

● write part of a research report: findings and discussion

● analyze and use research data and information

Further practice in:

● using rhetorical markers for adding/listing points

● talking about numbers and quantities

Introduction

Write up the table below on the board. Give some example phrases and ask students to say approximately what percentage they represent, e.g., a large majority = 80% approximately?

	overwhelming large significant slight small insignificant tiny	majority	
A/An		minority	(of + noun)
		number	
Over		half a quarter a third	
More	than		
Less		x%	

Note that *of* is needed if the category for the numbers is given: *A slight minority of respondents said that* … but *A slight minority said that* …

Ask students: what is the difference between *many and most?*

Exercise A

Set students to work in pairs to talk about the key elements of the numbers shown in the charts. If you wish, ask students to write some sentences. Feed back with the whole class, writing some example sentences on the board. Ask the class what these results show about Robins Transport (some of its strengths).

Answers

Possible answers:

Figure 1

A majority (60%) of respondents said that Robins transport was punctual.

60% of respondents said the services were punctual.

A significant minority (30%) said the services were not punctual.

A very small minority replied that they did not know if the services were punctual or not.

227

Figure 2

55% of respondents said they preferred RT to other companies.

An overwhelming majority of respondents (80%) said they thought Robins Transport provided good discounts compared to other companies.

A small minority (10%) disagreed that Robins Transport provided good discounts.

Exercise B

1 Set for individual work and pairwork checking. Remind students about linking words when giving a list of points. Tell students that each space may be for more than one word. They will also need to practise the expressions they used for quantity in Exercise A.

Feed back with the whole class, pointing out the use of past tenses when reporting findings.

2 Set for individual work. Remind students to use linking words and to begin with a topic sentence. This paragraph continues the *Findings* section of Report A.

Answers

Possible answers:

Findings

1 Firstly, on the negative side, a large majority (79%) of customers (*say*) said that Robins Transport's vehicles were too old. Only a small minority (10%) (*rate*) rated them as good quality. Although 43% of the respondents (*think*) thought that RT services covered enough routes in and outside the town, 57% did not agree. In addition, a significant minority (45%) (*state*) stated that services over the past five years (*deteriorate*) had deteriorated. Finally, most of the respondents (71%) (*want*) wanted RT to provide more frequent bus services.

2 The survey also revealed some positive aspects. Firstly, a majority of the respondents said that the services were punctual (60%) and that the staff were polite and helpful (70%). Moreover, although a small minority considered that the services were unreliable, an overwhelming majority (80%) were satisfied with the reliability. Secondly, in comparison with other companies, a very large majority thought that the discounts were good. Finally, a slight majority (55%) preferred Robins Transport to other companies.

Exercise C

1 Tell students to look at the notes on the right-hand page. These are the results of a student's Internet searches about the activities of some transport companies (as in Report B). They need to find the strategy word for the activities given, and also find why a company might do these things. Note that more than one answer might be possible. Set for pairwork discussion.

2 Refer students to page 102 of the Course Book, which gives the findings for Report B.

Tell students that the *Discussion* section of a report is where they can give their opinions on their findings. They should write a paragraph using the ideas they discussed in question 1. Set for individual work.

Answers

Possible answers:

1

Strategy	Activity	Reason/result?
joint venture	2 link-up with other companies	C improved transport networks; greater access to new technology
diversification	1 new or non-transport activities	B increased opportunities and profits
stock market flotation	4 sale of shares in the company to investors	A strong financial backing; able to take over other companies
internationalization	3 takeover of companies abroad	D more opportunities for expansion

2 Discussion

It is clear is that these companies have strong financial backing through stock market flotation, which has enabled them to take over other companies. Internationalization has increased the opportunities for expansion, through the purchase of foreign companies. Joint ventures with other companies have also enabled the companies to improve their connections with other networks as well as helping with access to up-to-date technical developments. Furthermore, diversification into other areas of transport and non-transport activities has increased the opportunities for growth and profitability of these companies.

See also the discussion paragraph in the model report (Resource 12E in the additional resources section), which has a few extra ideas.

Closure

1 Ask students to finish the model reports from Lesson 4, i.e.:

- the *Discussion* and *Conclusion* sections of Report A (the questionnaire survey of Robins Transport customers)
- the *Introduction* section of Report B (the Internet survey of transport companies' business strategies, in relation to Robins Transport)

After completing the work, students can compare their reports with the models in additional resources section (Resources 12D and 12E).

If you wish, students could investigate the companies mentioned (or other transport companies) to see what other information they could find:

www.go-ahead.com/

www.firstgroup.com/

www.stagecoach.com/

2 Ask students to work out the original questions used in the Robins Transport customer survey.

First, suggest some question types for questionnaires. Elicit the following:

- yes/no
- multiple choice
- open-ended

Tell students to concentrate on the *yes/no* or multiple choice types (open-ended questions will elicit qualitative information which is often hard to analyze) and to look at the data in Figures 1 and 2 and the sample *Findings* paragraph. They should try to formulate the actual questions given in the customer survey questionnaire.

Set for pairwork. Feed back with the whole class, writing examples of good questions up on the board. Refer to the model questionnaire in the additional resources section (Resource 12F).

3 Set a research report based on a questionnaire survey for homework. Students can use the ideas they have already discussed in this unit. They should write questionnaires, carry out the research amongst a suitable group of customers (20–40 respondents is fine) and then write up the report. See extra activity 4 for suggestions for topics.

Alternatively, students could choose to find out what the business activities of several global companies in the same sector are.

1 Work through the *Vocabulary bank* and *Skills bank* if you have not already done so, or as revision of previous study.

2 Use the *Activity bank* (Teacher's Book additional resources section, Resource 12A).

   A Set the crossword for individual work (including homework) or pairwork.

   Answers

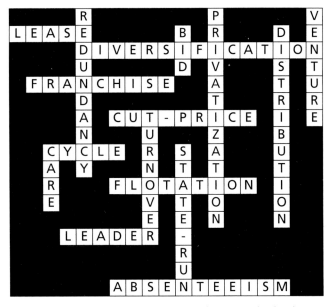

   B Set for individual work and pairwork checking.

   Answers

95%	the great majority
70%	a significant majority
53%	just over half
50%	half
48%	slightly less than half
10%	a small proportion
2%	a tiny minority

3 Set Resource 12G for individual work and pairwork checking.

   Answers

   Close Call Clothing Co. plc was losing money. It was under pressure from bankers and other lenders. <u>In addition</u>, shareholders were not happy when the share price dropped to an all-time low of 32p.

   <u>Consequently</u>, a decision was made to undertake a strategic review of the company. <u>First</u>, the management team set out to establish the views of all staff. <u>Next</u>, management were persuaded to agree to more ambitious targets.

Finally, progress-monitoring mechanisms were set up.

<u>As a result of</u> these measures, the company redesigned its manufacturing processes, which <u>led</u> to improved quality. Better organizational structures and delivery systems <u>also</u> enhanced customer relations.

These steps soon <u>resulted</u> in increased customer and retailer confidence, and sales quickly started to rise.

4 Ask students to practise making questionnaires for customer surveys. They could choose from the following topics (or other appropriate topics):

   ● Which of the two do customers prefer, e.g.,

   two local supermarkets

   two brands of mobile phone

   two brands of computer

   two brands of cosmetics

   two means of travel

   ● What do customers think of:

   Internet shopping

   a mobile phone brand

   a TV channel

   a new piece of personal entertainment equipment

   cosmetics for men

Activity bank

A Solve the crossword.

Down

1 The finance ... is concerned with the flow of money in and out of the business.
3 Operations management is concerned with production ... .
7 One of the four factors of production.
8 A person who buys goods.
10 Furniture, cars, computers, etc. are called ... goods.
11 Companies need to price their ... competitively.
13 The people who work for a company.
14 Money which is invested in a business.
16 The last stage of the transformation process.

Across

2 The first stage of the transformation process.
5 ... materials are necessary for manufacturing.
6 Sole ... can easily adapt to changing markets.
9 ... and equipment are part of the capital of a company.
12 Primary production uses the earth's natural ... .
15 Things that are sold by businesses.
17 We can ... businesses according to their production type.
18 The head of a company.

B Play noughts and crosses. Use the words in context or explain what they mean.

unlimited	strengthen	rethink
technological	relationship	financial
investment	community	competitive

marketing	human resources	research and development
finance	operations	limited liability
fiat money	secondary production	service industry

English for Business Studies – Copyright © 2008 Garnet Publishing Ltd.

Activity bank	

A Find 20 words from this unit in the wordsearch.

Copy the words into your notebook.

Check the definition of any words you can't remember.

K	Y	D	I	S	I	N	T	E	G	R	A	T	E	Q	N	L
D	E	L	E	G	A	T	E	D	L	K	T	N	W	G	A	H
B	N	E	N	V	I	R	O	N	M	E	N	T	K	N	L	L
C	O	M	P	L	E	X	B	T	N	T	D	P	O	X	N	Z
B	T	R	E	L	A	T	I	O	N	S	H	I	P	C	H	M
S	A	F	L	C	M	T	R	G	K	X	T	L	J	J	N	T
C	T	S	A	P	P	R	O	P	R	I	A	T	E	O	N	F
F	R	A	I	G	X	Y	Y	M	D	L	T	N	I	E	F	J
J	O	I	B	C	C	T	K	A	Q	Z	T	T	M	C	K	S
J	C	C	S	L	G	G	R	R	D	F	A	E	Z	V	F	H
X	Q	Z	U	I	E	T	F	I	L	R	V	K	T	E	L	X
H	V	K	V	S	S	F	G	A	E	E	T	K	I	Y	T	X
L	B	V	G	R	A	I	C	P	I	E	M	L	Y	N	H	T
T	A	Y	K	T	R	I	O	H	C	K	E	K	K	L	X	R
T	T	Y	S	K	P	O	C	R	R	B	L	G	T	W	R	T
Z	G	Y	E	Y	C	A	O	D	M	W	G	C	K	M	K	C
T	G	Z	T	R	L	F	K	V	I	S	I	O	N	N	T	R

B Do the quiz.

1 What is the word for:

a a group of people who work together

b someone who is highly skilled and knowledgeable

c getting rid of managers in the middle

2 Give adjectives which describe:

a a boss who is strict

b a boss who encourages people to contribute their ideas

3 Name the two types of organizational structure in Figures A and B.

4 List:

a five functional areas of a business

b three qualities of a good leader, according to Hooper and Potter

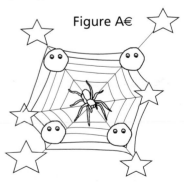

Figure A€

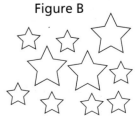

Figure B

In the first half of the 20th century, organizations tended to be controlled in rigid hierarchies.	In this type of structure there is one person at the top, the managing director or chief executive officer (CEO). There might be many layers of management. Information and orders are passed down through the layers. Typically, the company is divided into functional areas, such as sales, marketing, finance, etc. Each area has a manager in charge of a group of workers. Until recently, this arrangement was often accompanied by a division of labour at the lower levels. This means that each job is divided into clearly defined segments which can be carried out with little skill or training.
However, there are a number of problems with large, traditional hierarchies.	First of all, communication is often poor. Messages have to travel down from the top, and information from the bottom may never reach the top at all. Secondly, these systems often do not encourage people to take responsibility for the quality of their work or to use their initiative. Finally, companies with these structures may find it difficult to adapt to a changing business environment quickly.
As a result, some companies have moved towards flatter hierarchies, as recommended by Tom Peters in his book *Thriving on Chaos* (1987).	In other words, they have 'delayered', getting rid of people in the middle levels of management. In addition, many companies have adopted a team approach, with several people working together on a task.
However, different types of company may need different types of organizations.	For example, a traditional hierarchical structure is particularly appropriate for large government bureaucracies, where things need to happen according to fixed rules. This structure also suits big transport companies where, for safety purposes, people need to be trained to work according to strict standards. As Charles Handy points out, in this kind of structure everyone has a precise job description. There are routines, rules and procedures, and clear lines of management so everyone knows what should happen and there are no surprises.
There are other possible ways in which organizations can be structured.	For instance, according to Handy, in the 'club' structure, one individual leads a small group of perhaps 20 people. The leader chooses people who share her beliefs and values, and so the organization reflects the leader's personality. It is just like a club. The leader is like a spider at the centre of its web. There is a high level of trust, and communication is easy and informal because everyone knows what everyone else thinks. Communication lines are very short so these organizations can react quickly to change or new opportunities. However, if the leader is weak or leaves, the organization can disintegrate. This type of structure can be seen in new businesses or the art world or in politics.
In the 'task' structure, several people work together as a team, using their different skills.	There is little hierarchy but a lot of cooperation and discussion. Leadership of the teams can change from task to task. This structure is suitable for advertising agencies or product development, where there is a problem to solve. However, it is less useful for simple jobs because teams can be expensive and time-consuming.
Finally, a 'person' structure can be found where there is a group of people who are experts in their field.	They usually work individually rather than as a team. However, the experts also need administrators to help them. The administrators – often called secretaries or clerks – do not have any control over the professionals, and so an organization with a person structure may be quite difficult to manage. This type of organization – called a practice – is often used by groups of doctors or lawyers.
Of course, in real life, organizations rarely have just one structure.	In fact, most are a mixture of two or more types. But a hundred years ago, managers believed there was only one way to run all organizations, and that is certainly no longer the case.

Effective leadership is crucial for the success of a business.

According to Douglas McGregor, in his book *The Human Side of Enterprise* (published in 1950), managers tend to be divided according to their beliefs.

However, the style of leadership which is appropriate may depend on the situation.

It is also important to consider the relationship between leadership and teams.

In order for a leader to lead a team successfully, according to Hooper and Potter (in *The Business of Leadership*, 1997), there are some basic requirements.

Effective leadership is crucial for the success of a business.

According to Douglas McGregor, in his book *The Human Side of Enterprise* (published in 1950), managers tend to be divided according to their beliefs.

However, the style of leadership which is appropriate may depend on the situation.

It is also important to consider the relationship between leadership and teams.

In order for a leader to lead a team successfully, according to Hooper and Potter (in *The Business of Leadership*, 1997), there are some basic requirements.

Effective leadership is crucial for the success of a business.	It is the leader's job to make sure that everyone works towards the achievement of the organization's goals. But what is a good leader? Different people have different approaches to leadership. Some leaders are autocratic, which means that they make all the decisions and expect their staff to simply follow their orders. On the other hand, a democratic leader is more likely to involve staff in decisions, to delegate and to make use of teams in the organization of work.
According to Douglas McGregor, in his book *The Human Side of Enterprise* **(published in 1950), managers tend to be divided according to their beliefs.**	Theory X managers think that people are lazy, that employees need to be told what to do and have to be forced into doing their jobs properly. In contrast, according to McGregor, Theory Y managers believe that most people try hard to do their best, that they want to enjoy their work, and that everyone can have good ideas. As a leader, a Theory X manager is likely to be autocratic. A democratic leader will probably have Theory Y beliefs.
However, the style of leadership which is appropriate may depend on the situation.	For example, in a crisis, an autocratic style may be more effective because people may need a strong leader to tell them quickly what to do. On the other hand, in a stable situation where everyone understands their roles, and where time is not a problem, a democratic style can work well.
It is also important to consider the relationship between leadership and teams.	This is because recently there has been an increase in democratic management techniques which make use of team work. According to John Adair, in his book *Effective Teambuilding* (1987), the task of the team leader is to: • know what the job is and get it done • enable the team to work together • allow individuals to develop their abilities
In order for a leader to lead a team successfully, according to Hooper and Potter (in *The Business of Leadership,* **1997), there are some basic requirements.**	First, the leader must inspire trust and respect, not fear. This can only be done if the leader is open with team members and if the leader shows integrity. Second, the team needs to understand very clearly what is to be done, which means that everyone must have a 'shared vision'. In other words, orders are not imposed from above by the leader. Instead, everyone agrees the goals. Finally, there must be very good communications between all members of the team. Many problems in teams result from breakdowns in communication which cause misunderstandings.

Activity bank

A Solve the coded crossword.

Each number represents a letter. So 2 = C. Write C in all the number 2 squares.

Write I in all the number 3 squares. Write A in all the number 6 squares.

Look at the second word from the top. You can see CA _ A _ I _ I _ _ . What word is this? Yes, *capability*.

So 13 = P. Write P in the number 13 square on the right. Write P in all the number 13 squares in the grid.

Continue guessing the words.

B Play bingo.

Think of words for each of the categories and write them on card 1. Think of a word from another category for the last square ('another word').

Each student says one of their words. Cross the squares on card 2 when you hear a word from that category.

1

a motivator	a need	a means of communication
a hygiene factor	a verb	another word

2

a motivator	a need	a means of communication
a hygiene factor	a verb	another word

Activity bank

A Find 20 verbs from the first four units in the wordsearch.

Copy the verbs into your notebook.

Write the noun for each verb.

X	C	R	L	D	E	F	I	N	E	X	C	M	E	B	T
Q	P	C	O	O	P	E	R	A	T	E	K	T	W	W	R
M	L	C	X	V	E	X	E	N	G	D	A	Y	L	J	E
T	I	L	O	T	L	T	T	T	S	R	I	L	X	T	G
P	H	S	A	O	A	I	C	R	G	E	H	V	A	B	K
N	R	E	C	R	R	U	N	E	A	K	L	V	I	Y	G
T	R	O	A	A	R	D	T	N	T	N	I	E	N	D	B
C	Y	P	M	T	L	N	I	C	O	T	S	D	C	T	E
N	E	G	S	O	I	C	E	N	O	V	N	F	F	T	R
S	M	N	X	P	T	T	U	M	A	A	A	R	O	G	M
T	O	L	X	Z	O	E	N	L	P	T	Q	T	D	R	Z
C	O	P	E	R	A	T	E	X	A	N	E	G	E	C	M
K	T	R	P	D	T	Z	E	P	K	T	K	N	C	M	E
Y	I	N	T	E	R	A	C	T	J	J	E	F	M	V	G
M	V	M	T	M	P	W	J	E	X	P	L	O	I	T	C
D	M	R	S	A	T	I	S	F	Y	K	G	B	Q	N	W

B Play noughts and crosses. You must say the abbreviation or acronym and give the original words to place your symbol in a square.

FAQ	CAD	HTTP
MP3	RAM	CAL
ROM	PC	HTML

CAM	LAN	URL
WWW	CAM	ISP
CPU	RTF	PDF

Although we live in a time of technological change, the impact of new technology on business is nothing new.

New technologies have also always brought with them both opportunities and threats.

Another example was Richard Arkwright's (1732–1792) spinning machine.

The industrial revolution of the 20th and 21st centuries has been in information technology.

The new technologies are developing incredibly fast.

Although we live in a time of technological change, the impact of new technology on business is nothing new.

New technologies have also always brought with them both opportunities and threats.

Another example was Richard Arkwright's (1732–1792) spinning machine.

The industrial revolution of the 20th and 21st centuries has been in information technology.

The new technologies are developing incredibly fast.

HADFORD *University*

Faculty: Business Studies

Change or die!

The challenge of new technology

example {
Although we live in a time of technological change, the impact of new technology on business is nothing new. Technology has always been an important aspect of the macro-environment that is outside the control of companies. For example, in the 18th century in England – the beginning of the period known as the Industrial Revolution – several inventors made machine tools for

result of tech. {
working with steel which allowed others to make industrial machines. Mechanization enabled new production methods, which not only radically changed manufacturing but also society.

benefits of new tech. {
New technologies have also always brought with them both opportunities and threats. In the industrial revolution in England, many people made their fortunes through the establishment of companies that exploited the new technology, and great advances in living standards for people were achieved, particularly in western Europe and north America. Unfortunately, there were also

problems {
less positive social and political repercussions. For example, in the textile industry, the 'flying shuttle', invented by John Kay in 1733, resulted in increased production from a single machine, and so reduced the number of workers needed. This device was very much disliked by workers because of their fear of becoming unemployed, and, in 1755, Kay was attacked and one of his

more benefits {
machines destroyed by an angry crowd. However, many people realized that this invention would make cloth cheaper and more available, and would therefore actually improve people's lives.

change {
Another example was Richard Arkwright's (1732–1792) spinning machine. This machine changed spinning from a cottage industry to factory-based production since it required mechanical power to operate. Some people saw this development as a huge opportunity for

benefits + problems {
expansion of the industry, but others feared for their jobs. These people rioted and broke up the new labour-saving machinery. Clearly, they could not see that the machines would ultimately create new types of jobs, rather than reduce labour needs. These men were known as 'Luddites', a term which is still used today for people who refuse to accept new ideas or technology.

faster information {
The industrial revolution of the 20th and 21st centuries has been in information technology. The use of computers in partnership with telecommunications has resulted in a faster exchange of information so businesses can quickly take account of developments within their operating

Internet + business {
environment. In addition, the Internet is having a profound impact on the marketing mix strategy of organizations through new distribution and purchasing methods (consumers can now shop 24 hours a day comfortably from their homes). While the new 'dotcom' companies are exploiting

results of this
these new techniques, older companies are now having to adapt or lose their market shares.

implications for business {
The new technologies are developing incredibly fast. The product life cycle of some items, computer software for example, has shortened to less than a year. Obviously, this means that it is extremely important for companies to take technology's rapid advances into account and respond to changes if they wish to gain competitive advantage. Companies which are slow to react are likely to go out of business. However, as Rosabeth Moss Kanter, one of the world's

people = still more important {
leading business thinkers, points out in her book *Evolve!*, human relationships remain the key to business success, even in the digital age.

CAD	CAL
CAM	DVD
HTML	HTTP
ISP	LCD
PIN	ROM
URL	USB
WAN	WWW

Activity bank

A Solve the synonyms crossword. Find words with the same meaning as the clues.

Across

4 means (pl n)	**18** talk about
7 decline	**20** fall sharply
8 aim	**22** overview
11 type	**23** purchase
12 conclude	**24** satisfy
14 fundamentally	

Down

1 some people say	**10** requirements
2 firm (n)	**13** in fact
3 rise sharply	**15** client
5 promote	**16** naturally (2, 6)
6 task	**17** known as
9 crucial	**19** retail outlet
	21 principal

B Play opposites bingo.

Choose six words from the box and write one word in each square of your bingo card.

Your teacher will call out some words. If you have the **opposite** word on your card, cross it out.

The first person to cross out all the words on their card is the winner.

careful child easy elderly fall large
low luxury male poor professional
rigid sharply short single slightly
slow traditional unskilled

Marketing is not ...

... the same as _____ . This is only a small

_____ of marketing.

... just about selling. There are many other related

_____ which are involved.

So what is it?

There are four _____ aspects,

_____ the 'marketing mix' – also called the

'Four Ps' – to which _____ must pay attention.

1   The **Product** – must _____ the

_____ of the _____ .

2   **Promotion** – there are several _____ of

promoting a product, including advertising, special offers, mailing

and sponsorship.

3   The **Price** – this depends on the financial objectives as well as the

_____ of consumer being

_____ .

4   The **Place** – where do people _____ the

_____ ? This _____ both

means of distribution and type of _____ .

Verbs	Nouns	Adverbs	Adjectives
rise		gradually	
increase		sharply	
grow		slightly	
improve		markedly	
fall		significantly	
decrease		rapidly	
drop		steeply	
decline		steadily	

Which of the following brands of _____ do you usually buy?

Brand	Student A	Student B	Student C	Student D	Student E	Student F	Total

Which of the following brands of _____ do you usually buy?

Brand	Student A	Student B	Student C	Student D	Student E	Student F	Total

Poor contributions	Student A	Student B	Student C
disagrees rudely			
doesn't explain how the point is relevant			
doesn't understand an idiom			
dominates the discussion			
gets angry when someone disagrees with them			
interrupts			
is negative			
mumbles or whispers			
says something irrelevant			
shouts			
sits quietly and says nothing			
starts a side conversation			
other:			

Good contributions	Student A	Student B	Student C
allows others to speak			
asks for clarification			
asks politely for information			
brings in another speaker			
builds on points made by other speakers			
contributes to the discussion			
explains the point clearly			
gives specific examples to help explain			
is constructive			
links correctly with previous speakers			
listens carefully to what others say			
makes clear how the point is relevant			
paraphrases to check understanding			
says when they agree with someone			
speaks clearly			
tries to use correct language			
other:			

Student A

Previous research: primary research

Your research task:

Find out about **secondary research** and report back to your group. Say what this kind of research is, its advantages and disadvantages.

Your discussion task:

Contribute to the discussions on primary, qualitative and quantitative research, for example by asking for information or clarification, agreeing or disagreeing. If you have also researched any of these other types of research, say where you found your information.

Student B

Previous research: secondary research

Your research task:

Find out about **primary research** and report back to your group. Say what this kind of research is, its advantages and disadvantages.

Your discussion task:

Contribute to the discussions on secondary, qualitative and quantitative research, for example by asking for information or clarification, agreeing or disagreeing. If you have also researched any of these other types of research, say where you found your information.

Student C

Previous research: qualitative research

Your research task:

Find out about **quantitative research** and report back to your group. Say what this kind of research is, its advantages and disadvantages.

Your discussion task:

Contribute to the discussions on qualitative, primary and secondary research, for example by asking for information or clarification, agreeing or disagreeing. If you have also researched any of these other types of research, say where you found your information.

Student D

Previous research: quantitative research

Your research task:

Find out about **qualitative research** and report back to your group. Say what this kind of research is, its advantages and disadvantages.

Your discussion task:

Contribute to the discussions on quantitative, primary and secondary research, for example by asking for information or clarification, agreeing or disagreeing. If you have also researched any of these other types of research, say where you found your information.

Student A

1 <u>Secondary</u>

= info from sources, e.g.,
   books, Internet, trade
   mags, reports, etc.
   (i.e., already exists)

+ cheap; good overview of
   market; based on real
   sales statistics;
   relatively fast

− reports ⟶ sometimes
   expensive; poss. out of
   date

Student B

2 <u>Primary</u>

= new info: from (1) people,
   e.g., customers,
   retailers; (2)
   observation, e.g., of
   shoppers

+ info = recent; can ask
   specific questions
   (good method for
   psych. research)

− expensive; time-consuming

Student C

3 <u>Quantitative</u>

= statistical info, usually
   thro' questionnaires

+ good for factual info;
   overview of trends ∴
   large nos.

− sample <u>must</u> be v. big;
   people lie ∴ results
   may ≠ reliable; low
   response rate for
   questionnaires

Student D

4 <u>Qualitative</u>

M ≠ numbers; usually verbal
   info; used to find out
   attitudes, beliefs, etc.
   Methods inc. interviews,
   focus groups, etc.

+ reveal unknown probs;
   basis for quant. methods

− in groups, opinions easily
   led by one person; only
   small numbers ∴
   difficult to generalize

Activity bank

A Find 20 verbs from this unit in the wordsearch.

Copy the words into your notebook.

Write the noun for each verb.

Q	I	N	T	E	G	R	A	T	E	T	H	Q	D	L	T
R	F	D	W	N	W	W	L	W	C	H	R	C	W	A	T
L	G	Q	I	W	V	C	I	E	W	R	N	I	E	H	T
A	S	S	E	S	S	R	G	T	Z	G	E	F	A	R	F
N	L	D	H	X	P	A	I	H	H	E	E	A	V	L	W
P	R	A	K	S	K	L	T	N	V	D	Q	Z	T	M	K
C	R	N	U	C	A	C	A	E	C	C	R	R	X	E	M
W	M	K	A	N	I	T	I	Y	E	L	Q	A	E	D	N
F	J	P	D	D	C	H	U	T	B	C	U	T	W	E	P
Z	E	K	E	K	C	H	A	R	D	X	A	D	T	V	R
R	R	R	Y	A	Z	C	H	B	A	D	R	A	E	D	P
M	P	D	E	S	I	G	N	B	P	T	U	F	L	B	K
G	J	Y	N	D	K	R	H	U	Q	L	E	N	K	B	R
Z	L	Y	N	J	P	L	R	N	A	R	E	T	A	I	N
N	H	I	G	V	L	N	C	V	T	G	Y	T	M	Q	N
E	X	T	E	N	D	Z	E	R	S	P	O	N	S	O	R

B Think of a word or words that can go in front of each of the words below to make a phrase from business studies. Explain the meaning.

Example: market = *mature market, emerging market, target market, niche market*

_____ analysis		_____ cycle		_____ phase	
_____ approach		_____ edge		_____ portfolio	
_____ awareness		_____ flow		_____ range	
_____ benefits		_____ leader		_____ services	
_____ child		_____ led		_____ span	
_____ cost		_____ market		_____ strategy	
_____ cow		_____ message		_____ value	

1 Cash flow is _____ during the development phase.

2 In the _____ phase, unit costs are high.

3 Cash flow becomes positive in the _____ phase.

4 _____ sales mean that unit costs are reduced.

5 Sales are at their peak once the market has _____ .

6 Sales may start to _____ when the market reaches saturation.

1 Cash flow is negative during the development phase.

2 In the introduction phase, unit costs are high.

3 Cash flow becomes positive in the maturity phase.

4 Increasing sales mean that unit costs are reduced.

5 Sales are at their peak once the market has stabilized.

6 Sales may start to fall when the market reaches saturation.

a It is not until the maturity phase is reached that cash flow is no longer negative.

b Peak sales figures are achieved at the maturity phase.

c While the product is being designed and trialled, there are many expenses but no income.

d There may be a reduction in business if there are too many competitors.

e It costs a lot to produce each unit early in the cycle.

f Once the products start to sell, the company can make them more cheaply.

Original sentence	Student A	Student B
A business also needs to identify where a product, is in its life cycle, once it has been introduced.	A business needs to know where an item is in its life-span after it has been launched	Having launched the the product, it is important to monitor its progress through the life cycle.
	not satisfactory: not enough changes: this is patch-writing *progress through the*	*acceptable paraphrase: time clause changed to participle phrase ('once it has been introduced' 'Having launched the product'); use of empty 'it' ('A business also needs to' 'it is important to'); phrase in place of clause ('where a product is in its life cycle' 'its* *life cycle'). All words changed except 'life cycle', which is acceptable*
At what point, for example, will the market stabilize?	For instance, when will sales fall?	Have sales levelled off, for instance?
	not acceptable: although the words have been changed, the meaning is different from the original	*acceptable paraphrase: note that although there is a tense change here, ultimately this makes no difference to the meaning in the context*

Original sentence	Student A	Student B
If sales start to fall, does this indicate a decline phase?	If sales drop, does this mean a decline phase?	It is possible that a reduction in sales means that the market has started to shrink.
	not satisfactory: not enough changes: this is patch-writing	*acceptable paraphrase: use of empty 'it' ('If' → 'It is possible that'); clause changed to phrase ('sales start to fall' → 'a drop in sales'); phrase changed to clause ('a decline phase' → 'the market has started to shrink'). The only word the same as the original is 'sales', which is acceptable*
If so, the company may have to take action to try to extend the life-span of the product.	If so, the company should try to extend the life-span of the item.	In this case, there could be a need for extension strategies to prolong the product's life cycle.
	not satisfactory: not enough changes: this is patch-writing *vocab:'product' is the*	*acceptable paraphrase: replacement subject 'there' ('the company may have to take action to' → 'there could be a need for') verb phrase to noun phrase ('try to extend' → 'extension strategies')* *same as the original but this is acceptable*

Central to the marketing mix is the product itself.

Firstly, what is a product?

Having defined the product, the company will also need to be aware of its probable life cycle (PLC).

A business also needs to identify where a product is in its life cycle, once it has been introduced.

Finally, a company needs to carry out an analysis of its product portfolio.

Central to the marketing mix is the product itself.

Firstly, what is a product?

Having defined the product, the company will also need to be aware of its probable life cycle (PLC).

A business also needs to identify where a product is in its life cycle, once it has been introduced.

Finally, a company needs to carry out an analysis of its product portfolio.

	Main subject	**Main verb**	**Main object/ complement**	**Other verbs + their subjects + objects/ complements**
A	the name (of the cleaning product)	was changed	(to) Cif	which was known as Jif
B	Three of the many ways	will be described		in a which a product can be analysed
C	You	can also send	text messages	1. ... which are so useful 2. ... that this benefit has played an important part in the speed 3. ... at which the mobile phone market developed.
D	a company	must be	fully aware (of the qualities of its products)	As well as understanding its target markets, ...
E	the company	saw	a satisfactory increase in revenue.	Having taken these steps as part of an integrated marketing approach, ...

A portfolio	A problem	A extra
A brand	A cash	A life
A integrated	A mature	A text
A product	A brand	A added
A marketing	A unit	A decline
A customer	A market	A life
A competitive	A cash	A product
B analysis	B cow	B benefits
B cycle	B edge	B flow
B leader	B led	B child
B message	B awareness	B phase
B portfolio	B range	B approach
B market	B span	B strategy
B cost	B services	B value

Activity bank

A Solve the crossword.

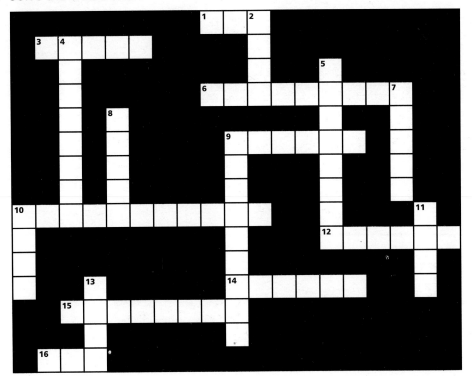

Across

1 In ... production, making the object is seen as one operation.

3 In ... production, many products can be made simultaneously.

6 A ... ... different factors affect planning decisions.

9 I'd like to make two ... .

10 ... for customers is a major factor.

12 The whole operational sequence is known as the ... chain.

14 A high ... attracts top managers.

15 A business needs to reduce costs if it is to ... profits.

16 Let me ... it another way.

Down

2 We must ... in mind that businesses need to be profitable.

4 In ... to costs, we need to examine qualitative factors.

5 Look ... ... way.

7 A business has both ... costs and variable costs.

8 The difference between the cost of raw materials and the income from sales is the ... added.

9 Gantt charts show what ... are happening at any one time.

10 ... flow refers to money received and spent by a company in a given period.

11 In ... production, there are no delays.

13 The ... of the matter is that inefficiency affects profitability.

Activity bank

Student A

B Play 'battleships'.
Answer Student B's questions about this grid.

	A	B	C	D	E	F	G	H	I	J	K	L
1					D	R	A	W	I	N	G	
2	R		P									
3	V	E		R			F	I	X	E	D	
4	A		S		O			L				
5	R			O		T				O		L
6	I				U.		O			A		O
7	A				E	R		T		N		C
8	B			T			C		Y			A
9	L		I					E		P		T
10	E	S		R	E	N	T		S		E	I
11												O
12	I	N	G	R	E	D	I	E	N	T	S	N

Ask Student B questions to find the following words from this unit:

four words for production types
two verbs ending in ~ate
four words which can be nouns or verbs

Ask: *Is there a letter in 1C?*
Use this grid to mark the letters/words you find. Mark empty squares with a cross.

	A	B	C	D	E	F	G	H	I	J	K	L
1												
2												
3												
4												
5												
6												
7												
8												
9												
10												
11												
12												

Activity bank

Student B

B Play 'battleships'.
Answer Student A's questions about this grid.

	A	B	C	D	E	F	G	H	I	J	K	L
1	B		D	E	L	A	Y	F				
2		A						L		J	O	B
3	S		T					O				
4	U			C				W		E		H
5	P				H				T			A
6	P					N		A		M		N
7	L				G		L			A		D
8	Y			I		U				S		L
9			S		C					S		E
10		E		L								
11	D		A		E	V	A	L	U	A	T	E
12		C										

Ask Student A questions to find the following words from this unit:

    two ways to show an idea for a new product
    four types of cost from a location
    two ways to refer to raw materials
    two words for the place of business

Ask: *Is there a letter in 1C?*
Use this grid to mark the letters/words you find. Mark empty squares with a cross.

	A	B	C	D	E	F	G	H	I	J	K	L
1												
2												
3												
4												
5												
6												
7												
8												
9												
10												
11												
12												

	Fixed phrase	Followed by ...	Actual information (suggested answers)
1	An important concept (is) ...	a new idea or topic that the lecturer wants to discuss	
2	What do I mean by ... ?	an explanation of a word or phrase	
3	As you can see, ...	a comment about a diagram or picture	
4	Looking at it another way, ...	a different way to think about the topic	
5	In financial terms, ...	a general idea put into a financial context	
6	Say ...	an imaginary example	
7	The point is ...	a key statement or idea	
8	In this way ...	a concluding comment giving a result of something	

Student A

Business location

1 **Fixed costs**
   don't vary with level of production activity

The cost of the site is important. Is it in the city or the country? What is the rent? How much will the interest be on a loan to buy the site? What is the cost of services, e.g., water, electricity?

Management salaries: salaries may depend on the place. For example, a high salary is needed to attract managers to an unpopular place.

However, costs may be reduced if there are government grants for establishing a business, for example in a poor area.

Student B

Business location

2 **Variable costs**
   vary with level of production activity

Transporting products to markets: businesses should locate near the market if the product is 'heavier' or 'bulkier' than the raw materials needed to make it (e.g., bread, soft drinks). Services (e.g., shops) must locate AT the marketplace.

Getting raw materials: businesses should locate near the source of the raw material if it is 'heavier' than the product (e.g., food production is located near farming areas).

Labour: costs will vary according to place and production levels.

Student C

Business location

3 **Revenue**

Convenience for customers: higher prices can be charged if a place is convenient.

Quantity of sales: some places may result in increased sales. Therefore high fixed costs may be justified.

The 'image' of the location: if a place has an 'upmarket' image high prices can be justified (e.g., holidays in parts of the Caribbean).

Local economy: if a shop is located in an area which is in decline, there will be poor sales.

Student D

Business location

4 **Qualitative factors**

Is there room for expansion? Businesses need to consider possible market growth.

Environmental effects: is the production process safe for the environment?

Quality of life: is it a good area? Will managers be happy to move there?

Local transport systems: are there road and rail links, ports, airport, etc.?

Activity bank

A Find 15 words from this unit in the wordsearch. All the words are uncountable nouns in the texts in this unit.

Copy the words into your notebook.

Check the definition of any words you can't remember.

D	E	L	I	M	I	N	A	T	I	O	N	T	P	B
W	M	A	N	A	G	E	M	E	N	T	G	Y	R	Y
U	T	I	L	I	Z	A	T	I	O	N	R	Q	T	L
F	V	O	L	U	M	E	M	G	N	E	Y	I	V	L
E	C	A	P	A	C	I	T	Y	N	C	L	Y	A	K
K	F	T	E	K	W	K	P	I	N	I	Q	V	K	R
M	P	F	L	X	D	J	H	E	B	W	I	N	P	Y
N	Y	U	I	Q	I	C	T	A	T	V	A	F	R	T
K	B	P	T	C	A	S	T	Q	R	B	R	S	J	P
V	Y	K	J	M	I	I	T	U	U	C	D	D	T	R
H	F	Q	T	S	F	E	S	E	R	A	V	M	R	E
P	C	V	N	O	Y	T	N	T	N	L	L	H	K	N
K	N	O	R	V	B	Z	B	C	D	C	Y	I	H	F
G	C	P	X	N	Y	Y	R	C	Y	T	E	W	T	B
P	R	O	D	U	C	T	I	O	N	F	V	L	K	Y

B Rearrange the letters in the words to form a correctly spelt word from this unit.

Jumbled word	Correct spelling
bamslase	
cuaarclstep	
ecpas	
eeialtrr	
feetcd	
frwookecr	
mireseep	
quetchnie	
tineer	
tskco	

Activity bank

A Solve the crossword.

Down

Down

1 Money gained from a business activity after paying all costs is …

2 … is keeping records of, and interpreting, financial transactions.

3 A … is a list giving the amount of money to be spent and the likely revenue for the coming year.

4 … are what an individual or a company owes to others.

6 … are the property of a person, company or business.

7 … is the gross revenue or the total business done by a company or organization.

9 The money spent in running the business, including wages and resources (but excluding tax and interest on loans) is called … costs.

10 The percentage measure of profitability, calculated as: net income / revenue is the profit ….

Across

3 A financial statement, summarizing a company's assets, liabilities and net value at a specific point in time is called a … sheet.

5 The money that goes into and out of a company is the cash …

8 … analysis is a technique used to compare the various costs associated with an investment with its possible benefits.

11 … is money or other assets, owned or used in operating a business.

12 … is ownership - usually a synonym for stock or shares in a company

13 A financial statement giving income, costs and expenses incurred during a specific period of time is called a profit and … account.

14 is putting money or capital into an enterprise or business, with the expectation of profit.

B Are the nouns in the box countable or uncountable? Use a dictionary to check.

asset	cash	cost	economy	liability
loss	margin	profit	sale	share	taxation

Review reduce + recite + review	**Notes** record
Here you write only important words and questions; this column is completed after the lecture. Later this column becomes your study or revision notes. You can use it by covering the right hand column and using the cue words and questions here to remember the contents on the right.	This column contains your notes. You should underline headings and indent main ideas. After the lecture or reading you need to identify the key points and write them in the review column as questions or cue words.

Summary
reflect + recite + review
After the class you can use this space to summarize the main points of the notes on this page.

Review	Notes
2 types of accounting are...?	Accounting in companies: management accounting (MA) and financial accounting (FA)
Why MA + FA important?	Attention to financial matters vital for *success* of company
	MA
Main purpose of MA ...?	1) *Forward* planning
Information supplied by ...?	● information given in *annual budgets*
Aims of MA?	● aim is to help company
(5 specific aims)	a) decide how to *spend* its money
	b) decide whether/how to *borrow funds* (e.g., to invest in a product, to *buy new equipment*, to employ more staff)
	c) keep a check on *cash flows* & value of *investments*
	d) predict *profits*/losses
	e) help monitor performance (incl staff)
Required by law?	2) Not a *legal* requirement
Management tool	3) Internal management mechanism
(advantages: why used?	● good *practice*
by whom?)	● powerful → *decisions* are based on
	● the data

Summary

There are two types of accounting: management and financial.

Management accounting is a useful management tool.

It's not a legal requirement. It's used internally.

Further definitions can be found at the following web pages

1 Cash flow statement

www.theaccountspayablenetwork.com/html/modules.php

www.disability.qld.gov.au/budget/05_06/mps/glossary.html

cfdccariboo.com/glossary.htm

wps.prenhall.com/wps/media/objects/213/218150/glossary.html

www.tdbanknorth.com/bank/glossary_sb.html

www.ibgbusiness.com/glossary_of_terms.htm

www.delawarecountybrc.com/glossaryterms.htm

www.reversemortgageofamerica.com/reverse_mortgage_terms.htm

www.indiainfoline.com/bisc/jama/jmmc.html

en.wikipedia.org/wiki/Cash_flow_statement

2 Break-even chart

www.gcsaa.org/mc/benefits/glossary.asp

http://en.wikipedia.org/wiki/Break_even_analysis

www.bized.co.uk/virtual/vla/theories/break_even_change.htm

3 Contribution

http://en.wikipedia.org/wiki/Contribution_margin

www.investopedia.com/terms/c/contributionmargin.asp

4 Budget

http://en.wikipedia.org/wiki/Budget

www.better-credit.com/glossary.html

www.mah.gov.on.ca/userfiles/HTML/nts_1_7042_1.html

https://remax-headinghome.com/Glossary.aspx

www.georgetown.edu/uis/ia/dw/GLOSSARY0816.html

data2.itc.nps.gov/budget2/glossary.htm

www.unisys.com/common/investors/glossary/b.asp

5 Investment appraisal

www.indiainfoline.com/bisc/jama/jmmi.html

www.bized.co.uk/cgi-bin/glossarydb/browse.pl?glostopic=0&glosid=1348

http://answers.yahoo.com/question/index?qid=1006041902699

More definitions can be found at:

www.bizhelp24.com/

www.chartfilter.com/glossary/c31.htm

www.learnthat.com/define/view.asp?id=280)

Amounts in millions of US dollars

	Jan 06	Jan 05	Jan 04
Assets			
	6,414	5,488	5,199
Net receivables	2,662	1,715	1,254
	32,191	29,447	26,612
	79,290	68,567	58,530
Other current assets	2,557	1,841	1,356
Total assets	123,114	107,058	92,951
Liabilities			
	40,178	35,107	31,051
Short-term debt	8,648	7,781	6,367
	30,171	23,669	20,099
Other liabilities	6,019	4,270	3,772
Total liabilities	85,016	70,827	61,289
Shares outstanding	4,165	4,234	4,296

US dollars ($) millions

DELL

Year	Revenue	Gross profit	Total net income
Apr 06	14,216.0	2,472.0	762.0
Jan 06	15,183.0	2,709.0	1,012.0
Oct 05	13,911.0	2,251.0	606.0
Jul 05	13,428.0	2,499.0	1,020.0
Apr 05	13,386.0	2,491.0	934.0

NIKE

Year	Revenue	Gross profit	Total net income
Nov 06	3,821.7	1,657.1	325.6
Aug 06	4,194.1	1,849.2	377.2
May 06	4,005.4	1,753.4	332.8
Feb 06	3,612.8	1,574.1	325.8
Nov 05	3,474.7	1,511.4	301.1

source: http://www.hoovers.com

US dollars ($) millions

DELL

Year	Revenue	Gross profit	Total net income
Apr 06	14,216.0	2,472.0	762.0
Jan 06	15,183.0	2,709.0	1,012.0
Oct 05	13,911.0	2,251.0	606.0
Jul 05	13,428.0	2,499.0	1,020.0
Apr 05	13,386.0	2,491.0	934.0

NIKE

Year	Revenue	Gross profit	Total net income
Nov 06	3,821.7	1,657.1	325.6
Aug 06	4,194.1	1,849.2	377.2
May 06	4,005.4	1,753.4	332.8
Feb 06	3,612.8	1,574.1	325.8
Nov 05	3,474.7	1,511.4	301.1

source: http://www.hoovers.com

Activity bank

A Complete the table.

→ Identify the part of speech (n, v or both).

→ Say whether nouns are countable (C), uncountable (U) or both.

→ Say whether verbs are transitive (T), intransitive (I) or both.

Word/phrase	Part of speech	Noun – countable or uncountable?	Verb – transitive or intransitive?
account			
bankruptcy			
bill			
borrow			
cheque			
client			
depreciation			
insolvency			
lend			
merger			
overhead			
stock exchange			
stock market			
stocks			
takeover			

B Think of a word or words that can go after each of the words or phrases below to make a phrase from business studies. Explain the meaning.

Example: *bank = bank loan, bank account*

asset

bank

bank overdraft

capital

corporate

fixed

personal

shares

trade

working

Introduction	Examples of ideas
introduce the topic area give the outline of the essay	

Body		
	Para 1: situation/problems (general)	
	Para 2: problems (specific examples)	
	Para 3: solutions	
	Para 4: evaluations of solutions	

Conclusion	

Carson J.G. & Carrell P.L. (1997). Extensive and Intensive Reading in an EAP setting. *English for Specific Purposes* Volume 16: Pages 47-60

Kotler, P. and Armstrong, G 2003 *Principles of Marketing* 10th edn. Pearson/Prentice Hall (London)

Nigel Slack, Stuart Chambers,, (2004) **Operations Management**. 4th ed. Prentice Hall Financial Times, Harlow

P.G.A.Howells & K.Bain 1990 Financial Markets and Institutions. Longman London

Bob Ortga. 1998: IN Sam we Trst. NY Times books

P Atrill and E. McLaney 5th edit 2006 Accounting and fnance for non-specialists. New Prentice Hall

Carson J.G. & Carrell P.L. (1997). Extensive and Intensive Reading in an EAP setting. *English for Specific Purposes* Volume 16: Pages 47-60

Kotler, P. and Armstrong, G 2003 *Principles of Marketing* 10th edn. Pearson/Prentice Hall (London)

Nigel Slack, Stuart Chambers,, (2004) **Operations Management**. 4th ed. Prentice Hall Financial Times, Harlow

P.G.A.Howells & K.Bain 1990 Financial Markets and Institutions. Longman London

Bob Ortga. 1998: IN Sam we Trst. NY Times books

P Atrill and E. McLaney 5th edit 2006 Accounting and fnance for non-specialists. New Prentice Hall

Activity bank

A Find 20 words from this unit in the wordsearch.
  → Copy the words into your notebook.
  → Check the definition of any words you can't remember.

  Match them in pairs to make 10 two-word phrases.

Q	M	F	M	C	P	R	O	D	U	C	T	I	O	N
W	L	C	C	R	L	T	Q	P	M	D	M	N	G	M
E	N	E	R	G	Y	I	M	R	Y	W	O	J	G	D
L	P	J	O	N	G	N	M	L	K	I	Q	R	N	L
F	L	O	Q	F	N	L	D	A	T	N	A	I	A	C
V	A	K	L	O	F	N	O	A	T	L	W	I	L	R
M	G	R	B	L	E	S	V	B	O	E	R	T	E	W
N	C	R	M	I	U	R	E	S	A	T	Q	W	L	X
B	A	X	R	W	E	T	T	T	S	L	O	N	N	H
C	K	F	M	S	A	N	I	U	T	P	M	K	J	M
C	H	A	N	G	E	S	D	O	L	I	Z	E	R	O
V	T	O	G	I	T	N	T	G	N	P	N	P	L	B
C	C	Q	M	B	I	C	D	E	K	N	G	G	K	R
E	N	V	I	R	O	N	M	E	N	T	A	L	L	Y
T	W	A	R	M	I	N	G	B	L	E	A	N	T	V

B Match a word in the first column with a word in the second column to make a two-word phrase. Make sure you know what they mean.

elderly	changes
European	employees
demographic	force
immigrant	labour
labour	market
skilled	Nations
United	Union
youth	workforce

According to Peter Drucker (2001), a well-known business thinker, there are many demographic changes which will affect businesses profoundly over the next 25 years. Firstly, the population is ageing and so patterns of employment will diversify. For example, provision of pensions for retired people is becoming an ever more serious problem for governments. As a result, many people will have to continue in their jobs until they are in their 70s. In addition, these elderly employees are not likely to work for companies on a full-time basis but as consultants, part-timers or temporary staff.

Secondly, there are the effects of fewer young people in many parts of the world. One result of this is that many of these countries will have to rely increasingly on an immigrant labour force. Another point is that markets will need to change: since the falling numbers of younger people mean fewer families, businesses which have built their markets on the basis of the family unit will now have to rethink their approach. Moreover, up to now there has been an emphasis on the youth market; from now on, the middle-aged segment is likely to dominate. Finally, because the supply of younger workers will shrink, businesses will have to find new and different ways to attract and retain staff.

Activity bank

A Solve the crossword.

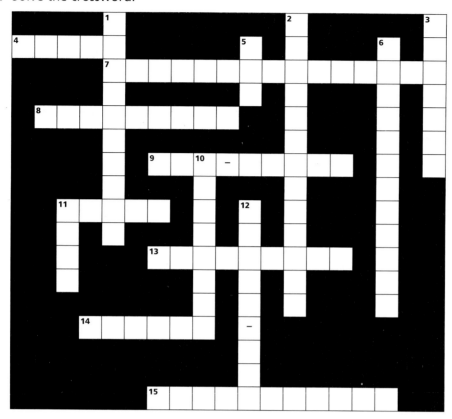

Down

1 I have decided to take voluntary …
and I am leaving the company at the end of the month after 26 years.

2 The company suffered badly after the … of the transport industry.

3 Are you going into a joint … with Acme Industries?

5 Acme Industries … for Evans Trading but lost out to Jenkins plc.

6 Their … channels were badly affected by the postal strike last month.

10 What is the annual … of the company? How much do they make every year?

11 How good is the customer … in that company? Do they have good after-sales service?

12 In some countries, transport is … , and in other countries it has been privatized.

Across

4 Do you own the factory or do you … it?

7 … protects a company from a sudden market change in demand for one product.

8 We are going to start to … the service from next year. Expansion will be very fast then.

9 They provide a … product but it is very good.

11 We are at the bottom of the economic … . The economy should pick up next year.

13 We are aiming for a stock market … at the end of the year.

14 The market … in a sector can usually charge a premium for their product.

15 In some industries, … is a big problem, because of low salaries or because of the stress of the job.

B Match the percentages with a suitable phrase to describe numbers of respondents.

95%	a significant majority
70%	a small proportion
53%	half
50%	a tiny minority
48%	just over half
10%	slightly less than half
2%	the great majority

SWOT analysis

When a company's performance is looking poor, it may need to make some changes. However, before the company can do this, it should establish where it is now through a strategic analysis. A commonly used technique for this is the SWOT analysis. In this method, managers carry out an 'external audit' in which they examine their business and economic environment as well as the market conditions they face in order to understand the opportunities and threats to the company. Secondly, the organization needs to complete an 'internal audit' in which its strengths and weaknesses are compared with those of the competitors. This means that managers should look at all the functional areas: finance, HR, marketing and operations. The results of such audits are presented in a four-box summary of the business's current strengths and weaknesses, and the opportunities and threats which will affect its future development.

A contract for transporting schoolchildren was given to Robins.

Robins borrowed £250k for the second time.

Robins Transport began operating.

Robins bought more taxis and minibuses.

Robins decided to start providing bus travel in Hadford.

Robins leased some taxis and minibuses.

Robins lost his job.

The company's gross income exceeded £2 million.

A contract for transporting schoolchildren was given to Robins.

Robins borrowed £250k for the second time.

Robins Transport was began operating.

Robins bought more taxis and minibuses.

Robins decided to start providing bus travel in Hadford.

Robins leased some taxis and minibuses.

Robins lost his job.

The company's gross income exceeded £2 million.

Questionnaire survey of Robins Transport customers

Introduction

For a long time, Robins Transport has been a highly successful business. However, because the company has lost market share recently, it is important to know what the customers think of the services provided. This report will describe a survey undertaken to find out customers' attitudes towards Robins Transport. Recommendations will also be made as to how the company can improve its customer care.

Method

A written questionnaire was designed to find out perceptions of RT's quality of service and how RT was seen in relation to its competitors. Two thousand questionnaires were sent to a random sample of RT bus customers, of which 150 were returned. In addition, 130 people were interviewed while waiting at bus stops during one day in June. Seventy percent of the whole sample were women.

Findings

Firstly, on the negative side, a large majority (79%) of customers said that Robins Transport's vehicles were too old. Only a small minority (10%) rated them as good quality. Although 43% of the respondents thought that RT services did not cover enough routes in and outside the town, 57% did not agree. In addition, a significant minority (45%) stated that services over the past five years had deteriorated. Finally, most of the respondents (71%) wanted RT to provide more frequent bus services.

However, the survey also revealed some positive aspects. Firstly, a majority of the respondents said that the services were punctual (60%) and that the staff were polite and helpful (70%). Moreover, although a small minority considered that the services were unreliable, an overwhelming majority (80%) were satisfied with the reliability. Secondly in comparison with other companies, a very large majority thought that the discounts were good. Finally, a slight majority (55%) preferred Robins Transport to other companies.

Discussion

It is clear from the results of this survey that Robins Transport is perceived by its customers in rather unfavourable ways. It seems that the vehicles are felt to be too old and on the whole the services do not meet the needs of the customers. Even where the majority view was positive, there is still room for some improvement.

A limitation of the research was that only 7.5% of the questionnaires were returned, which is a low return rate.

Conclusion

This survey has revealed some weaknesses, and to a more limited extent some strengths, in Robins Transport. Meanwhile, it is clear that in order to improve services and to remain competitive, Robins Transport needs to invest in new vehicles and increase the services which it provides. In order to do this, financial backing will have to be found to enable a sufficient level of investment.

Internet survey of transport companies' business strategies (in relation to Robins Transport)

Introduction

For a long time, Robins Transport has been a highly successful business. However, recently the company has lost market share to other bigger competitors. In order for Robins Transport to consider opportunities for developing and building its operation, it is useful to know what activities other successful transport companies are engaged in. This report will describe an investigation into three such companies. Strategies for the development and improvement of Robins Transport will be suggested.

Method

In order to find out the business activities of some successful transport companies, a survey of their websites was undertaken during the first week of June. The companies which were investigated were First Group, Go Ahead and Stagecoach.

Findings

Key findings are as follows. Firstly, all three of the companies studied have several features in common, such as being public limited companies and bidding for other transport companies. They all emphasize that they use the latest technology, both for passenger information systems and also to meet environmental concerns on emissions. They have a strong focus on safe, secure and relaxing travel.

Secondly, there are a few differences between the three companies. Go Ahead has diversified into other areas such as aviation and aviation services, and car parking. It has also gone into joint ventures with companies in Europe. First Group has been active in the USA where it has bought up companies and been involved in transport management systems. Stagecoach is providing hovercraft services in Scotland.

Discussion

Although the overall picture is quite complex, what is clear is that these companies have strong financial backing through stock market flotation, which has enabled them to take over other companies. Internationalization has increased the opportunities for expansion, through the purchase of foreign companies. Joint ventures with other companies have also given the companies the logistical advantages of connections with other networks as well as helping with access to up-to-date technical developments. A heavy emphasis on meeting the needs of their customers has also contributed to their success. Furthermore, diversification into other areas of transport and non-transport activities has increased the opportunities for growth and profitability of these companies. Finally, having very clear aims – for example, to increase the specific number of bus journeys undertaken, to improve safety and security targets, to meet emission controls – is clearly crucial.

Conclusion

To conclude, it is clear that transport businesses which have prospered and grown are now offering a wide range of services, including non-transport services. In addition, in order to maintain success, a company needs to have strong financial control and to consider strategies such as joint ventures, internationalization and flotation on the stock market. In our opinion Robins Transport should consider such strategies and look closely at the methods adopted by its competitors. Unless action is taken urgently, the company is in danger of going out of business. However, there is no reason why the company should not have a bright future if the right decisions are taken.

Robins Transport Customer Survey

Please help us to improve our services to you by completing this questionnaire.
The first 10 questionnaires we receive will receive a free 1-month Hadford bus pass.

Please indicate your answer by circling your choice.

1 How do you rate the Robins Transport (RT) vehicles?
   A good quality　　　　　B satisfactory　　　　　C too old

2 What do you think of our bus services? Are they:
   A punctual　　　　　not punctual　　　　　don't know
   B reliable　　　　　not reliable　　　　　don't know

3 What do you think of our services over the last five years?
   Have they:
   A improved　　　　　B deteriorated　　　　　C neither

4 Do you think RT staff are polite and helpful?
   yes　　　　　no　　　　　don't know

5 Do you think RT cover enough routes inside and outside the town?
   yes　　　　　no　　　　　don't know

6 Would you like RT to provide more frequent bus services?
   yes　　　　　no　　　　　don't know

7 Do you prefer RT to other transport companies in Hadford?
   yes　　　　　no　　　　　don't know

8 Do you think RT offer good discounts?
   yes　　　　　no　　　　　don't know

9 Any other comments?

Thank you for your help!

Use the words and phrases in the box to complete the text.

| also   as a result of   consequently   first   in addition   next   led   resulted |

Close Call Clothing Co. plc was losing money. It was under pressure from bankers and other lenders. _____ , shareholders were not happy when the share price dropped to an all-time low of 32p.

_____ , a decision was made to undertake a strategic review of the company. _____ , the management team set out to establish the views of all staff. _____ , management were persuaded to agree to more ambitious targets. Finally, progress-monitoring mechanisms were set up.

_____ these measures, the company redesigned its manufacturing processes, which _____ to improved quality. Better organizational structures and delivery systems _____ enhanced customer relations.

These steps soon _____ in increased customer and retailer confidence, and sales quickly started to rise.

Use the words and phrases in the box to complete the text.

| also   as a result of   consequently   first   in addition   next   led   resulted |

Close Call Clothing Co. plc was losing money. It was under pressure from bankers and other lenders. _____ , shareholders were not happy when the share price dropped to an all-time low of 32p.

_____ , a decision was made to undertake a strategic review of the company. _____ , the management team set out to establish the views of all staff. _____ , management were persuaded to agree to more ambitious targets. Finally, progress-monitoring mechanisms were set up.

_____ these measures, the company redesigned its manufacturing processes, which _____ to improved quality. Better organizational structures and delivery systems _____ enhanced customer relations.

These steps soon _____ in increased customer and retailer confidence, and sales quickly started to rise.